Rosemary

Simplify, digens,

Boxes, fraternaly,

Direct a one act — program

one act

3-5 minutes on sc

See and critic 4 play

Prompt book

Directing for the Theatre

To the memory
of
W. David Sievers

Directing for the Theatre

Third Edition

W. David Sievers
(Deceased)

Harry E. Stiver, Jr.
California State University
Long Beach

Stanley Kahan
California State University
Long Beach

WM. C. BROWN COMPANY PUBLISHERS
Dubuque, Iowa

Contents

Preface

This revision of the late W. David Sievers' book, *Directing for the Theatre*, attempts to preserve the basic philosophy and integrity of the original text. The author's vast penetration of and significant contributions to the art of the theatre mandate that his work not only be preserved but enriched.

This text was originally designed to provide the theoretical and practical bases for understanding what the potential artistic director needs to do in the preparation and rehearsal of a theatrical production. As stated by W. David Sievers, "It follows no one theory or system, but is indebted to many. It would not have been possible without the teachings and example of notable directors such as Erwin Piscator, Thomas Wood Stevens, James Light, F. Cowles Strickland, Samuel Selden, and Stella Adler. The book draws heavily upon the Stanislavski method, but equally upon Alexander Dean's technical analysis of stage mechanics, ... The creation of inner truth and the technical control of form are not mutually exclusive, but in fact two sides of the same coin. The working director needs to know both approaches, and should never mistake either part for the whole. This book integrates the two approaches in a way that has been found workable. . . ."

With these underlying principles in mind, the book has been reorganized to enable the director to follow from chapter to chapter a logical sequence of theory and techniques. The director is required to apply these principles artistically and practically as described in the final chapter on production execution. Naturally, updating and expansion of bibliographies, text, illustrations, and appendices have been necessary in order to make the book more pertinent to today's theatre. Importantly, new materials have been added which concentrate on directing in various types of theatres other than the prosecenium. Because the previous editions primarily concentrated on the educational theatre, but by no means were limited to it, this edition has been revised considerably to make it more applicable to all levels of theatre—professional, university/college, community, and secondary.

We are fully aware that no text can completely assure the knowledge-able director success with a production. Experience, talent, as well as numerous other assets must also be significantly present. We therefore submit this revision as an effort to further the probability that a memorable theatrical experience will occur between artists and audiences.

HES & SK

Acknowledgements

(The Acknowledgements from the first two editions have been reprinted intact in the interest of preserving the continuity and evolution of this book.)

It is with warm appreciation that I acknowledge my great indebtedness to Dr. Kenneth L. Graham, Professor of Speech and Theatre Arts at the University of Minnesota, who served as editorial advisor for the manuscript. I also wish to express my thanks to my colleagues in the Speech and Drama Departments of California State College at Long Beach; to Dr. John H. Green for his reading of the manuscript and the drawing of the ground plan for *The Barretts of Wimpole Street;* to Dr. Leo Goodman-Malamuth, Milton Howarth and Herbert Camburn for their valuable comments on the various chapters. I am also grateful to Dr. Frank Nelson of our English Department for permission to quote from his translation of Ibsen's *Pillars of Society,* and to Dr. Josephine Burley Schultz of the Art Department for assistance in locating art reproductions. Isabel Thomason and Aileen Alvich graciously served as models for the photographs of stage positions, and the latter also did the art work for the drawings and diagrams. Bill Coleman of Long Beach did the photography for the cover and many of the plays illustrated throughout the book. Above all, I am indebted to the many directors and designers who kindly furnished me with pictures of their productions and granted permission to use them as illustrations; those responsible for each picture are acknowledged and special thanks are due as well to George Freedley of the Theatre Collection, New York Public Library, to Mrs. Florence Vandamm of Vandamm Studios, and to Eileen Darby of Graphic House, Inc. Where not otherwise indicated, photographs are of productions at California State College at Long Beach.

For permission to quote from plays, I wish to acknowledge my thanks to the following:

Random House, Inc. for THE DIARY OF ANNE FRANK, by Frances Goodrich and Albert Hackett. Copyright 1954, © 1956 by Albert Hackett, Frances Goodrich Hackett and Otto Frank. Reprinted by permission of Random House, Inc. For HEDDA GABLER by Ibsen, translated by Eva LeGallienne in the Modern Library Book, *Six Plays by Henrik Ibsen*, Copyright, 1957.

Holt, Rinehart and Winston, Inc., for Robert Whitelaw's translation of Sophocles' *Antigone* in *An Anthology of Greek Drama*, Vol. I, and for Dudley Fitts and Robert Fitzgerald's translation of *Antigone* in *Greek Plays in Modern Translation*, Copyright, 1947.

Little, Brown and Company for *The Barretts of Wimpole Street*, by Rudolph Besier.

Hamilton Russell Corp., London, for *Blithe Spirit* by Noel Coward.

Reinheimer and Cohen for *You Can't Take It With You*, copyright by George S. Kaufman and Moss Hart.

Howard Richardson for his play, *Dark of the Moon*.

Viking Press, Inc. for *Death of a Salesman* and *The Crucible* by Arthur Miller. All rights reserved. Reprinted by permission of the Viking Press, Inc.

Harper and Brothers for *Our Town* by Thornton Wilder.

Robinson Jeffers for his play, *Medea*.

Anderson House for *Winterset* by Maxwell Anderson. Copyright, 1935, by Anderson House.

Samuel French, Inc., for *The Late Christopher Bean*. Copyright, 1932 (under the title *Muse of All Work*) by Sidney Howard, Copyright, 1933, by Sidney Howard, Copyright, 1959, (in renewal) by Polly Damrosch Howard. All rights reserved.

New Directions for *Summer and Smoke* excerpt, reprinted from *Summer and Smoke* by Tennessee Williams. Copyright, 1948, by Tennessee Williams. By permission of New Directions, publishers.

The second edition incorporated valuable suggestions made by Professor Donald D. Fogelberg of the University of Minnesota. I am indebted too to The Tyrone Guthrie Theatre of Minneapolis for permission to use the photograph of *The Three Sisters*, and to Frederic McConnell, director emeritus of the Cleveland Playhouse, for his production photograph of *The Crucible*. The section on the ground plan was expanded with the assistance of Dr. Maxine Merlino, Professor of Art and Theatre Design at California State College, Long Beach, whose drawing of sample ground plans are a contribution which is most sincerely appreciated.

W.D.S.

The authors of this revised edition wish to thank the Mark Taper Forum for permission to use the photograph of its theatre and the following at California State University, Long Beach, for their additional contributions: the Audio-visual Center for the reproduction of production photographs, the Department of Theatre Arts for permission to use production photographs, Dr. John H. Green for the photograph of the Department of Theatre Arts new Studio Theatre, and T. William Smith who graciously provided the art work for the figures in Chapter 4.

HES & SK

CABARET California State University, Long Beach. Directed by G. L. Shoup. Designed by Ralph W. Duckwall (Sets), William French (Costumes), Bernard J. Skalka (Lights), and T. William Smith (Makeup).

1 The Directing Challenge

I. Introduction.

Some critics have accused theatrical production of being time-consuming, expensive, and irrelevant. Theatre artists today must therefore be prepared to justify their work to administrators, management, and the public. To do this they should be clear as to the values of theatre to society and the purposes which it may serve; successful theatre directors not only understand these values—they believe in them fervently.

II. The heritage of theatre.

Many of the greatest minds of western civilization have written for the theatre. Together with mountebanks and humble entertainers, the theatre has attracted Aeschylus and Sophocles with their majestic vision of man's role in the universe; Euripides with his compassionate humanitarianism; Shakespeare with his vibrant characters and his poetry; Molière, Sheridan, and Shaw with their catalytic satire of human foible; Goethe, the last of the universal minds; Ibsen with his still-pertinent challenges to a democratic society; Chekhov, who taught the world how to observe the minute detail that makes up human character; and Strindberg and O'Neill who broke beneath the surface of psychological motivation. The humanistic vision and enduring values of these writers are all the more accessible because

1

they are in a form that is irresistibly appealing—the drama, permitting of emotional participation as well as intellectual understanding. The theatre is the most human of all arts, for its subject has always been the life of men and the destiny of Man. For some 2,400 years before John Dewey, the theatre has been a means of learning through *doing*, through participation (the very word *drama* comes from the Greek verb *to do*).

A brief glance at the heritage of the theatre should serve to remind directors of the proud past and high calling of their profession. There should be no need to apologize for the theatre as one of the significant arts; although in the great reevaluation of American society since Sputnik theatre artists have repeatedly been placed on the defensive. With the current emphasis upon technical and scientific information, it is becoming clear that space-age technology could prove to be a monstrous Frankenstein unless it rests in the control of humanistic, artistically educated individuals. More than ever before in history, man needs to draw upon his inner resources and his ability to communicate with his fellow man to achieve an enriched life (or any life at all) now that science has given him incredible power and more leisure than his ancestors ever dreamed of enjoying. A clear and unequivocal awareness of the opportunities in the theatre will be of invaluable aid to the potential director in developing his role in his chosen field.

III. Vocational opportunities for the theatre artist.

Appreciation for the theatre arts instilled on campuses has created a new generation of playgoers and participants. It is in providing leadership for those who seek the satisfactions of the theatre arts that many graduates of studios and theatre departments will find vocational opportunities. The most fertile fields lie away from Broadway and Hollywood, in the innumerable cities across the nation where the new theatre movement is growing from grass roots. As the cultural explosion expands, openings for well-trained theatre directors, teachers, designers, and technical personnel will increase in the following categories:

A. Secondary schools.

    1. High schools offer the most numerous opportunities for drama teachers and directors. A teacher's credential is required, and a broad background in other subjects is usually desired, as the drama program generally does not constitute a full teaching load. Although the pattern varies from state to state, many high schools find the following combinations workable:

ANTIGONE Millikan High School, Long Beach, California. Directed by Al Randall.

    a. Director of plays, generally combined with classes in English or speech; should have background in acting and dramatic literature.

    b. Technical director, teacher of stagecraft and scene designer for productions, generally combined with other subjects in art or industrial arts. Students with preparation in this combination are at present considerably in demand.

2. Junior high schools.

Although less specialization is required, a growing number of junior high schools will have opportunities for a teacher with some training in formal drama as well as the ability to use creative dramatics in other classes, which may include English, speech, or social studies.

Students interested in preparing for the secondary field should affiliate with and obtain further information from:

Secondary School Theatre Association, a division of the American Theatre Association. For address, see the latest issue of the *Educational Theatre Journal.* The placement services also service the high school field, although a student is most likely to hear of high school vacancies through the placement service of his school.

drama/comedy/problem

B. Junior colleges.

As school populations grow, more and more teachers will find placement in junior (two-year) colleges in states such as California and Texas. In addition to a teacher's credential and a major in drama, a Master of Arts degree in drama is recommended in many schools and required in some. Some specialization is desirable, either in acting-directing or technical theatre.

C. Colleges and universites.

Thousands of students are enrolled in colleges and universities throughout the country providing full-time and part-time instructional opportunities to qualified persons. A Master of Arts degree is usually required for such teaching positions, and the Ph.D., D.F.A., or M.F.A. degree or extensive experience in the professional theatre generally is a prerequisite for advancement on most university theatre faculties.

BERNARDINE University of Oregon. Directed by Frederick Hunter. Designed by Howard L. Ramey.

1. Specialization versus general background.
Smaller colleges require an all-around theatre person able to direct, design and build scenery and costumes, to teach acting, speech, and dramatic literature. The candidate with strong preparation in each of these fields will render himself more valuable to schools with limited faculties. In those colleges

with a large drama faculty, however, specialization is desirable; the most common combinations include:

   a. Acting-directing, voice.
   b. History of the theatre, dramatic literature, and playwriting.
   c. Technical theatre, scene design, and lighting.
   d. Costume design and construction, make-up.

2. Placement services.
   For college level positions, applicants should contact:

   a. American Theatre Association, contact placement service. (Also services high school, community, and children's theatre.) For current address, see latest issue of the *Educational Theatre Journal*.
   b. Speech Communication Association, placement service. For current address, see latest issue of *The Quarterly Journal of Speech*.
   c. The placement service of the student's college or university.
   d. Privately operated placement services.

D. Community theatres.

Throughout the country there is a mushrooming of community theatres which offer full or part-time employment to a director

SUDS IN YOUR EYE—COMMUNITY THEATRE   Long Beach Community Players. Directed and Designed by Dan Baurac.

and sometimes a technical director as well. Academic degrees are usually less important than a person's theatre skill, his ability to get along with volunteer workers, and his enthusiasm for the theatre. Insight into the problems and challenges of building and operating a community theatre can be gained from some of the books suggested at the end of this chapter.

Students interested in preparing for this field should affiliate with and obtain further information from:

American Community Theatre Association, a division of the American Theatre Association. For address see the latest issue of *Educational Theatre Journal*.

E. Children's theatre.

The children's theatre movement is developing throughout the United States and provides opportunity for part-time paid directors in some cases and volunteer directors in others. Organizations producing plays for children can be divided into:

SLEEPING BEAUTY—CHILDREN'S THEATRE California State University, Long Beach. Directed by Herbert L. Camburn. Designed by Herbert L. Camburn and Milton Howarth.

1. Groups using volunteer adult actors.
2. Groups using children as actors.
3. Professional adult groups producing for children.
4. Recreation groups.
   This is a sizeable and growing area offering opportunity for directors. Many communities employ drama directors through the municipal recreation department. Programs offered after

school and on Saturday include creative dramatics, puppetry, and formal dramatics for children and teen-agers.

Students interested in preparing for this field should affiliate with and obtain further information from the Children's Theatre Association, a division of the American Theatre Association. The address appears in the latest issue of *Educational Theatre Journal.*

F. Semiprofessional theatre.

There are more opportunities in this area than one might realize, and more are awaiting the imaginative director with the vision to organize such a theatre. Included in this category are many organizations offering experience for actors and backstage technicians which would be invaluable for future directors:

1. Outdoor summer pageants and historical dramas. Symphonic dramas begun by Paul Green have now spread from *The Lost Colony* at Manteo, N. C., to Williamsburg, Va., Cherokee, N. C., Berea, Ky., Blowing Rock, N. C., and the *Ramona* play at Hemet, Calif.

2. Summer Shakespeare festivals.
    Currently summer festivals offering Shakespeare include Boulder, Colorado, Ashland, Oregon, San Diego, California, Antioch, Ohio, as well as professional companies at Stratford, Ontario, and in Connecticut.

3. The so-called "off-Broadway" theatre, which now can be found in a number of cities other than New York, attempts to offer modest salaries to part or all of their company.

4. Summer theatres.
    Groups banding together to produce theatre during the summer, with either college or community affiliations, also form a growing opportunity for directors. Often the weekly receipts determine whether the group can be called semiprofessional, professional or a nonprofit organization.

G. Professional theatre.

When a strike of Actors' Equity Association in 1960 closed down all professional theatres in the United States, there were only 731 actors at work in New York City and another 175 on the road— an incredibly tiny proportion for a nation of over 192,000,000! There are more encouraging signs, however, in the burgeoning resident theatres and repertory companies outside New York which have sprung up or which have made the transition from community or semiprofessional to professional theatres thanks to subsidies from the Ford Foundation in cities such as Houston,

DEATH OF A SALESMAN—PROFESSIONAL PRODUCTION Directed by
Elia Kazan. Designed by Jo Mielziner.

San Francisco, Milwaukee, Oklahoma City, Minneapolis, Washington, D. C., and Los Angeles. Various states have established
Arts Councils to aid the performing arts, and the McKnight Foundation makes it possible for graduate students of drama to work
as apprentices at the Tyrone Guthrie Theatre in Minneapolis. The
decentralization of the professional theatre offers the most encouraging promise of vocational opportunity for talented and
well-trained young people interested in management, direction,
technical theatre, public relations as well as acting, and may
provide the pattern which will grow into the truly national theatre of the United States.

H. Creative writing.

Of all the skills within the broad field of the theatre arts, creative
writing is the least overcrowded as well as the most badly needed.
Directors of theatre at every level have a responsibility to seek
out and encourage new writing talent and to produce original plays

when possible. The person with an aptitude for playwriting should learn the theatre firsthand as an actor, director, or member of a backstage crew in addition to studying dramatic literature and the craft of playwriting. He will then find a variety of channels open to his talents—writing for the children's theatre, the high school theatre, musical comedy, possibly even television or motion pictures.

I. Television and motion pictures.

The best training for television and motion pictures is the living stage, offering the two-way communication between audience and performer which is unavailable in the other media. A strong preparation will permit the student to translate his basic skills in acting, directing, writing, costuming, or scenic design into the specialized requirement of TV and cinema. Like the professional theatre, however, these fields are fiercely competitive and unstable.

IV. Experiences the director should have.

A. Study in:

1. Acting
2. Stagecraft
3. Lighting
4. Costuming
5. Make-up
6. Dramatic literature and history of the theatre.

Work in these six areas is desirable before the person begins study in direction or play production—if not, as soon thereafter as possible.

7. Directing—laboratory experiences in directing scenes, then one-act plays and finally full-length plays.
8. Music and art appreciation.
9. Dance and movement for the stage.
10. Psychology.

B. Practical experience on productions.

There is no substitute for being involved in actual production. A person interested in *any* phase of the theatre should seek experience in *all* phases. A young person with ambition as an actor should not only welcome the opportunity to work backstage on technical crews—he should also seek out these opportunities; there is much he can learn about acting—timing, interpretation of lines, and audience response—by standing in the wings as a member of a prop, lighting, or stage crew. So too the student interested in creative writing should learn the theatre from backstage. Above all, a director needs to know every phase of backstage work from actual experience.

C. Attending the theatre.

It is not unheard of for a young theatre enthusiast to never have seen a professional production of a play. A student of the theatre should attend the theatre regularly, seeing all kinds of productions including professional companies, musicals, children's theatre, central staging, community theatre, and educational theatre. If a person (outside New York City) sees every professional company in his area, he will still see far too little theatre—much less, for example, than is available to a person in the average European city.

D. Keeping abreast of the field.

The theatre arts are a changing field in vocational opportunities, forms of staging, dramatic literature, and technical materials. The director needs to keep abreast of the field and should affiliate with professional organizations, receiving their journals and attending their conventions and conferences, often held locally, regionally, and nationally. Among the organizations working for the betterment of the theatre and theatre artists are:

1. American Theatre Association (ATA).
    Includes: Children's Theatre Association
    Secondary School Theatre Association
    American Community Theatre Association
    University and College Theatre Association
    University Resident Theatre Association
    National Association of Schools of Theatre

2. American National Theatre and Academy (ANTA).
    Chartered by Congress to foster a national theatre in the United States, ANTA receives no governmental subsidy as yet except for its overseas tours. ANTA is the American representative to the International Theatre Institute.

3. National Thespian Society (for secondary level).
    An organization with chapters in many high schools; publishes *Dramatics Magazine,* which is very valuable for high school drama teachers.

4. National Collegiate Players, publishers of *Players Magazine.*

5. National Theatre Conference, an association of community and college theatre directors (membership by election only).

V. Realization of the scope of the theatrical production.

Because theatrical production is today being carried on in small schools or communities where one person does everything and in large universities and theatre centers where all production supervision is by a staff of specialized artists, the neophyte director should not stand in awe or fear at the number of tasks that need to be performed for a smoothly running production; in many cases he will find help from unexpected sources if he will but seek it. The important thing is that before and during his preparation as a director he needs to be completely and constantly aware of the scope of all of the production elements.

A well-organized production team is indispensable, whether it be in high school, college, a community playhouse or on Broadway. Ideally, artistic unity can be fostered when a group of individuals come together to do creative work under effective leadership with clearly defined duties and lines of authority. This section therefore outlines the duties of a fairly extensive staff such as might be found within the scope of a large theatre operation. The director without a fully equipped theatre, a trained scene designer, and costume designer to work with or ample crews to draw upon, will be forced to adapt some of the concepts presented in this section to his particular needs. For a person in such a position, this section may serve as a valuable check-list of tasks to be done, even though he may have to keep changing hats and supervise them all himself.

A. The production staff.

    1. Producer.

        a. In the professional theatre the producer raises the money, obtains the rights to the play, hires the director and the cast, rents the theatre, and owns the production. In the educational theatre there is as a rule no producer; most of the production duties are assumed by the department of theatre arts.

        b. In the community theatre, the board of directors or its chairman often assumes many of the producer's responsibilities.

        c. In England the "producer" is what we call the "director," and the "manager" is what we call the "producer."

    2. Director.

        a. The director is responsible for staging the play, coaching the actors and integrating the entire production. In order to achieve a unified impression upon the audience, the director must be the final authority in all matters related to the production. Too many cooks have spoiled more than one theatrical broth.

b. The foregoing statement does not, however, preclude the directors using his authority sparingly and applying the best psychological principles of leadership, which include welcoming and encouraging creative contributions from others, consulting with his staff before making decisions, explaining his reasons rather than being arbitrary, respecting the special talents and training of his staff, and giving the entire team a sense of participation in the creative process.

3. Technical Director.

   a. The technical director is responsible for coordinating backstage activities that relate to scenery, lighting, properties, and sound.

   b. He may or may not serve as *scene designer* as well. Ideally he should, so that he can design with limitations of space, facilities, budget, and manpower in mind, and see the scenery through the construction and painting phases to final dress rehearsal. If the scenery is designed by someone else, he should work closely with the technical director to translate his concepts into realization.

   c. The technical director is responsible for the operation of the scene shop, including the purchase of materials and equipment.

4. Lighting Designer.
   Lighting is often done by the technical director or by a *lighting designer* who works closely under his direction in planning and executing the lighting.

5. Costumer.
   The costumer is responsible for all costumes worn in the play, including accessories such as gloves, jewelry, swords and wigs. The costumer may also be the *costume designer;* if the designs are done by someone else he should work closely with the costumer. In a modern realistic play costumes are usually not designed but selected and assembled by the costumer for the approval of the director.

6. Make-up Designer.
   It is sometimes a natural extension of the costumer's duties to assume responsibility for *make-up*. The head of make-up is responsible for planning or designing all make-ups and hair

styling, selecting colors of grease paint and powder, obtaining supplies, and supervising the make-up of the cast at each dress rehearsal and performance. Although actors traditionally make themselves up, they should be checked by the head of make-up each night before powdering.

7. Choreographer.

When a production involves dance or stylized movement, a choreographer works closely with the director.

8. Musical Director.

When a production involves live music, a musical director will work closely with the director. When recorded music is used, a music consultant will also be of invaluable aid to the director in selecting recordings.

9. Business Manager.

The business manager is responsible for expenditure of funds, keeping the production within its budget, handling ticket sales and receipts. In the absence of a staff business manager the director will generally assume these functions. A business manager usually handles or oversees crews responsible for: publicity, ticket sales and reservations, program editing, and bookkeeping.

B. The production crews.

1. Stage Manager.

a. The immediate right-hand man of the director, the stage manager is the most responsible position generally held on major productions and the best stepping stone to direction. During dress rehearsals and performances he assumes complete charge backstage. There may be several *assistant stage managers,* depending on the complexity of the production, for such tasks as getting crowds on and off, cueing lights or sound, prompting, or maintaining quiet on the opposite side of the stage from the stage manager.

2. Property Crew Head and Crew.

a. Responsible for the gathering, handling, shifting, and returning of all properties, which include three categories:

(1) Furniture.

(2) Trim props (those items desired by the designer to decorate the set, including drapes, rugs, lamps, pictures, bric-a-brac).

(3) Hand props (those items handled by the actors). When gloves, hats, etc., are discovered or left on stage, they are considered costume props, to be furnished by the

costume crew but shifted by the prop crew. As soon as the actors are free of books, important hand props (those handled a good deal by the actors) should be brought to rehearsal—or rehearsal substitutes provided —so actors can practice the use of them and save time at dress rehearsals.

b. Responsible to:

(1) The director for approval of each hand prop as to size, workability, and general effect.

(2) The designer for approval of each piece of furniture or trim as to color, style, and period.

(3) The stage manager for placement, shifting, and striking of all props and furniture during performance.

3. Stage Crew Head and Crew.

One crew may perform all of the following duties or may be subdivided into three separate crews. The head of the stage crew is often designated as *technical assistant* or shop foreman.

a. Responsibilities:

(1) Scene construction crew.
Responsible for building the scenery.

(2) Scene painting crew.
Responsible for painting the scenery.

(3) Stage crew.
Responsible for shifting scenery when more than one set is used. A *curtain man* will usually be designated from this crew. Where a counterweight system is used, this crew is often divided into: Grips—those handling set pieces on the floor; Flymen—those operating the counterweight system.

b. Responsible to: technical director (through stage manager for shifts during performance).

4. Lighting Crew Head and Crew.

a. Responsible for hanging the lights, operating the switchboard, shifting and electrical floor units, and where necessary, operating follow spots.

b. Responsible to: technical director or lighting designer who works under him during planning phase; responsible to stage manager during performance.

5. Costume Crew Head and Crew.

a. Responsible for gathering all costumes and accessories; some costumes may be constructed from designs, others may be rented, borrowed, bought either new or from salvage stores, or loaned by the cast. Fitting, alteration, cleaning, pressing, and returning costumes are part of this crew's duties. In addition some theatres check out costumes to each actor before every performance and check them in afterwards. In other theatres, the actor is made responsible for his costume once it is issued to him except for repairs and cleaning. On large costume productions the crew can be divided into:

(1) Costume construction crew.
(2) Wardrobe crew.
 During dress rehearsals and performances helps actors into costume, helps with quick changes, does emergency repairs, cleaning, and laundry.

 b. Responsible to: costumer; (wardrobe crew reports to stage manager for quick changes).

6. Make-up Crew Head and Crew.

 a. Responsible for supervising all make-ups, applying make-up to those actors unable to make up themselves, hair and wig dressing, purchasing supplies, maintenance, and clean-up of make-up and dressing rooms.

 b. Responsible to: Costumer or head of make-up.

7. Sound Crew Head and Crew.

 a. Responsible for obtaining and operating all sound effects, including recorded music. Simple sound effects such as door slams can be done by a member of the prop crew, but more complex productions may require a sound crew divided into:

(1) Manual.
(2) Recorded.

 b. Responsible to: technical director or director in planning; stage manager during performance.

8. Publicity Crew Head.

 a. Responsible for promotion and publicity of the play, including preparation of newspaper releases, radio and TV spots, publicity photographs, advertisements, posters, mailing pieces, banners, and marquee signs.

 b. *Poster and Program Designer* is often an artist who designs one unified layout for poster, mailing piece, and program cover subject to the approval of the director of the play.

 c. *Program Editor* is responsible for obtaining all names

(spelled correctly) for the program, acknowledgments, credits, program notes, and coming events; checks printer's proof.

    d. Responsible to: director, usually through business manager.

9. Box Office Staff.

    a. Responsible for reservations, ticket sales, and depositing of funds.

    b. Responsible to: business manager.

10. House Manager.

    a. Responsible for obtaining, training, and supervising the ushers. In charge of lobby and auditorium before and during performance.

    b. Responsible to: director, often through business manager.

C. The relationship between cast and crews.

A healthy relationship between the cast and the crews will do much toward insuring high morale backstage and a smoothly running production.

1. Recognition for the crews.

The unsung heroes of play production are the backstage crews, who rarely receive the acclaim of the public. The director and the actors should take every opportunity to give recognition and appreciation for the contribution of the crews. There is no place in the theatre for condescension toward the crews. Actors soon learn how dependent they are upon the support of the crews for a smooth performance.

2. Working together for the success of the production.

It should be explained to crew members that their *raison d'être*, their purpose for being backstage, is not an end in itself but rather one of service—to make sure that the actors go onstage able to do their best work and with all of the things they require. Because the success of the performance ultimately depends upon the ability of the actors to perform before a live audience where mistakes are irrevocable, crew members should support their cast, help them in every way possible so that they will not only go on stage with the right props, well-adjusted costumes, and effective make-up but also in the proper emotional state to concentrate upon their roles. A crew member who has acted himself will know the feeling of a cast member before curtain time; he will do nothing to upset an actor and jeopardize a performance. Instead, cast and crew should be given the feeling they are working together for the success of the production.

D. Responsibilities of the director.

1. Pre-production (prior to going into rehearsal).

   a. To bring together the production staff and in some operations a play selection committee for the purpose of selecting the play.
   b. To set the dates for the performances in consultation with the staff and other involved representatives.
   c. To be certain the rights to the play have been cleared.
   d. To be certain enough copies of the play have been secured.
   e. To check on the budget for the production in consultation with the technical director, the designers, and the business manager.
   f. To prepare for tryouts.
      (1) By setting a date for tryouts and publicizing it.
      (2) By making copies of the play available to the actors before tryouts.
      (3) By selecting scenes to be used for tryouts.
   g. To make a director's book in which his study of the play and his detailed interpretation are recorded.
   h. To clear the use of the theatre with the appropriate authority and to set up a rehearsal schedule, coordinating the times of all technical and dress rehearsals with the technical director and costumer.
   i. To schedule a series of production conferences with the technical director, costumer, and other members of the staff after all have had a chance to read and study the script.

2. Production conferences.
   The director takes the initiative in bringing together all the responsible staff and crew heads for planning conferences. Most of the headaches of production stem from decisions made when everyone who is affected has not been consulted.

   a. First production conference.
      (Note: in the following, the term "set designer" is meant to include the technical director if the two are not the same person.)

      (1) Director presents his interpretation of the play and his concept of style for the production (see Chapter 3). The staff may react to the director's interpretation or present their own interpretations. After a full and open

discussion, a common interpretation should be agreed upon. Although the director is the final authority he should try to incorporate as much as possible the concepts and feeling for the play contributed by the staff.

(2) The common interpretation should include a consideration of mood, style, and ways in which the author's intent can be reinforced by setting, lighting, costumes, properties, music, and actors.

b. Second production conference.

(1) After designers have had adequate time to prepare sketches, the director calls a second production conference with the set designer, costumer, lighting designer, and make-up designer.

(2) Set designer presents his preliminary sketches, ground plans and/or models to the staff. They are evaluated from the following aspects:

(a) Overall impression and mood.

(b) Effectiveness in furthering the author's intent and the agreed-upon interpretation.

(c) Placement of principal acting areas and ground plan.

(d) Feasibility of execution and shifting.

(3) Although the director is vitally concerned with the ground plan in its functional accommodation of his planned action for the play and the size, placement, and usability of furniture while the technical director (when different from the set designer) is concerned primarily with executing and shifting the sets with a given number of dollars and man-hours, the set designer should, as far as possible, have his wishes respected in regard to:

(a) Color

(b) Form

(c) Composition of the total visual picture

(d) Choice of materials

(4) On the basis of the foregoing factors, the final decision to accept, modify or redo the designs is made by the director after adequate discussion, exploration of alternatives, and respect for the integrity of the designs which can be modified only so far without destroying the basic intent of the designer.

(5) Costumer submits costume sketches (if a period play)

or discusses the costume requirements of the play with the director (if a modern dress play). Any possible clashes in color or design between settings and costumes can be noted and remedied at this time.

(6) The director should rely upon the costumer's more thorough research and knowledge of:

    (a) The period and the fashions worn at the time.

    (b) Color, style, and silhouette which would be appropriate.

    (c) Combinations of colors for characters who have scenes together.

    (d) Choice of fabrics.

    (e) Cost of construction or renting.

(7) The director's concern with the costumes includes:

    (a) The general impression of the costume and the reflection of the character who wears it.

    (b) The freedom of movement and gesture which the costume permits for the stage business the director has in mind.

    (c) The time required for quick changes of costume.

c. Third production conference.

1. Designers submit revised designs, color sketches and/or models, and scale ground plans to the staff.

2. Director, designers, technical director, and choreographer (where applicable) agree in final detail upon the designs.

3. Overlay tracings of the ground plan should be given to the director, stage manager, property crew head and lighting designer by the technical director, who also supervises the laying out of the ground plan on the floor of the stage or rehearsal hall with paint or masking tape prior to the first blocking rehearsal.

4. Further production conferences.
The director should continue to confer with the technical staff, either together or individually, until all questions are resolved. *These conferences should not be held during rehearsal,* however, when the director should be free to concentrate on his cast. The director should make sure that he covers each item on this check list if applicable:

a. Discusses the costumes in further detail with the costumer (in some cases the physique of the actors cast in the roles may alter the final design). When designs are not used, each character should be discussed in detail and what he is to wear in each act listed on the costume plot. In the latter method, the costumer will assemble the costumes over a period of weeks; some directors prefer to see and approve each costume before the first dress rehearsal.

b. Confers with the business manager to make sure that:
   (1) Tickets have been ordered in ample time.
   (2) Copy approved for publicity releases.
   (3) Design of poster, mailing pieces, and advertisements approved.
   (4) Publicity photographs scheduled and date coordinated with costumer and actors concerned.
   (5) Program copy and layout approved, and proof checked at last possible moment.
   (6) Royalty check sent to play-leasing company in ample time.
   (7) Production photographs scheduled at time agreeable to staff.

c. Confers with head of prop crew on hand props, particularly those involved in the action of the play, and makes sure that crew head has conferred with designer on each item of furniture and trim needed.

d. Confers with lighting designer to discuss in detail the mood, intensity, acting areas, and motivation for the light.

e. Confers with the make-up designer to discuss in detail the make-up of each character and coordinating it with the lighting so that the color of the light does not destroy its effect.

f. Confers with the sound effects crew head to discuss in detail each sound effect, how it will be made, and where it begins and ends.

g. Coordinates the schedule for the use of the stage, making sure that the technical director and lighting technician have adequate time on stage for setup and technical rehearsals. The director often can work successfully in a rehearsal hall if he has planned ahead with this in mind.

h. Makes sure that everyone is informed as changes occur during rehearsal. The stage manager can help in this liaison, notifying the prop crew head of new props added or changed placement of props.

VI. Summary.

The theatre arts offer a *total* experience involving the intellectual, emotional, spiritual, and physical aspects of human beings. Vocational opportunities exist in various areas of theatre and in various types of theatre organizations for those individuals who dedicate themselves to thorough preparation in the theory and practice of the arts of the theatre. The potential director, however, must have a complete perspective of his role of authority within the scope of the total production framework. He must realize that a well-organized production team with each person clear as to his responsibilities and lines of communication, is indispensable to successful unity of artistic expression in a production.

A. The heritage of the theatre is humanistic and artistic.
B. There are numerous vocational opportunities for the theatre artist.
  1. Secondary schools.
  2. Junior colleges.
  3. Colleges and universities.
  4. Community theatres.
  5. Children's theatre.
  6. Semiprofessional theatre.
  7. Professional theatre.
  8. Creative writing.
  9. Television and motion pictures.
C. The potential director should have numerous experiences.
  1. Study.
  2. Practical experience on productions.
  3. Attending the theatre.
  4. Keeping abreast of the field.
D. He must realize the total scope of the theatrical production.
  1. The production staff.
  2. The production crews.
  3. The relationship between cast and crews.
  4. Responsibilities of the director.

Selective Bibliography

"The Arts in the Comprehensive Secondary School." *Bulletin of the National Association of Secondary-School Principals,* 46, 275, Sept., 1962.

ATA Annual Directory. Washington, D. C.: American Theatre Association.

Benner, Ralph. *The Young Actor's Guide to Hollywood.* New York: Coward McCann, 1964.

Bentley, Eric. *What Is Theatre? A Query in Chronicle Form.* Boston: Beacon Press, 1956.

Borum, May Rose, and McGee, Barry. *Stage Production.* Los Angeles: Los Angeles City College, 1956.

Chorpenning, Charlotte B. *Twenty-One Years with Children's Theatre.* Anchorage, Ky.: The Children's Theatre Press, 1954.

Cohen, Robert. *Acting Professionally.* Palo Alto, Calif.: National Press Books, 1971.

Davis, Jed H., and Watkins, Mary Jane. *Children's Theatre: Play Production for the Child Audience.* New York: Harper and Brothers, 1960.

Farber, Donald C. *Actors Guide: What You Should Know About the Contracts You Sign.* New York: Drama Book Specialists, 1971.

———. *From Option to Opening: A Guide for the Off-Broadway Producer.* New York: Drama Book Specialists, 1970.

Gard, Robert E., and Burley, Gertrude S. *Community Theatre: Idea and Achievement.* New York: Duell, Sloan and Pearce, Inc., 1959.

Gassner, John. *Producing the Play.* New York: Holt, Rinehart & Winston, Inc., 1953.

Gruver, Bert. *The Stage Manager's Handbook.* New York: Drama Book Specialists, 1972.

Halstead, William P. *Stage Management for the Amateur Theatre.* New York: F. S. Crofts, 1937.

Harmon, Charlotte. *How to Break into the Theatre.* New York: The Dial Press, Inc., 1961.

Hartke, Gilbert V. "Educational Theatre," *Educational Theatre Journal,* vol. 8 no. 1, March, 1956.

Heffner, Hubert. "Theatre and Drama in Liberal Education," *Educational Theatre Journal,* vol. 16, no. 1, March, 1964.

———. Selden, Samuel, and Sellman, H. D. *Modern Theatre Practice.* New York: Appleton-Century-Crofts, 1973.

Hirschfeld, Burt. *Stagestruck: Your Career in Theatre.* New York: Messner, 1953.

International Theatre Institute (editors). *Theatre 4; the American Theatre, 1971-1972.* New York: Charles Scribner's Sons, 1972.

Joels, Merrill E. *How to Get into Show Business.* New York: Hastings House, Inc., 1969.

Langer, Susanne K. *Problems of Art.* New York: Charles Scribner's Sons, 1957.

Mearns, Hughes. *Creative Power.* New York: Dover Press, 1959.

Motter, Charlotte Kay. "A Method of Integrating the High School Drama Program," *Educational Theatre Journal,* vol. 12, no. 2, May, 1960.

———. "The Dramatic Arts, A Comprehensive Teaching Medium," *Educational Theatre Journal,* vol. 13, no. 4, December, 1961.

Novick, Julius. *Beyond Broadway.* New York: Hill and Wang, 1968.

Reiss, Alvin H. *The Arts Management Handbook; a Guide for Those Interested in or Involved with the Administration of Cultural Institutions.* New York: Law-Arts Publishers, Inc., 1970.

Savan, Bruce. *Your Career in the Theatre.* Garden City, N. Y.: Doubleday and Co., 1961.

Selden, Samuel, ed. *Organizing a Community Theatre.* Cleveland: National Theatre Conference, 1945.

Shaffer, James F. *The Director, The Actor and the Stage.* Portland, Oregon: Allied Publishers, 1956.

Stratman, Carl J. *American Theatrical Periodicals, 1798-1967; A Bibliographical Guide.* Durham, N. C.: Duke University Press, 1970.

Summer Theatre Directory. Washington, D. C.: American Theatre Association.

Taylor, Harold. "Education by Theatre," *Educational Theatre Journal,* vol. 15, no. 4, December, 1963.

Ward, Winifred. *Theatre for Children.* Anchorage, Ky.: Children's Theatre Press, 3rd ed. rev., 1958.

Wickham, Glynne. *Drama in a World of Science.* Toronto: University of Toronto Press, 1962.

Wright, Edward A. and Downs, Lenthiel. *A Primer for Playgoers.* Englewood Cliffs, N. J.: Prentice-Hall, Inc., 1969.

Young, John Wray. *The Community Theatre and How It Works.* New York: Harper and Brothers, 1957.

THE TEAHOUSE OF THE AUGUST MOON University of Nebraska. Directed by Harry E. Stiver. Designed by Charles Lown.

THE QUEEN AND THE REBELS California State University, Long Beach. Directed by Ralph W. Duckwall. Designed by Herbert L. Camburn (Sets and Costumes) and John H. Green (Lights).

2 Play Selection

I. Introduction.

The problem of play selection is critical in the theatre, where wrong choices may spell disaster. The director must therefore be widely read in dramatic literature, and must keep abreast of the field by reading new plays and rereading old ones. It is a wise practice never to select a play for production on the basis of having once read or seen it, but to read it afresh with the specific production in mind.

II. Criteria for play selection.

In order to maintain his perspective in the face of various pressures from segments of his audience with special tastes, actors with favorite roles, and the many practical limitations in production facilities, the director needs to keep in mind a well-defined set of criteria for play selection. These criteria can be divided into two main categories: those relating to the merits of the play itself and those relating to the practical problems of staging it.

A. The drama itself—is it a good play?
   This should be the overriding consideration in play selection. The director must be able to read a play and evaluate it on the basis of its literary and theatrical values, knowing that his actors will look better if their vehicle is substantial. Even professional stars

often fail to save a weak play; non-professionals should not be asked to do so.

It was Aristotle who first observed that there are six major elements for consideration in most plays (although each is certainly not of equal importance or receives the same emphasis in different plays): (1) plot or story, (2) characters, (3) theme, (4) language, (5) spectacle, and (6) melody or music. With the exception of music, which forms a category of its own in our theatre, Aristotle's ingredients can hardly be improved upon:

1. The plot or story.
   The author's story, and how interestingly he tells it, is the skeletal structure of the drama from which the other elements grow. A strong plot—as in melodrama or farce—may overcome weaknesses of characterization, language, or theme. A play without a strong plot—for example *The Cherry Orchard, The Member of the Wedding*—must rely heavily on characterization, theme, and language as compensation. Some questions to consider in evaluating a plot include:

   a. Is the story sufficiently large in scope to absorb one, two, or three hours of the audience's time?
   b. Does the story grow believably and logically from its original premises?
   c. Does the action seem lifelike and well-motivated, or farfetched and contrived by the hand of the author?
   d. Is there sufficient action and change of situation to engage, sustain, and finally satisfy the audience's interest?
   e. Are there sufficient obstacles or complications placed between the protagonist and his desire or wants so that the audience can empathize or participate in his struggle?
   f. Are the individual episodes integrally related to the main story? Are they properly prepared for, do they "build" effectively to a climax and then move the story forward?

2. The characters.
   Many classic writers including Shakespeare freely re-used old plots; it was in the richness of the characterizations that their plays rose above their sources. The great dramas of every period survive because their characters are alive—even when their themes become dated (as with Ibsen). It is characterization too which attracts actors to want to play the roles, and which sustains them when their lack of experience or technique might show through in a one-dimensional character. In evaluating character, the factors which should be considered include:

    a. Are the characters recognizable and real—do we believe in them as people who might exist in life?

    b. Are the characters interesting as people—colorful, contrasting, memorable, vital—in short, human? Do they have many facets or has the author oversimplified his observations of real people?

    c. Do we feel that we know these people intimately by the time the play is over?

    d. Is there at least one major character whom we like—with whom we can identify?

    e. Is the motivation of the characters logical, convincing—based on a deep insight into human psychology? Does the author illuminate behavior or merely describe it?

3. The language.

    Poetic drama because of its embellishment of the language has always contained inherent dramatic values. Although poetry *per se* has largely disappeared from our realistic theatre, we still look to our best playwrights to use language that is emotionally charged, selected for its eloquence, memorable in organizing ideas more expressively than everyday speech. We remember Arthur Miller's "Attention, attention must be finally paid . . ." and the superbly tooled verbal gems of Oscar Wilde, Giraudoux and Albee. These questions regarding language will help distinguish worthwhile plays from pot-boilers:

    a. Do the characters speak with heightened expressiveness?

    b. Has the author captured the rhythm, color, and even **poetry** of everyday speech?

    c. Are there lines or passages that express ideas worth quoting—lines which make the audience say, "I wish I had said that."

    d. Is the choice and arrangement of words fresh and unhackneyed, appropriate for the characters?

    e. Will the language help the actors in characterization or stand in their way?

4. The theme or meaning.

    What the play is "about," what the author is saying, is quite often the quality which attracts us to the play. We should beware, however, of plays which are weak in the three foregoing ingredients—plot, character, and language—relying too heavily on the message, no matter how deeply felt by the author. The great plays dramatize their message, not merely state it. Suffusing the humanistic classics is a theme of the dignity of each individual's life and the value of struggle to overcome obstacles. The problem of whether or not the theme can be made relevant to a contemporary audience is of utmost importance. A check list for evaluating the theme of a play might include:

a. Has the author observed a segment of life with honesty and integrity, and reported his conclusions fairly?
b. Does the play have something worthwhile to say?
c. Is the author's theme worth saying? Are there lasting values which would justify the time spent in producing it?
d. Does the author's theme touch upon universal human experience? Is it true to life? Does he relate specific situations to a larger frame of reference? Does the theme enlarge our view or understanding of life?

5. Spectacle.
We can include here more than Aristotle could have envisioned, broadening his concept to include primarily all those visual elements which make a play "good theatre."

a. Will the play come alive on the stage so as to absorb the interest of an audience—will it be theatrically effective?
b. Does the play take full advantage of the theatrical elements of scenery, costuming, lighting, make-up, and music for the aesthetic satisfactions which they can offer?
c. In short, does the play have to be seen on the stage rather than read to be fully appreciated?

B. The practical problems of staging which affect play selection.
Assuming the play under consideration is a good play by most of the aforesaid criteria, there are a number of practical factors which may affect its choice for production. Essential as it is to consider these limiting factors, the director should not settle for a play which merely presents no production problems—it should also be a good play.

1. Is the play appropriate for its audience and participants?
Play selection is a sensitive and often delicate matter; the director should be aware of the potential problems and must share with his fellow artists the obligation to raise the tastes and appreciations of his audience gradually, to overcome intolerance and narrowness, and to challenge and develop an audience in his theatre.

a. The director must know his audience.
A play that would be acceptable in a sophisticated community might not have appeal in a less urbane one.
b. The director should have the courage of his convictions.

Some boards, managements, and administrators tend to be overly fearful of public reactions to some plays. The theatre director may need to plan a tactful, long-range campaign to convince his superiors that an innocuous but safe drama program does not fulfill the responsibilities of good theatre. His superiors should rely upon his good taste, judgment, and integrity and not attempt to censor or screen each play before it may be produced, nor should one crank letter be a cause for panic.

   c. To enjoy this freedom, the director must accept the responsibility for mature judgment.

      (1) His aim must not be to shock for its own sake, or to make a test case at the expense of his long-range objectives.

      (2) The playwright's intent should be a guiding consideration, and the director should be faithful to this intent.

      (3) A controversial play should be defensible for its literary or dramatic values. The director should consider the overall impact which the play might have; he should educate his audience by easy stages rather than startling jumps. There may be times when his long-range dedication to fostering appreciation for the theatre must take priority over his personal preferences in play selection.

      (4) The director should decide whether some few deletions are justified. Certain actions and words often can be omitted without doing violence to the play. However, it is better not to do a particular play than to cut it to the point of destroying the playwright's intent.

2. Can the play be cast adequately?

   a. Is the distribution of male and female roles suitable for the group?

   b. Are there too many mature roles for a group of young actors?

   c. Does the play's success depend upon one major role being brilliantly played?

   d. Do the roles present challenge to the actors?

3. Can the play's scenic requirement be handled?

   a. How many sets does the play require?

   b. How complete or realistically detailed must the sets be?

    c. What are the problems of scene shifts and off-stage storage?

    d. Are there sufficient man-hours available to construct the sets?

4. Is the available budget adequate for the play?
Items which substantially affect the budget include:

    a. Scenery—where a large stock does not already exist.

    b. Costumes.

       (1) If the play is a period play, can the costumes be constructed, rented, or taken from stock?

       (2) How large a cast will have to be costumed?

    c. Wigs (usually costly to rent).

    d. Properties.
Certain drawing room plays require elegant furniture and trim props which may have to be rented or purchased.

    e. Publicity.
Less well-known plays will require a more extensive publicity campaign than others in order to draw audiences.

    f. Royalty.
The director must consider it his ethical responsibility to pay the required royalty. There can be no justification for evading this requirement.

       (1) Royalty is rarely a burden and never the major percentage of the total budget. To seek out "Budget Plays" or "Ten-Dollar Plays" at the sacrifice of dramatic merit is a short-sighted policy.

       (2) The director or business manager should write to the play-leasing company well in advance, stating the size of his auditorium and the price of his tickets. The play-leasing companies are usually cooperative in giving minimum royalty quotations where justified.

       (3) An American play may be copyrighted for twenty-eight years and renewed for twenty-eight. If it is more than fifty-six years old it will normally be in the public domain and hence royalty-free. Translations, adaptations, and musical versions may be copyrighted, however. The royalty for a good new translation of a classic may be almost as much as for a new play, but it is well worth the investment.

5. Is the play available?
Recent releases of Broadway successes play a large part in the programming of many theatres. The director can never assume that he has the right to produce a play merely because it is

listed in a catalogue. Plays are sometimes released to non-professionals in one part of the country and not in another. In other cases rights are withdrawn when the play is sold to motion pictures or made into a Broadway musical. It often takes months of correspondence to locate and obtain the permission of the copyright holder. The director *must always* obtain the permission of the copyright holder or his agent before announcing the play, purchasing scripts or going into production.

6. Does the play fit in with the rest of the season?[1]

   a. A well-balanced season should have variety, appeal to many different tastes, and draw upon the rich heritage of dramatic literature.

   b. A classic should be chosen, when possible, for its timeliness —for the pertinence of its theme or story to the needs and interests of contemporary audiences.

   c. The season should have a balance among serious and light plays, classics and modern drama, plays for the box office and plays for the aesthetic satisfaction of the discriminating.

   d. Plays which make heavy demands upon the technical director or the costumer should be alternated with plays which are less demanding.

   e. Each generation of students should be exposed, during their three or four years in a school, to some of the enduring classics of dramatic literature. A theatre in a high school or college which lets students graduate without having seen Shakespeare, Molière, the Greeks, or Ibsen can hardly claim the name of educational theatre.

   f. Play selection should take into account what has been performed recently by all of the theatres in the community.

7. Will the type of theatre in which the play is to be produced *best* accommodate the director's particular concept of and approach to the production? (See Chapter 3.)

8. Lastly does the play appeal to the director, the actors, and the production staff, exciting their imaginations and making them want to produce it?

---

1. The following criteria are intended for the educational theatre. The community theatre, semiprofessional, and professional theatre necessarily place stronger emphasis upon the play's box office appeal. Most commercially successful producers discover, however, that in the long run audiences can be attracted profitably to plays that meet most of these criteria.

III. Resources for play selection.

To build a season of plays which takes cognizance of the criteria given, the director should be aware of the resources upon which he may draw. He should first of all be familiar with the conventional classification of plays by type.

A. Types of plays.

Although elements of one type may be found in another—and generally are in modern drama—the types following are the most clearly distinguishable:

1. *Tragedy:* a serious work of some significance in which the hero strives to overcome formidable obstacles but in the end is overcome by them.

    Examples: *Othello, Oedipus Rex*

OTHELLO—TRAGEDY California State University, Long Beach. Directed by W. David Sievers. Designed by Milton Howarth (Sets), Herbert L. Camburn (Costumes) and John H. Green (Lights).

2. *Comedy:* a humorous work in which the hero succeeds in overcoming his obstacles.

    Examples: *Twelfth Night, Arms and the Man*

    a. *High comedy* or *comedy of manners:* a work which generally draws its characters from the upper strata of society and depends for its humor upon verbal wit.

        Examples: *The Rivals, The Importance of Being Earnest*

ARMS AND THE MAN—COMEDY California State University, Long Beach. Directed by Harry E. Stiver. Designed by Beala B. Neel (Sets) and Herbert L. Camburn (Costumes).

      b. *Low comedy* or *farce:* a work which depends less upon verbal wit than upon physical action, ludicrous situations and unexpected happenings.

         Examples: *Charley's Aunt, Room Service*

  3. *Drama:* a play which is basically serious but does not necessarily result in the death of the hero. Most modern plays fall in this category.

         Examples: *The Glass Menagerie, Six Characters in Search of an Author*

  4. *Melodrama:* a serious play, usually with a happy ending, in which there is a maximum of physical action, suspense, and overt conflict.

         Examples: *Ten Nights in a Barroom* (Period), *Dial "M" for Murder*

B. Categories from which to choose.

  1. Classics.

    a. Greek and Roman

    b. Medieval

SIX CHARACTERS IN SEARCH OF AN AUTHOR—DRAMA California State University, Long Beach. Directed by Harry E. Stiver. Designed by Ralph W. Duckwall (Sets and Lights) and Herbert L. Camburn (Costumes).

TEN NIGHTS IN A BARROOM—MELODRAMA (PERIOD) California State University, Long Beach. Directed by Stanley Kahan. Designed by Bernard Skalka (Sets) and Herbert L. Camburn (Costumes).

    c. Shakespeare and Elizabethan
    d. Molière
    e. Restoration and eighteenth century
    f. Oriental
    g. Nineteeth century European
    h. Early American

2. Modern classics of Europe, including (but not limited to):

    a. Ibsen and Strindberg
    b. Bernard Shaw
    c. Wilde, Coward, and English school
    d. Irish school
    e. Chekhov and Russian school
    f. Twentieth century continental writers

3. The best of the modern American playwrights, including (but not limited to):

a. Eugene O'Neill	k. Arthur Miller
b. George Kelly	l. Tennessee Williams
c. Clifford Odets	m. William Inge
d. Maxwell Anderson	n. James Baldwin
e. Lillian Hellman	o. Edward Albee
f. Elmer Rice	p. Le Roi Jones
g. Kaufman and Hart	q. Neil Simon
h. Thornton Wilder	r. Lorraine Hansberry
i. William Saroyan	s. John Guare
j. Sidney Kingsley	t. Megan Terry

4. Recent Broadway successes.
5. Contemporary European plays of note.
6. Standard mysteries and comedies.
7. Plays for children.
8. Musicals.
9. One-act plays.
10. Original plays.
    Whenever possible, new creative talent should be encouraged by the production of original plays by local or undiscovered writers. In many cases the material may compare favorably with the old-hat plays in the catalogues, and the group will have the satisfaction of staging a *première* and giving a new writer an opportunity to see his work come to life.

C. Play-leasing companies.
    The director should be on the mailing list of the play-leasing companies so as to receive their latest catalogues, which are helpful in play selection. Translations and acting versions of classics are

often listed by several companies and should be compared before selecting the most theatrically effective one to produce.

D. Other sources.

1. To keep current, find out what other groups are doing, and draw upon the insights of dramatic criticism, a director should constantly refer to such periodicals as *Educational Theatre Journal, Theatre World, Dramatics, The Drama Review, New York Times* (Sunday Drama Section), *Theatre 4* and others which he might find meaningful from time to time.
2. Consult library sources such as anthologies, indexes, guides to play selection similar to some of those which are recommended in the Selective Bibliography at the end of this chapter.
3. Refer to Appendix on Play Selection in back of this book.

IV. Summary.

A. The criteria for play selection include the following considerations:
1. The drama itself—is it a good play?
2. The practical problems of staging.
B. Resources for play selection.
1. Types of plays.
2. Categories from which to choose.
3. Play-leasing companies.
4. Other sources.

EVALUATION FORM FOR PLAY SELECTION
(Use 5 x 8 card)

Name of play ....

Author .... Translator (if foreign play) ....

Type of play .... Style of play ....

Full-length ...... One-act .... Number of characters .... Men. ....Women.

Number of sets .... Int. .... Ext. Period of costumes............................

Levels of theatre for which appropriate ....

Play-leasing company .... Royalty ....

Production problems if any ....
....

Theme of play ....
....

Brief summary of plot (use this space and reverse side of card) ....
....
....

Selective Bibliography

Barnat, Sylvan, Berman, Morton, and Burto William. *Aspects of the Drama.* Boston: Little, Brown and Co., 1967.

Brockett, Oscar G. *The Theatre, An Introduction.* New York: Holt, Rinehart & Winston, Inc., 1969.

Brooks, Cleanth and Heilman, R. B. *Understanding Drama.* New York: Holt, Rinehart & Winston, Inc., 1955.

Chicorel, Marietta, ed. *Chicorel Theater Index to Plays in Anthologies, Periodicals, Discs, and Tapes.* Vol. 1: Plays in print available in the English language. New York: Chicorel Library Publishing Corporation, 1970.

–––. *Chicorel Theater Index to Plays in Anthologies, Periodicals, Discs, and Tapes.* Vol. 2: Plays not indexed in Vol. 1 available in the English language. New York: Chicorel Library Publishing Corporation, 1971.

Corrigan, Robert W., and Rosenberg, James L. *The Context and Craft of Drama.* San Francisco: Chandler Publishing Co., 1964.

Hartnoll, Phyllis, ed. *The Oxford Companion to the Theatre.* London: Oxford University Press, 1967.

Hatch, James V. *Black Image on the American Stage: A Bibliography of Plays and Musicals* 1770-1970. New York: Drama Book Specialists, 1970.

Hatlen, Theodore W. *Orientation to the Theatre.* New York: Appleton-Century-Crofts, 1962.

Kerr, Walter. *Tragedy and Comedy.* New York: Simon and Shuster, 1967.

Kienzle, Siegfried. *Modern World Theater; A Guide to Productions in Europe and the U.S. since 1945.* Trans. A. and E. Henderson. New York: Frederick Ungar Publishing Co., Inc., 1970.

Lovell, John Jr. *Digest of Great American Plays.* New York: Thomas Y. Crowell Co., 1961.

Matlaw, Myron. *Modern World Drama: An Encyclopedia.* New York: E. P. Dutton & Co., Inc., 1972.

Melchinger, Siegfried. *The Concise Encyclopedia of Modern Drama.* New York: Horizon Press, 1964.

Ottemiller, John H. *Index to Plays in Collections.* New York: Scarecrow Press, 1957.

Plummer, Gail. *Dramatists' Guide to Selection of Plays and Musicals.* Dubuque: Wm. C. Brown Company Publishers, 1963.

Rowe, Kenneth Thorpe. *A Theatre in Your Head.* New York: Funk and Wagnalls Co., 1960.

Shank, Theodore J. *A Digest of 500 Plays.* New York: Crowell-Collier, 1963.

Tennyson, G. B. *An Introduction to Drama.* New York: Holt, Rinehart & Winston, Inc., 1967.

THE VISIT California State University, Long Beach. Directed by Harry E. Stiver. Designed by Ralph W. Duckwall (Sets), Herbert L. Camburn (Costumes), John H. Green (Lights) and T. William Smith (Makeup).

3   The Director's Interpretation of the Play

I. Introduction.

Before the director can begin his work with the cast (or even choose a cast intelligently) he needs to evolve and crystallize in his mind an interpretation of the play. This interpretative study may take a week for a light comedy or a year for a classic. A person who does not find this phase of theatre art rewarding and stimulating should go no further in his plan to become a director.

The two basic processes which go on during the director's interpretative study of a play are: (1) to determine what the play means, and (2) to find a form in which to project this meaning to the audience. To accomplish these two aims, the director will need to reread the play many times, each with a different purpose.

II. Determining what the play means.

This is a much more complex process than may at first be apparent. It includes discovering the theme of the play, studying what critics have written about the play, re-creating the background of the play through research, analyzing the characters and their motives, dividing the play into actions and beats, crystallizing the particular emphasis the director wishes to give the production, and preparing the text for production on the basis of this interpretation.

A. Discovering the theme or meaning of the play.
   1. From what is stated explicitly in the play itself.

      Some playwrights are fairly specific as to the meaning of their plays, or at least provide strong clues which the director may take as a significant statement of meaning. Others are less apparent, and the director may have to search for hints, phrases, images, symbols, and key speeches which suggest meaning. Some of the following lines may be revealing in the director's search for meaning.

      a. "He had the wrong dreams. All, all wrong. . . . He never knew who he was." *Death of a Salesman.*
      b. "This is the glory of earth-born men and women, not to cringe, never to yield, but standing, take defeat implacable and defiant, die unsubmitting. . . ." *Winterset.*
      c. "Greed, Hannah, Greed." *The Late Christopher Bean.*
      d. "I love them, Tony. . . . I love them deeply. Some people could break away, but I couldn't. I know they do rather strange things. . . . But they're gay and they're fun and . . . I don't know . . . there's a kind of nobility about them." *You Can't Take It With You.*

   2. From what is shown implicitly through the action of the characters.

      a. In *The Cherry Orchard,* the characters are emotional, generous, impulsive, but never take positive action to save themselves.
      b. In *The Time of Your Life,* the good people find that there are times when they must rise up and put a stop to evil by whatever means they can.
      c. In *The Crucible* a community is caught by hysteria when its individuals are frustrated and thwarted in their various personal needs.

   3. From what the playwright has written elsewhere that may help illuminate the play. For example:

      a. Shaw's lengthy prefaces are unique in dramatic literature for the light they shed upon his plays.
      b. Eugene O'Neill kept a diary while he was at work on *Mourning Becomes Electra* in which he states his purpose in the play: ". . . to get modern psychological approximation of Greek sense of fate . . . which an intelligent audience of today, possessed of no belief in gods or supernatural retribution, could accept or be moved by."[1]

1. Quoted in Barrett H. Clark, *European Theories of the Drama* (New York: Crown Publishers 1947), p. 530.

c. A full understanding of Blanche in *A Streetcar Named Desire* requires a study of Alma in *Summer and Smoke*, for the two characters suggest the same repressed Southern lady at different stages of her life.

d. William Inge has written about *Picnic:* "I was fascinated to find out how . . . the women seemed to have created a world of their own, a world in which they seemed to be pretending men did not exist. It was a world that had to be destroyed, at least for dramatic values."[2]

B. Studying what critics have written about the play and the author.

1. Before staging a classic or an important modern drama, the director should steep himself in the dramatic criticism of the play. Although literary analysis and theatrical interpretation are not synonymous, the director's insights can be deepened by his study of dramatic criticism; conflicting critical viewpoints can help bring his own interpretation into focus, and he may discover values in the text which he had overlooked.

2. In the case of Shakespeare an imposing bibliography (see Ebisch and Schuecking, *A Shakespearean Bibliography*, 1931) need not cause the director to shy away. A good reading list might begin with:

a. A. C. Bradley, *Shakespearean Tragedy.*
b. H. C. Granville-Barker, *Prefaces to Shakespeare.*
c. Howard Furness, *The New Variorum Edition of Shakespeare.* (Several now in paperback, Dover Publications.)
d. E. K. Chambers, *Shakespeare: A Survey.* A Drama book.
e. Webster, Margaret, *Shakespeare Without Tears.* A Premier paperback.

3. For other playwrights, the *Reader's Guide to Periodical Literature*, the *International Index* and the *New York Times Index* will lead the director to useful critical material. For plays staged in New York since 1939, the *New York Theatre Critics' Reviews* provides the most complete critical summary, but the director should also consult the published work of leading dramatic critics. Knowing the critical response to a play may help the director to tighten weak acts, eliminate obsolete references, clarify ambiguities, and anticipate the reactions of his own audience.

2. William Inge, "Picnic from 'Front Porch' to Broadway," *Theatre Arts*, vol. 38, no. 4, April, 1954, p. 33.

C. Re-creating the background of the play through research.

1. Whenever the play is set in any period or environment other than the one in which the director has lived, considerable research will be necessary by the director so he can steep himself in the period and locale. This phase can be one of the most absorbing for the director, and he may make assignments to his cast so that they can share in the research and become familiar with the background of the play. Among the questions that may need to be answered are these:

   a. Who are the people the playwright describes?
   b. Where do they live—in what kind of houses and towns?
   c. What do they do for a livelihood?
   d. How do they dress?
   e. Because of occupation and dress, how do they move and gesture?
   f. What do they eat and drink, and how are they served?
   g. How are their names pronounced?
   h. What is known about their special institutions treated in the play—courts, hospitals, armies, churches?
   i. What else should the director and actors know about them in order to understand the author's play fully?

2. Sources for this particular kind of research.

   a. Talking with people of the same background—Welshmen in the community for *The Corn is Green,* the Oriental community for *Teahouse of the August Moon,* Pennsylvania Dutch for *Papa is All,* police officers for *Detective Story.* Often someone contacted in this way will be willing to serve as "research consultant" for the production and even to lend properties.
   b. Visiting actual locations if practical—the French quarter of New Orleans for *A Streetcar Named Desire,* a waterfront for *Anna Christie,* a small Southern town for *Inherit the Wind.*
   c. Reading history, biography, manners, customs, and fiction written during or about the period. In preparing *The Crucible,* for example, the director might find it helpful to read Cotton Mather, Perry Miller's *The Puritan Mind,* and Lion Feuchtwanger's *The Devil in Boston.*
   d. Painting, architecture, arts and crafts of the period.
   e. Travel books, postcards, and photographs.
   f. Old fashion magazines, Sears-Roebuck catalogues, newspaper advertisements, back issues of *Life,* and family albums for costumes and accessories.

3. The theatrical history of the play.

Knowing the kind of theatre, audience, scenery, costumes, and theatrical conventions that were typical of the period in which the play was written and first produced will give the director an understanding of the particular form of the play. For example, familiarity with the painted wings and backdrops in use at the time of *The School for Scandal* or *Fashion* may suggest a stylish modern treatment that requires no delays for scene-shifting. Knowing of the repressive government censorship in force at the time *He Who Gets Slapped* was written in Russia would aid the director in interpreting Andreyev's deliberately vague symbols. Even the knowledge that a particular actor created a certain role may help the director clarify his impressions of the character. Certainly a knowledge of Shakespeare's Globe Theatre is necessary before the director can find a modern equivalent that will permit an unbroken flow of the scenes in Shakespeare's plays.

D. Analyzing the characters and their motives.

The central meaning of a play very often is stated in terms of the main action or goal of the principal character or characters. Before the director can crystallize his interpretation, he will need to analyze each character in the play, his motivation, and his relationship to all the other characters. A complete analysis of a character should include all the facets treated in Chapter 8.

1. The use of *verbs.*

Although sound character analysis can be done in many ways, directors trained in the Stanislavski method tend to seek out verbs which express the basic action or struggle of the characters. This is a practical application of both the Aristotelian system which defines drama as an "imitation of an *action*" and of the contemporary, post-Freudian psychology which attempts to understand individuals in terms of their basic drives, wants, or goals and how they are achieved or thwarted.

2. The *spine* of the play.

Harold Clurman popularized the use of the term "spine" (which was Richard Boleslavsky's translation of Stanislavski's term "super-objective"[3]). As Clurman phrases it:

> . . . *what fundamental desire does the plot of his*

3. Richard Boleslavsky, *Acting: The First Six Lessons*, (New York: Theatre Arts, Inc., 1933), Third Lesson.

> *play symbolize, what deep struggle gives it*
> *shape and direction. What is the play's CORE?*[4]

When he directed Odets' *Night Music* for the Group Theatre, Clurman found the spine in the idea that the characters were *searching for a home.* When Robert Lewis directed Saroyan's *My Heart's in the Highlands,* he found the spine in the idea of people trying eagerly to give things to other people. The spine can thus be defined as the unifying or all-embracing action or impulse which motivates the characters and drives them to the final denouement. Like the spine of the body, it can be thought of as a trunk line which brings together the separate parts and carries them forward as a unit.

3. The spine of each character.

The spine of the play usually bears a close relationship to the spine of the principal character or characters. The spines of the other characters (also stated in terms of verbs) will bear some relationship to the spine of the protagonist, either negatively or positively, furthering or blocking the basic action. Examples:

a. Stanislavski tells how his whole interpretation of *The Imaginary Invalid* was clarified when he realized that the protagonists spine was not "I wish to be sick," but "I wish to be thought sick."[5]

b. In the article previously referred to, Clurman illustrates the value of verbs rather than adjectives to describe character by examples from Odets' *Awake and Sing.*

(1) Bessie Berger, the mother, constantly wants "to take care of everything." (This is more helpful for the actress playing the part than to be told she is "meddlesome.")

(2) Ralph, the son, wants "to get away from his environment." (This is more helpful for the actor than to tell him he is playing a "young idealist.")

c. Elia Kazan, the noted Broadway director who staged *A Streetcar Named Desire,* has analyzed the spines of the principal characters in a lucid article which should be read by every student director.[6]

4. Harold Clurman, "Principles of Interpretation," in *Producing the Play,* by John Gassner, (New York: The Dryden Press, 1953), p. 277.

5. Constantin Stanislavski, *An Actor Prepares* (New York: Theatre Arts, Inc., 1936), p. 257.

6. Elia Kazan, "Notebook for A Streetcar Named Desire," in *Directors on Directing: A Source Book of the Modern Theatre,* ed. Cole and Chinoy (Indianapolis: The Bobbs-Merrill Company, Inc., 1963), pp. 364-379.

(1) Blanche...............to find protection.
(2) Stella...................to hold onto Stanley.
(3) Stanley...............to keep things his way.
(4) Mitch..................to get away from his mother.

E. Dividing the play into actions and beats.

If the *spine* tells what the character wants in the play (and in life), the *actions* tell the various things he does to achieve his spine, and the *beats* are the detailed ways he goes about furthering his actions. Each action and beat somehow relates to the spine; a group of beats make up an action, and a group of actions make up the spine.

1. Because some of the translators and followers of Stanislavski have used different terms to describe these concepts, the following diagram may prove helpful:

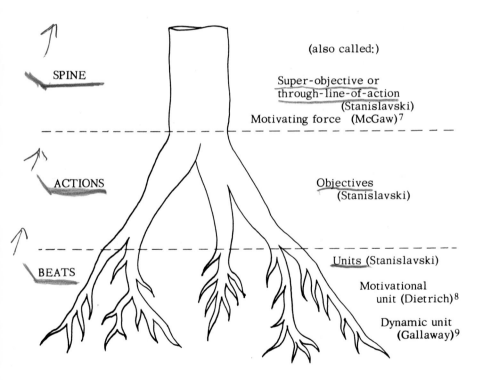

SPINE

ACTIONS

BEATS

(also called:)

Super-objective or through-line-of-action
(Stanislavski)
Motivating force (McGaw)[7]

Objectives
(Stanislavski)

Units (Stanislavski)

Motivational
unit (Dietrich)[8]

Dynamic unit
(Gallaway)[9]

7. Charles McGaw, *Acting Is Believing* (New York: Rinehart and Co., 1955), Chapter 7.
8. John E. Dietrich, *Play Direction* (New York: Prentice-Hall, Inc., 1953), Chapter 6.
9. Marian Gallaway, *The Director in the Theatre.* (New York: The Macmillan Co., 1963).

2. Identifying the beats.

When the director has selected the spine of the play and of each of the characters, he is ready to proceed with the detailed analysis of each act and scene, breaking the play down moment by moment into its beats and actions. This is an essential prerequisite to blocking, for *where the beat or action changes, the visual picture should also change.*

a. Separate the beats by drawing a line across the page of the director's book each time the beat changes. For each beat, the director should ask himself, "What is the character trying to do here?" "What does he want here?" Why is he saying that?" Record the answers to these questions in the margins of the director's book. (Be sure to find the *character's* reasons and not the *playwright's*, which may be entirely external—the need to reveal information to the audience, for example.)

b. How to tell when a new beat begins.

A new beat may begin:

(1) When a new character enters, bringing with him a new want or desire. (Every entrance—the so-called "French scene"—does not mark a new beat; a character may merely participate in the existing beat.)

(2) When a character begins a new approach or gets a new idea.

(3) When another character assumes the initiative. At any given moment, one character is apt to be more aggressive, to dominate, while other characters react or respond to him. When another character takes the initiative or begins "to carry the ball," it may denote a new beat. In older theatre parlance, this determines "whose scene it is."

(4) After a climax has been reached.

c. Selecting strong verbs.

In analyzing what the character is trying to do, the director should wherever possible select strong and active verbs which will stimulate the actor rather than weak, passive, or indifferent verbs. Examples:

STRONG AND ACTIVE VERBS	WEAK AND INACTIVE VERBS
to goad	to tell
to defy	to get angry

STRONG AND ACTIVE VERBS	WEAK AND INACTIVE VERBS
to needle	to suggest
to tease	to hint
to blow off steam	to inform
to force his hand	to wonder
to "mother"	to be sorry

    d. Verbs that reveal *motivation* and *character.*

The director should seek verbs that reveal inner emotional needs and motives—what the character is thinking and feeling rather than what he is saying; the audience will hear the latter for itself. The beats should get beneath the surface of dialogue and express the dynamics which motivate the character to say the given words. The director therefore needs a deep insight into the psychology of human motives, even unconscious motives. If this phase has been done thoroughly, the task of inventing business, movement, and picturization will later come easily. For illustration see the examples given from *Romeo and Juliet* and *The Glass Menagerie* in Chapter 8.

3. Structuring the beats toward climax.

The director should select beats with a sense of progression, growing from weaker to stronger until a climax is reached. A number of beats can be grouped together until they form one main action which culminates in a strong climax. Then a new main action begins. (Climax is treated more fully in Chapter 9.) To illustrate the concepts of the previous page, *The Diary of Anne Frank* could be broken down as follows into spine, actions, and beats; the beats of one scene are given in detail as they might appear in the director's book in preparation for actual blocking.

THE DIARY OF ANNE FRANK
Dramatized by Frances Goodrich and Albert Hackett

SPINE: to hold together as a family and preserve their faith, humor and courage under extreme pressure.

MR. FRANK'S SPINE: to hold his family together and preserve some semblance of normal daily life.

ANNE'S SPINE: to find some meaning for the life she is forced to lead.

THE DIARY OF ANNE FRANK
Act and Scene Breakdown

Act I

Scene 1. (Prologue) Mr. Frank: to keep from breaking down as he sees the room for the last time and tells Miep goodbye.

Scene 2. The two families: to get settled and acquainted.

Scene 3. Anne: to tease young Van Daan. Mr. Frank: to make room for another person and make him feel welcome.

Scene 4. Mr. Frank: to keep Anne from hurting her mother's feelings.

Scene 5. To make Hanukkah a happy festival. Mr. Frank: to keep their courage up when almost discovered by a thief.

Act II

Scene 1. Miep: to cheer them up for New Year's. Peter: to seek Anne's companionship for the first time.

Scene 2. Anne and Peter: to discover their love for each other.

Scene 3. Mrs. Frank: to release her pent-up feelings against Mr. Van Daan. Miep: to bring the good news about the invasion.

Scene 4: Anne: to share her faith with Peter at the moment of crisis.

Scene 5. Mr. Frank: to tell Miep and Kraler that he knows Anne is gone.

(from Act I, Scene 3)

ANNE: to tease young Van Daan.	ANNE: (Enters, dressed in Peter's knickers, jacket and cap.) Good evening, everyone. Forgive me if I don't stay. I have a friend waiting for me in there. My friend Tom, Tom Cat. Some people say that we look alike. But Tom has the most beautiful whiskers...and I have only a little fuzz. I am hoping...in time...
PETER: To get even with her.	PETER: All right, Mrs. Quack Quack! ANNE: Peter! PETER: I heard about you...How you talked so much in class they called you Mrs. Quack Quack. How Mr. Smitter made you write a

composition... "'Quack, Quack,' said Mrs. Quack Quack."

ANNE: Well, go on. Tell them the rest. How it was so good he read it out loud to the class and then read it to all his other classes!

ANNE: To give him the dickens for teasing her back.

PETER: Quack! Quack! Quack...Quack... Quack...

ANNE: You are the most intolerable, insufferable boy I've ever met!

MRS. VAN DAAN: That's right, Anneke! Give it to him!

ANNE: With all the boys in the world...Why I had to get locked up with one like you!

MRS. FRANK: to put a stop to the kidding before it goes too far.

MRS. FRANK: Anne, dear...your hair. You're warm. Are you feeling all right?

ANNE: Please, Mother.

MRS. FRANK: You haven't a fever, have you?

ANNE: No. No.

MRS. FRANK: ....Let me see your tongue.

MR. FRANK: To restore peace between Anne and her mother.

MR. FRANK: I think there's nothing the matter with our Anne that a ride on her bike, or a visit with Jopie de Waal wouldn't cure. Isn't that so, Anne?

F. Crystallizing in words the particular emphasis, point of view, or approach which the director wishes to give the production for his particular audience.

1. The director is ready to do this only after he has done the research indicated into the play itself, the critical commentary, the backgrounds of the play and its theatrical history, the analysis of character, and the breakdown of the play into actions and beats.

2. The director should now summarize his approach in a one sentence concept that begins with: "This is a play about ———" or "This is the story of ———." The concept should not be a literary or moral theme such as "The wages of sin are death," but a theatrical concept of the basic action or spine of the play as the director perceives it. *If a director cannot do this on the basis of sound analysis, he is not prepared to direct his selected play.*

3. The staging, cutting, scenery, even casting, may hinge upon the way the foregoing sentence is completed. For example:

a. *The Diary of Anne Frank* could have become oppressive

and gloomy if the director's approach had been, "This is a tragedy about what the Nazis did to a group of Jews." Instead, the spine suggested, emphasizing the family feeling, faith and humor, makes for a more touching and human performance.

b. The Laurence Olivier film of *Hamlet* began with the clear concept that "This is the story of a man who could not make up his mind."

c. If the director of *Romeo and Juliet* interprets it as the story of "star-crossed lovers," he might conceivably cut the last scene of the reconciliation of Capulet and Montague. If however, he interprets it as "the story of two lovers blighted by family enmity," then the last scene cannot be cut. Today's director, moreover, may see the timeliness of throwing the final accent upon the parents who failed to understand their impetuous, headstrong, "mixed-up teen-agers."

d. During the Hitler period, Erwin Piscator interpreted *King Lear* for a New York production as the story of an aging authoritarian who attempts to maintain a balance of power by dividing his kingdom.

e. The Moscow Art Theatre's 1958 staging of *The Cherry Orchard* interpreted it as a comedy foretelling an optimistic future rather than a nostalgic picture of a dying order.

4. No two directors will see precisely the same values in a play nor state their interpretation in the same terms. The director's affinity for certain subjects and environments may be a key to a valid and exciting interpretation. Harold Clurman emphasizes this personal connection between the director and his script. It is this subjective element in play interpretation that makes directing creative and the theatre varied and fascinating. The neophyte director should read some of the best available interpretations which successful directors have written concerning their productions. A suggested list is given at the end of the chapter.

G. Preparing the text for production.

The final phase of the director's interpretative study is the preparation of the text. In the case of contemporary plays from Samuel French or Dramatists Play Service, this may be a relatively simple matter. In the case of classics and translations, however, the editing of the text is a major reflection of the director's insight into the play. Included in this phase are:

1. Developing a feeling for the language of the play.
   Before he can coach the actors in the interpretation of lines,
   the director will need to discover for himself the special qualities of the language used by the playwright, by:

   a. Appreciating the poetic quality of the dialogue, where ap-
      plicable.
   b. Feeling the rhythm and tempo of the dialogue, especially
      if any cutting is contemplated.
   c. Singling out particularly eloquent speeches which the di-
      rector will want to have pointed.
   d. Deciding, if the play involves dialect, the extent to which
      it should be used by the actors.
   e. Knowing the meaning and pronunciation of every word
      used in the dialogue.

2. Selecting the most effective translation in the case of a foreign play. All available translations should be compared, for
   the translator has a large influence upon our appreciation of
   an author's style and language—whether it is colloquial or
   archaic, sprightly or heavy, prose or verse, British or American. Compare these translations and note how different is the
   feeling conveyed in each case:

(from the opening scene of Antigone by Sophocles)

"O Sister-Life, Ismene's, twin with mine,	"Ismene, dear sister,
Knowest thou of the burden of our race	You would think that we had already suffered enough
Aught that from us yet living Zeus holds back?	For the curse on Oedipus:
Nay, for nought grievous and nought ruinous,	I cannot imagine any grief
No shame and no dishonour, have I not seen	That you and I have not gone through. . . ."[11]
Poured on our hapless heads, both thine and mine."[10]	

10. Translated by Robert Whitelaw, in *An Anthology of Greek Drama*, Vol. I. Reprinted by permission of Holt, Rinehart and Winston, Inc.
11. Translated by Dudley Fitts and Robert Fitzgerald in *Greek Plays in Modern
Translation*. Reprinted by permission of Holt, Rinehart & Winston, Inc.

(from Act III of Ibsen's *Pillars of Society*)

"Do not condemn me without bearing in mind how things stood at that time. . . . I came home and found my mother involved in a mesh of injudicious undertakings; we had all manner of bad luck—it seemed as if misfortunes were raining upon us, and our house was on the verge of ruin. I was half reckless and half in despair. Lona, I believe it was mainly to deaden my thoughts that I let myself drift into that entanglement that ended in Johan's going away."[12]

"Don't condemn me until you remember the situation I was in. . . . When I came home I found my mother involved in a whole series of unwise deals. Then we had a streak of bad luck. We seemed to be caught in a flood of misfortunes and the family business was on the verge of ruin. I was half reckless and half desperate. Lona, I think the real reason I let myself get involved in that affair was to get away from my troubles."[13]

3. Selecting the acting edition to be used by the cast.

   Acting editions should always be compared with the full text so as not inadvertently to choose a chopped-up version which was edited by a squeamish director of bygone days or one with a quite different interpretation of the play. (*The Rivals* and *The Importance of Being Earnest,* for example, have been subjected to heavy-handed editing; Baker's Plays carry the least truncated versions.) Each director will want to do his own cutting and editing.

4. Cutting and editing the text.

   Although the copyright laws protect the author's material,[14] the director who has paid the stipulated royalty fee need not hesitate to make minor cuts or changes so long as they do not violate the author's intent nor destroy the over-all effect of the play. He should not, however, attempt to rewrite the play or insert "gag lines" for local consumption. Legitimate cutting and editing of a text includes the following:

   a. Shortening or eliminating scenes that are too long, repetitious, or static. A good cut is one which makes a smooth and logical transition, bridging the omitted material within an

---

12. William Archer translation.
13. Translated by Professor Frank G. Nelson of California State University, Long Beach for a production at this university, and used by permission.
14. The Dramatists Play Service contract with a producing group, for example, stipulates that "The play must be presented substantially in its published form, as per the playbook furnished you."

actor's speech, blending to a later speech of the same actor or to a response by another actor. The director should trust his first impressions—if a scene seemed too long on first reading it, it may also seem so to the audience. When a beat seems to be played out or characters repeating themselves, it is time for a new beat to begin. A cut should *not* be made, however, if the material does any one of the following:

(1) Furthers the plot.

(2) Adds significantly to our understanding of a character.

(3) Contains notable language or humor.

(4) Provides motivation for a following speech.

b. Cutting or clarifying lines that are so obscure or archaic that the particular audience would not understand them. It seems legitimate, for example, in staging *The Importance of Being Earnest* in an American school to change Lady Bracknell's exclamation:

> "Untruthful! My nephew Algernon? Impossible. He is an Oxonian."

to

> "Untruthful! My nephew Algernon? Impossible. He is an Oxford man."

Shakespeare, especially in the comedies, presents a special problem because of his fondness for the Elizabethan "conceit" or play on words, the meanings of which are often lost on a modern audience. Unless a meaning can be suggested by gesture or pantomime, it often is better to cut the obscure passage. It would be presumptuous to attempt to rewrite Shakespeare. (The director may, however, consult the Variorum edition and choose from the various folios, quartos, and standard editions, the word that seems most meaningful.)

c. Eliminating minor characters or combining several into one. In *Romeo and Juliet,* for example, a director short of male actors can combine the lines assigned to Officer in Act I, Scene 1, Citizen in Act III, Scene 1, and Chief Watchman in Act V, Scene 3. The first and second servants in Act IV, Scene 2, also can be combined with Peter and Gregory or Sampson.

d. Changing the gender of minor characters when appropriate, because of a shortage of either men or women from whom to cast. Merriman, the butler in *The Importance of Being Earnest,* could, for example, become a maid.

e. Reducing the number of scene changes, where it can be

done without weakening the impact of the play. The third act of *The Importance of Being Earnest,* for example, could be played in the garden setting of the second act; a few lines would have to be modified, but for a group with limited stagecraft facilities the compromise might be worth making.

f. Placing of intermissions in multi-scene plays where they can be of the most help in scene-shifting, remembering, however, that intermissions should follow scenes of strong suspense or climax.

g. Adding speeches or even scenes from another translation (if a foreign play) or from the full text (if using an acting edition). A translation is often far from literal, and would more accurately be called an adaptation. The director may discover desirable values in speeches which a translator omitted. Even an acting edition of a recent American play may omit speeches which the director might see a value in restoring. The acting edition of *Summer and Smoke,* for example, omits the prologue with the children and the effective father-son dialogue (used as an illustration in Chapter 5) which are to be found in Williams' full published text.

h. Clarifying the author's intent where confusion might occur. For example, the prologue to *The Dairy of Anne Frank* ends with Mr. Frank's reading Anne's diary to Miep. The epilogue begins with a return to this scene, but Mr. Kraler has joined the others. In order to help the audience identify the flashback framework, it might be desirable to bring Mr. Kraler into the prologue just before the reading of the diary begins, so that the prologue ends on the same visual picture with which the epilogue begins.

i. Checking misprints, typographical errors, and even incorrect assignment of speeches which sometimes occur in acting editions.

j. Modifying the dialogue where necessary to fit the action and physical blocking. Incidental references to the ghost standing near the piano in *Blithe Spirit* may be changed, if the set is too small to accommodate a piano, to a mantelpiece or buffet. Many times a director will have occasion to change lines such as "Don't just sit there" to "Don't just stand there."

5. The following are examples of judicious cuttings which eliminate nothing essential in plot, characterization, language, or motivation, and which make smooth transitions:

a. *Romeo and Juliet,* II, 3.

Friar Laurence

Holy Saint Francis, what a change is here!
Is Rosaline that thou didst love so dear
So soon forsaken? Young men's love then lies
Not truly in their hearts, but in their eyes.
Jesu Maria, what a deal of brine
Hath washed thy sallow cheeks for Rosaline!
How much salt water thrown away in waste
To season love, that of it doth not taste!
The sun not yet thy sighs from heaven clears,
Thy old groans yet ring in mine ancient ears,
Lo here upon thy cheek the stain doth sit
Of an old tear that is not washed off yet.
If e'er thou wast thyself, and these woes thine,
Thou and these woes were all for Rosaline.
And art thou changed? Pronounce this sentence then,
Women may fall, when there's no strength in men.[15]

b. *Summer and Smoke,* by Tennessee Williams, Part II, Scene 5. Although the following lines undoubtedly were written to show Alma's beat of "straining to make conversation" to cover up her embarrassment and excitement at seeing John again, a director might feel that the lines are not sufficiently interesting or revealing to warrant delaying the tempo of the scene and could cut as follows:

ALMA: No greetings? No greetings at all?
JOHN: Hello, Miss Alma.
ALMA: Those new glass cases — ah! Such glacial brilliance!
JOHN: New equipment.
ALMA: Everything new but the chart.
JOHN: The human anatomy's always the same old thing.
ALMA: And such a tiresome one! I've been plagued with sore throats.
JOHN: Everyone has here lately. These Southern homes are all improperly heated. Open grates aren't enough.
ALMA: They burn the front of you while your back is freezing.
JOHN: Then you go into another room and get chilled off.
ALMA: Yes—yes—chilled to the bone.
JOHN: But it never gets quite cold enough to convince the damn fools that a furnace is necessary, so they go on building without them.

---

15. In cutting Shakespearean poetry, the director should avoid cutting half of a rhymed couplet or words necessary to complete a line of iambic pentameter.

ALMA: Such a strange afternoon.
JOHN: Is it? I haven't been out.
ALMA: The Gulf wind is blowing big, white—what do they
call them? Cumulus?—clouds over! It seemed deter-
mined to take the plume off my hat—like that fox
terrier we had once named Jacob, snatched the plume
off a hat and dashed around and around the back
yard with it like a trophy.
JOHN: I remember Jacob. What happened to him?
ALMA: Oh, Jacob. Jacob was such a mischievous thief. We
had to send him out to some friends in the country.
Yes, he ended his days as—a country squire! The tales
of his exploits—
JOHN: Sit down, Miss Alma.
ALMA: If I'm disturbing you—?
JOHN: No.

III. Finding a plan by which to project this meaning to the audience.

When the director has crystallized for himself what the play means
both in general terms and in scene-by-scene analysis, he is ready to
think of ways to translate this analysis into theatrical impressions that
will specifically articulate his concept to his audience. He should
have completed all of the steps detailed in determining what the
play means *before* his first production conference with his designer.
Sometimes the playwright helps the director in this respect; at other
times the director must do the creative work of finding a plan of
execution. Tennessee Williams has anticipated the director's problem
and visualized *The Glass Menagerie* in production:

> The play is memory. Being a memory play, it is dimly
> lighted, it is sentimental, it is not realistic. In memory
> everything seems to happen to music. That explains the
> fiddle in the wings.

A. Selecting a *style* for the production.

The director's first problem in projecting the meaning of the play
is to find a style which will best express his concept and which
can be reflected in acting, scenery, properties, costumes, and
make-up.
Style can be defined as an expression of (1) the author's personal
way of translating life to the stage, and (2) the theatrical conventions in use during the historical period in which he wrote. If
"holding the mirror up to nature" can be considered to be the
aim of all dramatic art, who holds the mirror, how he holds it,

where he focuses it, and the kind of mirror he holds can be thought of as factors which determine style. Because of changing theatrical conventions, what seemed real in one century may seem artificial in another.

The director may select theatrical conventions of a specific historical period allowing these to dictate in part his style approach. He may superimpose a personal or a contemporary style upon the period style in which case he must unify at least two stylistic approaches. Or he may merely adhere to a contemporary style treatment. Whatever his decision, in most cases he should strive for consistency in style.

The extent to which the playwright attempts to photograph or mirror real life gives a basis for a discussion of some of the various historical and contemporary styles.[16]

1. Presentational styles.

    Until the advent of modern realism, actors played directly to the audience; conventions such as asides, soliloquies, and enlarged movement were freely used even though they are not normally part of everyday life, and poetic language was used to heighten emotion beyond the powers of normal speech. The play was "presented" directly to the audience rather than disguised as an illusion of life itself.

    a. *Classic Greek drama.*
        Action was centered largely in a circular dancing area with the audience sitting on three sides. Emotions needed to be larger than life size, and they were often reinforced by music and choral responses.

    b. *Oriental drama.* With no attempt at realism, the audience is well aware that it is watching a symbolic distillation of life rather than a picture of life itself.

    c. *Medieval theatre.* Wagons or simultaneous platforms furnished a minimum of background while the actors often played to and among the audience.

    d. *Shakespearean theatre.* The large forestage made possible intimate contact with the audience, with a number of other acting areas where the audience's attention could shift without pause. The background was largely conventional, with the actual locale described in the poet's words.

16. For a fuller treatment of styles, see: H. D. Albright, William P. Halstead, and Lee Mitchell, *Principles of Theatre Art* (Boston: Houghton Mifflin Company, 1955), Chapters 13, 14, 15; Mordecai Gorelik, *New Theatres for Old* (Samuel French, Inc., 1940); John Gassner, *Producing the Play* (New York: The Dryden Press, 1953), Chapters 3, 4, 5; Frank McMullan, *The Director's Handbook* (The Shoe String Press, Inc., 1964), Part V.

THE TROJAN WOMEN—CLASSIC GREEK DRAMA California State University, Long Beach. Directed by David MacArthur. Designed by Marguerite Seethaler (Sets and Costumes).

BENTEN THE THIEF (KABUKI)—ORIENTAL DRAMA California State University, Long Beach. Directed by Onoe Kuroemon II. Designed by Ralph W. Duckwall (Sets), Herbert L. Camburn and Gail Crellin (Costumes) and T. William Smith (Makeup and Wigs).

ANDROCLES AND THE LION–MEDIEVAL WAGON STAGING California State University, Long Beach. Directed by Kenneth Rugg. Designed by Ralph W. Duckwall (Sets) and Richard Levering (Costumes).

MERRY WIVES OF WINDSOR–SHAKESPEAREAN PRODUCTION California State University, Long Beach. Directed by David MacArthur. Designed by Ralph W. Duckwall (Sets) and Herbert L. Camburn (Costumes).

e. *Molière, Restoration, and eighteenth century drama.* Although painted backgrounds were used, the actors tended to play on the forestage, retaining a frank sense of confiding their emotions and wit to the audience.

THE AFFECTED YOUNG LADIES—MOLIERE   California State University, Long Beach. Directed by W. David Sievers. Designed by Milton Howarth (Sets) and Inge Schmidt (Costumes).

2. Representational or illusionistic styles.

   With the advent of the scientific attitude in the nineteenth century together with advances in lighting and stagecraft, the theatre began to strive for an illusion of real life on the stage. The proscenium arch was thought of as a picture frame or "fourth wall," behind which all action became stage-centered rather than audience-centered.

   a. *Realism.* An attempt to convey the illusion of reality through careful attention to detail, the use of everyday language, and the elimination of asides, soliloquies, and direct contact between actor and audience. The actors presume not to know the audience is present, and the audience presumes to be watching real life. (Ibsen, Chekhov, Hellman, Stanislavski in acting.)

PICNIC—REALISM California State University, Long Beach. Directed by Stanley Kahan. Designed by Ralph W. Duckwall.

   b. *Naturalism.* An extreme form of realism which attempts to give a complete photograph of reality—a "slice of life"—without eliminating or selecting details or structuring the material into a complex plot. (Zola, Gorki's *The Lower Depths*, Hauptmann's *The Weavers.*)

DEAD END—NATURALISM Broadway Production. Directed by Sidney Kingsley. Designed by Norman Bel Geddes.

THE TRIAL OF THE CATONSVILLE NINE—SELECTIVE REALISM
California State University, Long Beach. Directed by Harry E. Stiver. Designed by
Bernard Skalka (Sets) and Buckley C. Jeppson (Costumes).

c. *Selective or suggestive realism.* A style which selects realistic details as needed without cluttering the picture with a complete depiction of reality. Part of a room, a window, or fragment of a wall may be sufficient, hence full walls and ceilings can be eliminated. A gothic arch may suggest a whole cathedral. (*Billy Budd, Darkness at Noon, No Time for Sergeants, The Trial of the Catonsville Nine.*)

LOOK HOMEWARD, ANGEL—SUGGESTIVE REALISM   California State
University, Long Beach. Directed by W. David Sievers. Designed by Milton Howarth
(Sets) and Herbert L. Camburn (Costumes).

3. Revolts against representationalism.

   The twentieth century has seen many efforts to free the theatre from the limitations of realism and restore greater artistic freedom to the playwright and director. Although our theatre today remains basically realistic, the trend away from realism is still going on, and realistic elements are often juxtaposed with nonillusionistic styles.

   a. *Symbolism.* The use of symbol(s) to convey meaning, mood, or emotion. Gordon Craig and Adolphe Appia furthered this "new stagecraft" movement by attempting to synthesize within this style all of the arts in the theatre, including painting, music, lighting, and dance. (Maeterlinck, Yeats, Andreyev, Lorca.)

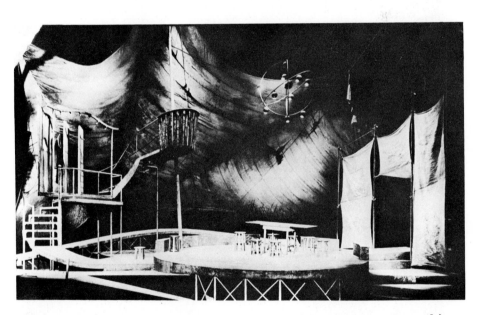

J. B.—SYMBOLISM Broadway Production. Directed by Elia Kazan. Designed by Boris Aronson.

   b. *Neo-Romanticism.* A return to the poetic form in costume drama which permits a heightening of effect and language not possible in realism. (Rostand, Maxwell Anderson, Christopher Fry.)

   c. *Expressionism.* Purposeful distortion of reality usually as seen by the playwright or a leading character to express inner meaning or the impact of twentieth century mechanization upon the individual. (*The Adding Machine, The Great God Brown, Beggar on Horseback, The Visit.*)

THE LADY'S NOT FOR BURNING—NEO-ROMANTICISM California State University, Long Beach. Directed by Clayton Garrison. Designed by Lillian Garrison and John H. Green.

THE VISIT—EXPRESSIONISM California State University, Long Beach. Directed by Harry E. Stiver. Designed by Ralph W. Duckwall (Sets), Herbert L. Camburn (Costumes), John H. Green (Lights) and T. William Smith (Makeup).

d. *Constructivism.* Elimination of external surfaces in order to penetrate to the skeletal construction, showing ramps, levels, steps, and joists. All elements of theatre are functional and represent aesthetic complexities of a machine. (Primarily Meyerhold and his influence on contemporary theatre.)

MARAT/SADE—CONSTRUCTIVISM California State University, Long Beach. Directed by Kenneth Lyman. Designed by Warren Travis (Sets), and Agnes Rodgers (Costumes).

e. *Subjective realism.* The influence of Freudian psychology in attempting to express man's inner and even unconscious life through dream symbols, psychological distortion, and the "free association" of ideas. (*Death of a Salesman, Dream Girl, The Glass Menagerie.*)

f. *Theatricalism.* Calling the audience's attention frankly to the fact that they are in a theatre rather than watching a slice of life. Deliberate breaking of the "fourth wall," often with the use of imaginary properties, or scenery shifted in view of the audience. (*Our Town, The Skin of Our Teeth,* numerous musical comedies.)

g. *Formalism.* A return to permanent architectural settings based on classic or abstract forms. (Jacques Copeau, "Globe Theatre" staging of Shakespeare, the use of unit sets, and "space-staging.")

PHILADELPHIA, HERE I COME—SUBJECTIVE REALISM California State University, Long Beach. Directed by Edward A. Wright. Designed by Ralph W. Duckwall (Sets), Warren Travis (Costumes) and John H. Green (Lights).

NOAH—THEATRICALISM Broadway Production. Directed by Jerome Mayer. Designed by Cleon Throckmorton, Animals and Masks by Remo Bufano.

THE CRUCIBLE—FORMALISM Cleveland Playhouse. Directed by Frederic McConnell. Designed by William A. McCreary.

h. *Epic theatre*. The "learning-theatre," which rejects realism, empathy, and illusion in favor of teaching a sociopolitical thesis through the use of narration, projection, slogans, songs, and direct contact with the audience. (Primarily Brecht and Piscator and their influence on twentieth-century theatre.)

THE PRIVATE LIFE OF THE MASTER RACE—EPIC THEATRE Hunter College. Directed by Bernard Dukore. Designed by Robert Guerra.

i. <u>*Absurdism.*</u> The works of such writers as Genet, Ionesco, Beckett, and in some cases Albee, which on first glance have no rational meaning have been referred to by Martin Esslin as "the theatre of the absurd." Elements of surrealism and symbolism are utilized along with absurdity and irrationality in order to suggest the meaninglessness of life and the difficulty of human communication. (*Waiting for Godot, Rhinoceros, Tango.*)

BIEDERMANN AND THE FIREBUGS—ABSURDIST DRAMA Illinois State University. Directed by Harry E. Stiver. Designed by Bernard Skalka.

j. <u>*Current styles.*</u> Needless to say our contemporary eclectic theatre has produced and is producing numerous styles in its search for audience communication and/or participation. Multi-media and mixed media presentations, theatre of cruelty, transformation dramas, happenings, environmental theatre, and other experimental patterns are each presenting a challenge to the director to become aware of and use an individualized approach to the particular style treatment required. (Josef Svoboda, Artaud, Megan Terry, Kaprow.)

B. Planning for the most effective use of the theatrical elements.

The director's concept and his selected stylistic approach must be related to each of the elements of the theatre in planning the production. As Gordon Craig has advocated, the director must unify all of the elements of the theatre in order to create an inte-

JULIUS CAESAR–MIXED MEDIA California State University, Long Beach. Directed by Stanley Kahan. Designed by Ralph W. Duckwall (Sets and Lights) and Warren Travis (Costumes).

grated impact upon the audience. The elements of the theatre through which the director projects the play to the audience are:

1. Actors
2. Scenery
3. Lighting
4. Properties
5. Costumes
6. Make-up
7. Music
8. Sound
9. Dance

1. Actors.

 a. Preparation for casting.

   As the director analyzes the characters, their spines, actions, and beats, he will begin to form specific impressions of the kind of people his playwright has created. Before try-outs he will need to prepare brief paragraphs describing each character. (Refer to Chapters 8 on Characterization and 10 for casting.) It is often helpful for the director to maintain a picture file for make-up studies and as an aid in casting. (Use only candid photographs of real people, not sketches or posed pictures of models or actors.) It would help crystallize the director's images of the characters to find a photograph that suggests each person in the play.

b. After casting.
What the director does with his cast after he has selected it is of course the essence of play direction, and is dealt with in all of the succeeding chapters.

2. Scenery.

The director should rely heavily upon his scene designer to find the visual form that will best express the interpretation of the play. He should guard against trying to design the sets for him. The director can, however, save the designer many hours of wasted time and later frustration if at the very beginning of the production conferences the director supplies the unifying statement of interpretation and spark that will ignite the imaginations of scene and costume designers as well as choreographer and composer, if involved. The director should therefore be clear in his own mind on the following points and be prepared to discuss them at the first production conference.[17]

a. The kind of background or environment which will make the action of the play seem logical and best convey the interpretation of the play to the audience.
b. The style of production that will best express the director's concept for a contemporary audience.
c. The general mood or atmosphere which the scenery should convey.
d. Simplifications in setting which might be practical without losing the over-all impression desired.
e. Shifting problems, if any.
The director should be aware of the time that might be necessary for each shift. It is detrimental to the tempo and over-all effect of the play to lower the curtain for more than thirty seconds to shift scenery. The placement of one or two ten-minute intermissions may solve the problem, but they cannot always be placed primarily to satisfy shifting requirements; they must occur only after strong climaxes in the story. Some ways which have been found effective in dealing with the multi-set play include:

17. This discussion of scenic problems relates primarily to the proscenium stage. Other possible solutions to visual design are discussed in Chapter 6.

(1) Permanent settings.
   (a) Multiple sets, with several areas simultaneously on stage and shifting accomplished by light.
   (b) Utilizing side areas outside the proscenium arch for short scenes if space is available.
   (c) Unit sets. Changes are accomplished by opening and closing arches, windows and doors by drapes, plugs, etc.

(2) Flying the sets.
   This method requires a counterweight system and sufficient height above the proscenium arch so that the scenery can be raised out of sight. A small three-fold box set can be flown in and then opened up. If there is much furniture to shift, however, an act intermission may be required.

(3) Revolving stage.
   This method tends to be cumbersome and to require that masking pieces be brought in from the sides.

(4) Wagon stages.
   This is a very much-used method in which sets or parts of sets are wheeled into place on low platforms with casters, and all furniture and props are preset. It does, however, require off-stage storage space and may prove noisy in shifting.

(5) Projected scenery.
   This method offers exciting possibilities where literal realism is not required. Sufficient distance between projector and cyclorama is necessary (through which the actors cannot move) and a correction must be made for distortion, but designers are finding many ways to use projections effectively.

(6) Alternating between forestage and inner stage.
   A curtain (traveller or drop) divides the stage halfway upstage; scenes play on the forestage while the inner stage is being shifted. This is ideally suited for Shakespeare, and is frequently used for musicals.

(7) Black velour curtains.
   In front of an inconspicuous background minimal, suggestive scenic elements can be placed. If the light is kept off the curtains, the audience will be able to accept them as walls. Box sets can even be suggested in front of black velours, using such simple elements as a low wainscoting, door frames, etc.

(8) Shifting in view of the audience as part of the action. This method can be used with style and ingenuity for the enjoyment of the audience. Minor characters can move furniture, or actors can shift their own sets, as was done in the Lunts' production of *The Visit*.

(9) Space staging.

When a stage is large enough and the light can be carefully controlled, actors can be placed on a virtually bare stage except for platforms and steps and made to stand out three dimensionally against what seems to be an infinitely deep and black background. A shifting pattern of light and shadow can suggest a change of scene. Norman Bel Geddes has utilized space-staging brilliantly in his designs for *Hamlet*, *Lazarus Laughed*, and *The Divine Comedy*.

(10) Running the flats.

As a final alternative when none of the foregoing plans is feasible, the scenery (flats) can be unlashed, folded in sections, and carried offstage. The props and furniture are carried off after the scenery, then the new props and furniture are carried on, and the new flats then lashed into place. This method is slow and usually requires an intermission. However, ingenious design can sometimes work wonders in limited space, using double-faced flats which fold in or out to reveal a second set.

f. The ground plan.

The ground plan should not be copied from a previous production but should be a creative development of the con-concept and style arrived at for each given production. Both the director and the designer are vitally concerned with the ground plan of the set—the designer because it relates to balance, spatial relationships, and visual impact; the director because it dictates some of the blocking, movement, and the playing of the scenes. Before his first production conference with the designer, the director should know his play well enough so that he can discuss these problems intelligently with the designer:

(1) The principal acting areas called for by his planned action for the play.

(2) The placement of important furniture in the acting areas to enable the director to develop the action units in movement and blocking he desires.

(3) The possibility of grouping several pieces of furniture

COMMON MISTAKES IN ARRANGING GROUND PLANS

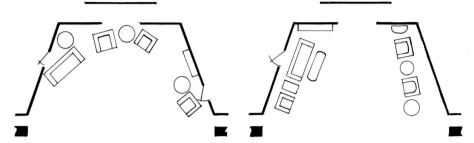

Do not block entrances nor weaken impact of characters' appearance by placement of furniture in front of doors.

Do not force actors to upstage one another by placing furniture at a sharp angle against the side walls.

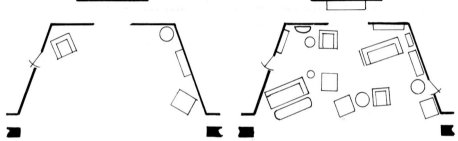

Do not create a barren effect by too little furniture, wasted space, or forcing the actors to play in a vacuum.

Do not inhibit the actors by cluttering the set with too much furniture.

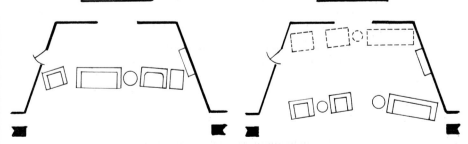

Do not force the actors to remain center stage by crowding furniture to center in a straight line.

Do not force the actors too far upstage or downstage by crowding furniture to either area.

as a unit in one area of the stage in order to permit people to talk together, as required by the particular scenes of the play.

(4) The number of actors who have to work together and the physical action required in restricted spaces, on ramps and platforms.

(5) The maximum utilization of the existing space without crowding, and (in the case of quick shifts) the minimum number of set pieces and furniture that have to be shifted.

(6) The best location for doors and windows if they figure prominently in the action.

   (a) There should be an unrestricted view of the door if entrances and exits are important.

   (b) Entrances are most effective through a door on the back wall, exits through a door downstage on the side walls.

   (c) Doors normally swing onstage if they lead to the outside and offstage if they lead to another room. On side walls they are hinged upstage.

   (d) Windows are most effective on the side walls if characters have to react to what is seen through them. A window on the back wall is most effective if the audience must see people through it.

(7) The offstage locations and where each door leads.

(8) The sight lines in the theatre for which the production is planned, so as not to locate significant furniture, doors or acting areas where they will not be seen from all seats (i.e., in the shaded areas on the following drawings):

After these items are discussed by director and designer, the designer should bring to the next production conference tentative sketches and ground plans. After further discussion and possible modification, the ground plan should be agreed upon at least ten days to two weeks prior to the first rehearsal in order to give the director time for his prerehearsal blocking.

3. Lighting.

The lighting of the set and the actors is usually conceived as an integral part of the scene design. It is sufficient at this stage of the director's study simply to consider:

a. Is the lighting to be predominantly brilliant or low-key?

b. Is the lighting to be predominantly warm or cool?

c. Will motivated light sources be necessary, i.e., lamps, chandeliers, or fixtures?

Stage Terminology[18]

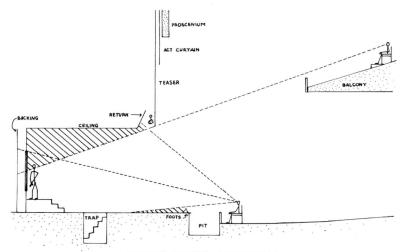

SIGHT LINES—VERTICAL

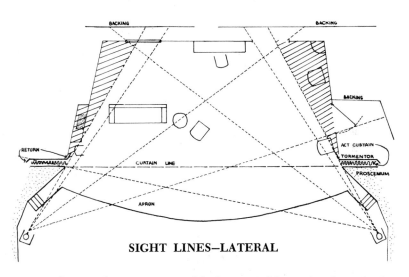

SIGHT LINES—LATERAL

    d. Are there any special lighting problems (such as the beautiful dawn that is referred to in *A Moon for the Misbegotten,* or the need for special flexibility in controlling light and dark areas in "space-staging" or simultaneous settings).

    e. Will the hats (if planned by the costume designer) present problems in placing lighting instruments so as to get light onto actors' faces?

[18]Students unfamiliar with stage terminology are referred to Bowman, Walter Parker and Robert Hamilton Ball, *Theatre Language; A Dictionary of Terms in English of The Drama and State from Medieval to Modern Times.* New York: Theatre Arts Books, 1961.

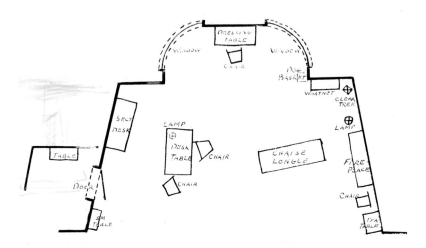

THE BARRETTS OF WIMPOLE STREET Conventional Ground Plan (See photograph of this set on page 138.)

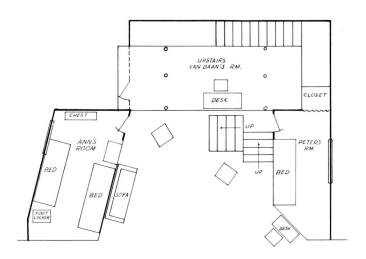

THE DIARY OF ANNE FRANK Conventional Ground Plan (See photograph of this set on page 106.)

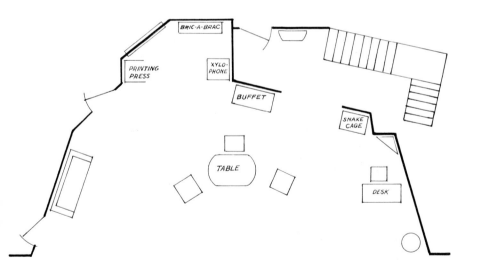

YOU CAN'T TAKE IT WITH YOU Conventional ground plan and setting. California State University, Long Beach. Directed by W. David Sievers. Designed by John H. Green.

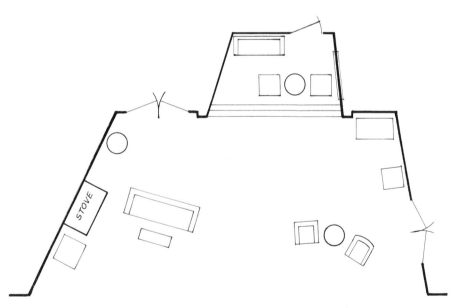

HEDDA GABLER Conventional ground plan and setting. California State University, Long Beach. Directed by W. David Sievers. Designed by Milton Howarth (Sets) and Herbert L. Camburn (Costumes).

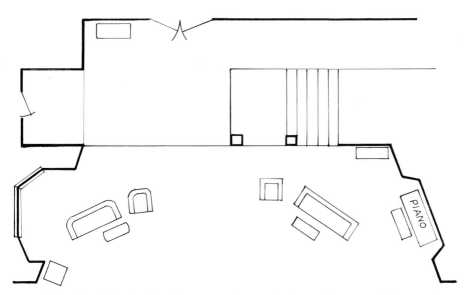

THE LITTLE FOXES Conventional ground plan and setting. California State University, Long Beach. Directed by Stanley Kahan. Designed by Milton Howarth (Sets) and Herbert L. Camburn (Costumes).

4. Properties.

   Dressing the stage is, like lighting, a function of design; the use of the furniture, however, needs to be considered by the director in his interpretation. Where a number of authentic properties are required, as for example in *Men in White, Detective Story, Stalag 17* or *You Can't Take It With You,* the director's research will not only reveal the kind of properties needed but will often suggest business for the actors using them. The director should be prepared to discuss with the head of the property crew:

   a. The kinds of properties needed.
   b. Whether "practical" or not (i.e., made to operate in view of the audience).
   c. The action involving them.
   d. Research sources for information on style and type of props.
   e. The placement of the props on stage or by whom carried on.

5. Costumes.

   Before the costumer can begin his research into the period and the actual creation of designs, he should be clear as to the following points, which the director should be prepared to discuss with him (preferably at the first production conference):

   a. How can the costumes help convey the meaning of the play to the audience?
   Costuming *Romeo and Juliet,* for example, in the hot colors and bold contrasts of fourteenth century Italy will make its impetuous love story more believable than if it were costumed in Elizabethan high fashion. Molière's *Affected Young Ladies* needs to be costumed in the height of absurd affectation in order to point Molière's satire. Anouilh's *Antigone,* originally played in tuxedos and evening gowns, can be made more timely by costuming Creon and the guards in the military uniforms of an Iron Curtain nation.

   b. In what period should the play be costumed?
   Hamlet has been costumed in every period from medieval Danish to World War II G. I. Often a 50 or 100 year variation in the period of the costumes will not disturb the audience and may add to the effect of the production. To modernize an older play may save on costume budget but lose some of its charm or meaning. *The Importance of Being Earnest,* for example, depends upon being costumed in a frothy and artificial elegance; modern young ladies

are hardly dependent upon Mama's permission to speak to a young man. *Hedda Gabler,* on the other hand, could be played in modern dress, as the unfulfilled woman Ibsen depicted has not disappeared from our culture.

c. How can the style and general effect of the costumes be integrated with the style, color, and mood of the settings? Should the costumes be literal, enlarged from realism, or fanciful?

d. How can each costume best reflect the character who wears it? In *Summer and Smoke,* for example, Miss Alma's dresses can aid in her characterization by being restrictive and prim. Juliet's costumes, however, need to permit free, impulsive, girlish movement.

e. What problems of quick change are there?

The Diary of Anne Frank offers a record number of quick change problems, requiring careful advance planning concerning which garments can be underdressed and which added; the set designer, too, should be aware that each off-stage area where characters exit needs to be accessible to the wardrobe crew. *Othello* illustrates another quick change problem: Othello's first appearance is in the informal garb of a honeymoon night. He exits and must reappear four lines later formally gowned to appear before the Duke in the Senate.

f. How large a budget is available for costume?

This will in many cases govern the number of extras and bit parts that can be included as well as the number of costume changes for the principals.

6. Make-up.

Make-up is as integrally related to costuming as lighting is to scene design. The director's original conception of the characters should include their facial characteristics and the general impression to be conveyed. Where quick changes of make-up are required, this should be taken into consideration in the placement of intermissions. There can be little specific planning for make-up until the play is cast and the facial features of the actors studied, with the following exceptions:

a. Wigs, where needed, should be considered early in the planning because of their high cost.

b. Haircuts of the cast should be checked, and where necessary, actors should be asked not to get haircuts until the performances are over.

c. When forced to cast young players in older parts, the director should be aware of which types of facial structures take character make-up best, and what can be accomplished with beards and mustaches.

7. Music.

The decision to use music and to what extent grows out of the director's interpretation of the play, coupled with the practical problem of covering scene shifts. The functions which music may serve include:

a. To provide emotional reinforcement for the actors.
b. To set the period and mood.
c. To bridge from scene to scene.
d. To contribute to tension and suspense.
e. To underscore or punctuate significant moments or climaxes.
f. To lead the audience from realism toward fantasy or any other style change.
g. To fill in the time needed for scene shifts and to cover the noise of shifting.
h. To take the place of the curtain in non-proscenium staging.
i. To provide an overture.

While the actual selection of music can be done later, the director should be conscious early in the planning of the potential contribution music could make to the production.

8. Sound effects.

The extent to which the director wishes to employ realistic sound is related to his conception of style. While some realistic plays such as *The Diary of Anne Frank* require detailed sound plots of recorded effects, others such as *Our Town* are better off with a rather obvious vocal imitation (of the rooster crowing, for example) than an authentic recording. An awkwardly managed sound effect or a late sound cue, however, destroy the mood of a tense scene—for example, the bellowing of cows in the last scene of *The Crucible*. The director should be aware of sound problems early enough to order or prepare special effects if necessary.

9. Dance.

Plays in the realistic style rarely offer opportunity for dance movement, but many plays which transcend realism offer possibilities for integrating dance within the drama. Among them are *Dark of the Moon, Dream Girl, Peer Gynt, Beggar on Horseback*, and *Happy Birthday*. As one of the theatre's most ancient forms of emotional expression, dance should be used as an enrichment and a means of heightening dramatic effect wherever the style of the play permits. Working closely with a choreographer, the director will want to consider:

   a. Ways in which rhythmic movement or movement beyond realism can enrich the production.
   b. Space requirements for movement in relation to the ground plan.
   c. Problems of casting dancers.
   d. Style and quality of movement.
   e. Selection of appropriate music for dance.
   f. Costumes that permit freedom for dance movement.

10. Other reflections of the director's interpretation of the play.

   As the director arrives at a unified interpretation of the play and crystallizes the "production idea" with his technical staff, he should also try to find an integrated style and treatment of:

   a. Posters and mailing pieces, coordinated with the design of the production.
   b. Promotion and publicity stories, based on those elements in the director's interpretation which best lend themselves to arousing interest in the production.
   c. Program design and program notes if desired.
   d. Lobby displays, growing out of research in the period, the playwright, settings, or costumes.

IV. Recording the interpretation in the director's book.

The director's book is the tangible result of all the foregoing study and research. It differs from the stage manager's prompt book in that the former is the projected or anticipated production and the latter the actual record of what is evolved in rehearsal.

Directors vary as to the extensiveness of their directors' books. Max Reinhardt's famous *regiebuch* was so detailed that it could be turned over to an assistant to conduct rehearsals. Mental notes may be sufficient for experienced directors or for simple productions. For the less experienced director, however, a carefully prepared book is not only an assurance that no step has been omitted from his interpretative study, but also a ready source of reference in rehearsal. The director should remember that clarity and detail in recording his pre-production planning will significantly increase his directorial efficiency and considerably reduce the amount of rehearsal time required. The book should not be thought of as a finished product to which the actors must conform however, but only as a tentative basis for conducting rehearsals, subject always to the exciting variations that grow out of a creative rehearsal.

A. Items that should be included in the director's book:

1. Critical commentary on the play.
2. Background material and research.
3. The type or form of the play.
4. A statement of the director's concept of the play.
5. A statement on the style of the production.
6. The basic action of the play and division of the text into actions and beats.
7. The relationship of each character to the basic action.
8. Analysis of characters. (See Chapter 8.)
9. The text itself, cut and edited.

   a. When acting editions are used, each page can be pasted onto a sheet of three-hole notebook paper with a center panel cut out to permit reading both sides of the page, or special pre-cut paper of this type is available.
   b. When working from manuscripts, extra wide margins should be left by the typist.

10. Notations on major and minor climaxes as they occur in the text. (See Chapter 9.)
11. Notations on tempo in the text. (See Chapter 9.)
12. If a multi-scene play, arrangement of scenes into acts and placement of intermissions. (See breakdown of *Othello* on page 90.)
13. A ground plan of the sets, to scale and one or two ground plans, one above the other, on a blank page opposite each page of the script on which to record and trace all movements, groupings, and positions of the characters. (See Chapters 4, 5, and 6 for this blocking preparation.)
14. Blocking of the scenes. (See Chapters 4, 5, and 6.)
15. Business and interpretative notations in the text. (See Chapters 5 and 7.)
16. Notations on the use of theatrical elements within the text and summarized at the end—a separate page for props, costumes, music, and so forth.
17. Bibliography and list of source materials for future reference.

B. For sample pages of a prepared script in a director's book for *Othello*, see the following: (Conventional symbols used in marking a director's book include X for Cross, Ent. for Enter, Ex. for Exit, CC for Counter Cross, a capital letter initial for each character and the terminology of the stage as given on pages 97, 98. If two ground plans are used opposite each page of the script, the one on the upper half should correspond roughly to the upper half of the page of dialogue, the one on the lower half to the lower half. The change of position made by each character is indicated by a number sequence and the numbers are also entered into the dialogue at exactly the place the movement is to occur.)

OTHELLO California State University, Long Beach. Directed by W. David Sievers. Designed by Milton Howarth (Sets), Herbert L. Camburn (Costumes) and John H. Green (Lights).

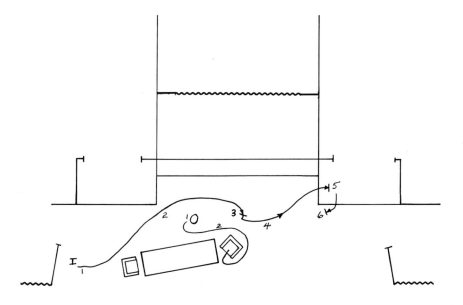

Exit DESDEMONA and EMILIA

It is, at this point, that the conflicting elements of the play come into direct contact and the formation of the tragedy begins. There is no violent urging of facts. It is the skillful maneuvering disguised by honesty. Remember that Othello has not read the play. He foresees no future catastrophe. He thinks at this point that Iago, Cassio, and Desdemona are the finest people in the world. There is no doubt or suspicion in his mind. There is no quick suspicion of jealousy. He is not yet ready to grasp at petty facts and turn them into woeful abundance.

	OTH ①	Excellent wretch! Perdition catch my soul. But I do love thee! and when I love thee not,	(said with a sense of well being. He is
X to Ch L Table	②	Chaos is come again. (reads from scroll)	happy)
Above and R of tables	IAGO ①	My noble lord—(Pause before saying line)	
	OTH	What dost thou say, Iago? (Pause and then he says this casually)	
X to C	IAGO ②	Did Michael Cassio, when you wooed my lady, know of your love? ③	(This is the first planting of the seed and must be done
	OTH	He did, from first to last. Why dost thou ask? (No heavy pointing here)	with great care)
X UL	IAGO ④	But for a satisfaction of my *thought;* No further harm. ⑤	(It is casual but yet with a *slight* hint of implication)
	OTH	What of thy *thought,* Iago?	(Notice the words *think and thought* through here. He must start Othello to thinking)
	IAGO	I did not *think* he had been acquainted with her.	
	OTH	O Yes, and went between us very oft. (Lightly with a laugh)	
X a step to C	IAGO ⑥	*Indeed?* (slightly more implication, but no melodramatic typifying)	

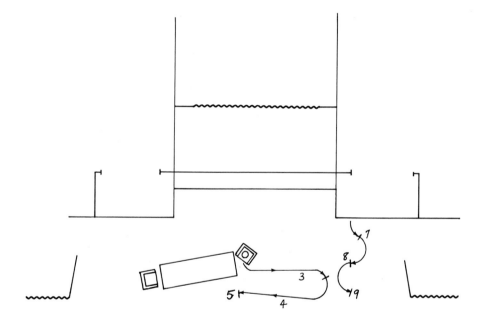

	OTH	Indeed? Ay, indeed. Discern'st thou aught in that? (Ordinary tone.) Is he not honest? (He is still reading)
Turns to L	IAGO ⑦	Honest, my lord? (He allies himself with Othello's elemental sense of honesty)
	OTH	Honest? ay, honest. (Othello's attention is as yet not arrested)
Turns to R	IAGO ⑧	My lord, for aught I know. (comes in quickly with this and gives it the tone of increduality)
	OTH	What dost thou think? (no sudden arrest here)
XDL	IAGO ⑨	Think, my lord? (slight pause in this line)
	OTH	Think, my lord! By heaven, he echoes me, As if there were some monster in his thought Too hideous to be shown. (Takes more notice. Pause Lifts eyes and puts mind to what is said. It is reflective Treats the last four lines with quiet humor)

Thou dost mean *something*, I heard thee say even now, thou lik'st not that, When Cassio left my wife.

Rises, XDL — What didst not like? ③
And when I told thee he was of my counsel
In my whole course of wooing, thou criedst
"Indeed?"
And didst contract and purse thy brow together
As if thou then hadst shut up in thy brain
Some horrible conceit.

X Back to Chair — If thou dost *love* me ④ Show me thy *thought*.
(Said with a smile as though the whole thing was ridiculous, continues to read from scroll) ⑤

OTHELLO

Production Scheme and Act Breakdown

SCENE # IN TEXT	OUR SCENE #	CONTENT OF SCENE	STAGE AREA	SCENIC REQUIREMENTS
ACT I Scene 1	ACT I Scene 1	Rousing of Brabantio	Full	A street in Venice, before Brabantio's house, with 2d story porch or window, under which Iago can hide.
Scene 2	Scene 2	Summoning of Othello	Shallow	Before the Sagittary Inn.
Scene 3	Scene 3	Hearing Brabantio vs. Othello	Full	Doge's Palace, Senate Chamber.
p. 23 lines 326-422.	Scene 4	Baiting Roderigo to follow to Cyprus.	Shallow	Merely close drape from previous scene.
ACT II Scene 1	Scene 5	Disembarkation at Cyprus	Full	Open place with high platform. Steps to descend from harbor. Things to sit on, bales, trunks.
Scene 2	cut			
Scene 3	Scene 6	Getting Cassio drunk & disgraced	Shallow	Servants carry in table and benches, wine barrel.
		1st INTERMISSION		
ACT III Scene 1	cut			
Scene 2	cut			
Scene 3	ACT II Scene 1	Planting 1st suspicion Handkerchief dropped.	Full	Garden or Patio within Cyprus castle. Place for eavesdropping.
lines 187-226 of III, Scene 4	Scene 2	Bianca-Cassio giving her the handkerchief.	Shallow	In front of drape.
ACT III, Scene 4	Scene 3	Demanding the handkerchief	Full	Same as II, 1, above, Garden or Patio of Castle.
ACT IV, Scene 1	go on, continuous	Epilepsy and Eavesdropping	Full	Same.
		2nd INTERMISSION		
ACT IV, Scene 2	ACT III Scene 1	Confronting Desdemona.	Full	Bedchamber, with heavy practical door, four-poster bed with curtains, drawn now.
lines 198-267 of IV, 2	Scene 2	Iago-Roderigo, needling Roderigo to kill Cassio	Shallow	Before drape.
ACT IV, Scene 3	Scene 3	Willow Song	Full	Same as III, 1. Bedchamber. Curtain around bed now open.
ACT V Scene 1	Scene 4	Killing of Roderigo & wounding of Cassio	Shallow	Street, needs "bulk" for Roderigo to hide behind.
Scene 2	Scene 5	Smothering of Desdemona, and resolution.	Full	Same as III, 1, Bedchamber.

V. Summary.

The director's interpretative study of a play, involving scholarly, critical, and creative aspects, is the period in which he becomes deeply absorbed with his play, and from which he evolves the ultimate unity of production. Interpretation involves the dualism of creative and technical aspects—internal and external, impression and expression— which will be reflected throughout the analysis of directing problems in succeeding chapters of this book.

The director's study is far from finished, however, when he enters rehearsal; new insights and values will or should emerge as he works with his cast. The processes involved in the director's interpretation are:

A. Determining what the play means. (Internal)

1. Discovering the theme or meaning of the play.
2. Studying what critics have written about the play and the author.
3. Re-creating the background of the play through research.
4. Analyzing the characters and their motives.
5. Dividing the play into actions and beats.
6. Crystallizing in words the particular emphasis, point of view, or approach which the director wishes to give the production for his particular audience.
7. Preparing the text for production.

B. Finding a plan by which to project this meaning to the audience. (External)

1. Selecting a style for the production.
2. Planning for the most effective use of the theatrical elements:

a. Actors	f. Make-up
b. Scenery	g. Music
c. Lighting	h. Sound
d. Properties	i. Dance
e. Costumes	j. Other reflections of the director's interpretation.

C. Recording the interpretation in the director's book.

1. Items that should be included in the director's book.
2. A sample page from a director's book.

Selective Bibliography
Directors' Interpretation of Plays

Bentley, Eric. *The House of Bernarda Alba,* in *In Search of Theatre.* New York: Alfred A. Knopf, Inc., 1953.

Brook, Peter. "A Realistic Approach to 'Eugene Onegin.' " *New York Times,* October 27, 1957.

Clurman, Harold. "Some Preliminary Notes for *The Member of the Wedding,*" in *Directors on Directing,* edited by Toby Cole and Helen Krich Chinoy. Indianapolis: The Bobbs-Merrill Co., 1963.

Gallaway, Marian. *The Playboy of the Western World,* in *The Director in the Theatre,* by H. Hunt. New York: The Macmillan Co., 1963.

Gielgud, John. "Staging *Love for Love,*" Theatre Arts, XXVII, 11, November, 1943.

Gorchakov, Nikolai M. *Stanislavski Directs.* New York: Funk and Wagnalls Co., 1954.

Kazan, Elia. Excerpts from a notebook on *Death of a Salesman,* in Kenneth Thorpe Rowe, *A Theatre in Your Head.* New York: Funk and Wagnalls, 1960.

————. "Notebook for *A Streetcar Named Desire,*" in *Directors on Directing,* edited by Toby Cole and Helen Krich Chinoy. Indianapolis: The Bobbs-Merrill Co., 1963.

Lewis, Robert. *My Heart's in the Highlands,* in John Gassner, *Producing the Play.* New York: The Dryden Press, 1953.

Miller, Arthur. "A Show Soliloquy," (Kazan's approach to *After the Fall*), *Show Magazine,* IV, 1, January, 1964.

Redgrave, Michael. *Uncle Harry,* in *Mask or Face,* by W. Archer. New York: Theatre Arts Books, 1958.

Robertson, Toby. "Directing *Edward II,*" *Tulane Drama Review,* VIII, 4, Summer, 1964.

Rossi, Alfred. *Minneapolis Rehearsals; Tyrone Guthrie Directs Hamlet.* Berkeley, Calif.: University of California Press, 1970.

Stanislavski, Constantin. *Stanislavski Produces Othello.* Trans. Helen Nowak. London: Geoffrey Bles, Ltd., 1948.

————. *The Seagull Produced by Stanislavski.* Trans. David Magarshack. New York: Theatre Arts, 1952.

General

Barry, Jackson G. "José Quintero: The Director as Image Maker," *Educational Theatre Journal,* XIV, 1, March, 1962.

Brook, Peter. *The Empty Space.* New York: Atheneum, 1969.

Canfield, Curtis. *The Craft of Play Directing.* New York: Holt, Rinehart & Winston, 1963.

Chekhov, Michael. *To the Director and Playwright.* New York: Harper, 1963.

Clark, Brian. *Group Theatre.* New York: Theatre Arts Books, 1971.

DeBanke, Cecile. *Shakespearean Stage Production: Then and Now.* New York: McGraw-Hill Book Company, 1953.

Gielgud, John. *Stage Directions.* New York: Random House, 1964.

Grotowski, Jerzy. *Towards a Poor Theatre.* New York: Simon and Shuster, Inc., 1968.

Guthrie, Tyrone. *A Life in the Theatre.* New York: McGraw-Hill Book Co., 1959.

Hawes, David S. "Preparation for Producing Moliére," *Educational Theatre Journal*, XIII, 2, May, 1961.

Hunt, Hugh. *The Director in the Theatre*. London: Routledge and Kegan Paul, 1954.

Joseph, Bertram. *Acting Shakespeare*. New York: Theatre Art Books, 1960.

Knight, G. Wilson. *Principles of Shakespearean Production*. Penquin Books, 1949.

McFarlane, James W. *Discussion of Henrik Ibsen*. Boston: D. C. Heath & Co., 1962.

McMullan, Frank A. *The Directional Image*. Hamden, Conn.: Shoe String Press, 1962.

———. *The Director's Handbook*. Hamden, Conn.: Shoe String Press, 1964.

Oxenford, Lyn. *Playing Period Plays*. London: J. Garnet Miller, Ltd., 1958.

Saint-Denis, Michel. *Theatre: The Rediscovery of Style*. New York: Theatre Arts Books, 1960.

Symons, James M. *Meyerhold's Theatre of the Grotesque*. Washington, D. C.: American Theatre Association, 1971.

Tairov, Alexander. *Notes of a Director*. Trans. William Kuhlke. Washington, D. C.: American Theatre Association, 1971.

Van Druten, John. "The Job of Directing." *Theatre Arts Anthology*. New York: Theatre Arts Books, 1950.

Watkins, Ronald. *On Producing Shakespeare*. New York: W. W. Norton and Co., 1951.

Webster, Margaret. *Shakespeare Without Tears*. New York: McGraw-Hill Book Co., 1942. Premier Paperback, 1957.

THE PRINCE AND THE PIRATES California State University, Long Beach.
Directed by Kenneth W. Rugg. Designed by Herbert L. Camburn.

4 Picturization

I. Introduction.

When the director has completed his interpretative study of the play, made up his director's book, and received a tentative ground plan from the scene designer (or made one himself if he is working without a designer), he is ready to begin his "blocking" of the play. Blocking can be defined as the physical arrangement of the actors on stage and their movement from place to place. The two aspects of blocking are (1) the advance blocking which the director does on paper prior to going into rehearsal, often with a scale ground plan or model and toy soldiers, golf tees, chessmen, stickpins, or pipe cleaners bent to represent the actors so that all positions can be plotted and recorded in the director's book, and (2) blocking rehearsals, in which the director tests out his preplanned blocking with the actors; the latter inevitably involves modifying the original conceptions, adjusting, changing, incorporating creative ideas advanced by the cast, and dealing with problems that had not been foreseen on paper. Nevertheless, even the most experienced directors find that preplanning of the blocking is an essential part of their "homework" in order to solve complex problems and save time in rehearsal. What most beginning directors fail to realize is that the blocking provides the basic visual structure for the articulation of their interpretation of the script. If it does not make a proper and unique creative statement in terms of

advanced Blocking prior to rehearsal

test preplanned blocking

95

meaning and style at each given moment, the audience will be visually confused.

A. Functions of Blocking:

1. To compose effective stage pictures,

(handwritten left margin: 1) To compose effective picture. 2) Visability. 3) to move from one picture to another)

Picturization can be defined as the imposition of visual pattern upon random life, the arrangement of the formless into a form that is meaningful and aesthetically satisfying. Even if a cast of outstanding stars were assembled, a director would still be necessary because:

   a. The actors cannot see themselves as they appear from the audience.

   b. It is not practical for each actor to arrange his own groupings with others—his concentration should be within his character.

   c. The actor, like the scenery, properties, costumes and lights, becomes an element in the total picture, and his position on stage at all times is the responsibility of the director; this explains why the profession of direction arose late in the nineteenth century concurrently with the growth of picture-frame realism and the decline of the star system. The proscenium director can benefit greatly from a study of great paintings, many of which have approximately the same proportions as the average proscenium opening.

2. To keep the actor visible to the audience when he has lines or important reactions.
   The actor's face is generally the most expressive part of his body, and audiences want to see it. As the dialogue progresses from character to character, the director must serve as a kind of "traffic cop" to make sure that the speaking actor is visible and the others subordinate or appropriately related to the speaker.

3. To move the actors from one picture to another.
   Although this chapter will analyze picturization as though the director composes a series of unrelated "stills," the practical application of these principles is always limited by the fact that one picture grows out of the preceding one and leads to the succeeding one. It is through the movement of the actors that the director links the stage pictures and gets the actors where he needs them at any given moment. As movement serves a number of other purposes in addition to linking the stage pictures, it will be treated separately in the next chapter.

B. The director's approach to picturization. *(handwritten: must say something to the death or and blind –)*

There is an old adage that there are two people in every audience for whom the director must plan—the deaf old lady and the blind old man. For the rest of the audience that can both see and hear, effects are doubly strong when one impression reinforces the other. The director thus has two media through which he can communicate with the audience—the visual and the auditory. It would be pedantic to attempt to decide which makes the stronger impression on the audience; we go to the theatre to *see* a play, but many of the greatest playwrights (including Shakespeare) make their strongest appeal through *oral* language. Although television separates the electronic components of "video" and "audio," any such separation in the theatre is purely for purposes of analysis. This chapter and the following chapter on movement present the means by which the director organizes or composes the visual picture primarily for the proscenium theatre (a form in which the director should probably learn to work first). There is little likelihood that the director will be working on the same production in several different types of theatres; therefore, to provide easier reference and avoid confusion, the special principles and techniques applicable to arena, thrust, and other forms of non-proscenium theatre are treated in Chapter 6. Chapter 7 presents the means of organizing the oral pattern.

C. Stage terminology used in blocking on the proscenium stage.

1. *Stage right* and *left* are always the actor's right and left as he faces the audience.
2. *Downstage* means nearer to the audience. The downstage foot is the foot nearer the audience. To *move down* means to move nearer the audience.
3. *Upstage* means farther from the audience. To *move up* means to move away from the audience.
4. *Cross down right* (abbreviated as XDR) means to move to the downstage right area. XULC means to cross to up left center.
5. *Onstage* means nearer to the center of the stage.
6. *Offstage* means farther from the center of the stage. To move several steps off is to go several steps away from center.
7. *Above* a person or object means on the upstage side.
8. *Below* a person or object means on the downstage side.
9. To *open up* means to turn more of the actor's body to the audience, i.e., from profile to one-quarter, or from one-quarter to full-front. (See body positions, II, B, 1.)
10. To *turn in* means to turn less of the actor's body to the audience, i.e., from one-quarter to profile, or from profile to three-quarter.

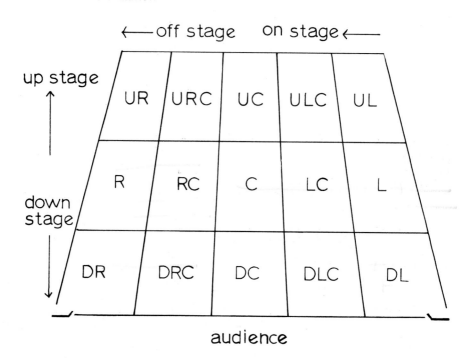

←—off stage   on stage←——

up stage ↑

| UR | URC | UC | ULC | UL |
| R | RC | C | LC | L |

down stage

| DR | DRC | DC | DLC | DL |

audience

11. To *cover* means to stand between another actor and the audience, or between a property and the audience. (There are times when the latter is necessary, as the covering of an oil lamp when it is being turned on.)

12. To *focus* means to look at another actor.

13. To *steal* means either (1) to attract attention illegitimately from one's partner or (2) to move unobtrusively to a new position, also called "easing down" or "dropping down."

D. The requirements of effective stage picturization.

Authorities in the field of painting generally agree that good visual composition should have the following attributes: *unity, balance, center of attention or emphasis,* and *variety.* For stage picturization we must add two more requirements: it must *tell the story,* and be *functional.* These six qualities are mutually interrelated and affect each other. The simplest to manage for the young director, however, is *center of attention or emphasis.*

II. **The stage picture should have a center of attention.**

The director in one sense may be said to direct not the play itself but the attention of the audience to the play, compelling the spectators to look where he wants them to and anticipating their emotional responses. Unlike the camera director who can compel the audience's attention by a close-up which excludes everything except what he wishes to emphasize, the stage director must use more subtle and complex means of subordinating that which is less important and direct the spectators' eyes where he wishes them.

SIX CHARACTERS IN SEARCH OF AN AUTHOR—CENTER OF ATTENTION California State University, Long Beach. Directed by Harry E. Stiver. Designed by Ralph W. Duckwall (Sets and Lights) and Herbert L. Camburn (Costumes).

Center of attention, or *visual emphasis* is perhaps the most important aspect of composition. An audience can look at only one center of attention at a time. A picture with no center of attention may confuse or bore an audience. It is even more bewildering when an audience hears a line of dialogue and cannot locate the speaker.

A. Kinds of visual emphasis.

    1. *Single emphasis* is upon one actor at a time, although two actors very close together (as in an embrace) may constitute one center of attention.

    2. *Shared emphasis* permits the audience to dart its eyes quickly from one actor to another in a fast repartee of dialogue. There should be nothing between the two characters which interrupts the easy shift of the audience's attention from one to the other.

    3. *Secondary emphasis* involves the creation of subsidiary centers of attention in addition to the principal one. It is useful

in crowd scenes to add variety and interest, but must be held within limits so as not to detract from the primary emphasis. Characters with secondary emphasis may later in the scene become the principal center of attention and should be so placed that attention can go easily to them. Often, too, a character gives a speech about another character who is silent, and the audience often glances briefly at him to see how he is reacting, then back to the speaker.

4. *Multiple emphasis* may be used in crowd scenes such as the prologue to *Carousel*, when there are moments in which there is no center of attention but a variety of groups of more or less equal interest. The audience looks from one to the other as at a three-ring circus; before long, however, the director will need to concentrate the attention of the audience.

5. *Offstage emphasis* is effective for certain moments such as in *The Diary of Anne Frank* when the family is intently listening toward the foot of the steps, or in *Ghosts* when the orphanage burns down. Although offstage emphasis makes a telling picture, it should be used for moments of limited duration.

B. Means of achieving emphasis.

These twelve means are not listed in order of importance. A director generally will use more than one at a time, depending upon his interpretation of the scene and the particular set in which he is working. Note how many different means were used by da Vinci in *The Last Supper*. Emphasis can be directed to the actor:

1. Through the actor's *body position*.

    a. Definition of the basic body positions for the individual actor: (Note: in the following the front edge of the stage is presumed to be on a straight line between the edges of the proscenium arch, 90 degrees from the center seats of the audience.)

      (1) *Full-front position*, in which the actor's body and head directly face the audience.

      (2) *One-quarter position*, in which the actor's upstage foot parallels the front edge of the stage and his downstage foot is brought comfortably back and turned at a 45 degree angle from his upstage foot. This pulls the actor's body around so that more is seen by the audience. His face is on the same axis as his upstage foot. *The one-quarter position is the "home position" and the actor usually should assume it when working with a partner until directed otherwise.*

[handwritten marginalia:]
1 actors body position
2 Through the area of the stage
3 Through the use of levels
4 Through the use of contrast
5 Through the use of isolation
6 Through the use of focus
7 Lines
8 triangles
9 Scenic reinforcement
10 lighting
11 Color
12 Movement & speech

THE LAST SUPPER—EMPHASIS

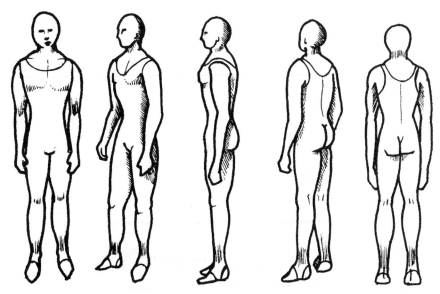

1. FULL-   2. ONE-   3. PROFILE   4. THREE-   5. FULL-
   FRONT   QUARTER   QUARTER   BACK

BODY POSITIONS

(3) *Profile position,* in which the actor's head and body parallel the front edge of the stage and both his feet are approximately 90 degrees from the audience.

(4) *Three-quarter position,* in which the actor's downstage foot parallels the front edge of the stage and his upstage foot is brought comfortably back, pointing upstage at a 45 degree angle.

(5) *Full-back position,* in which the actor's back is to the audience and he faces directly upstage.

b. Relative strength of the various body positions:
Other things being equal, the actor in the strongest body position will receive emphasis. An actor in a strong body position can usually dominate regardless of the area of the stage he uses.

(1) Full-front is the strongest position.

(2) One-quarter is next strongest.

(3) Profile is medium in strength.

(4) Three-quarter is a weak position.

(5) Full-back is a weak position.

(6) Standing is stronger than sitting.

(7) Sitting is stronger than lying down.

(8) Sitting or standing erect is stronger than slouching or leaning.

(9) Body positions can be strengthened or weakened by the direction the head is turned. A full-front position can be weakened by turning the head to profile; a three-quarter position can be strengthened by turning the head into profile.

(10) Kneeling, which generally is weak, can best be kept opened by kneeling on the downstage knee and keeping the upstage knee up.

c. Positions of two actors playing a scene together.

(1) *Shared* means that both actors are in one-quarter positions, equally visible and equally distant from the front edge of the stage.

(2) *Profile* means that the two actors are each in profile position facing each other and equally distant from the front edge of the stage.

(3) *Upstaging* means that one of the actors is in one-quarter position, upstage of his partner who must therefore turn his head and body to a three-quarter position to face his partner. The *upstage actor* has *taken* the scene and the downstage actor *given* it. Although there are

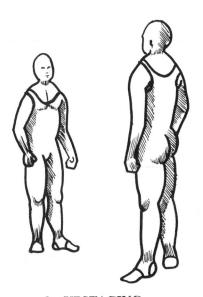

1. SHARED

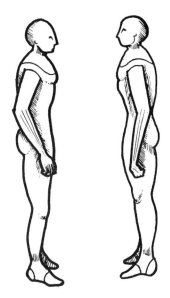

2. PROFILE

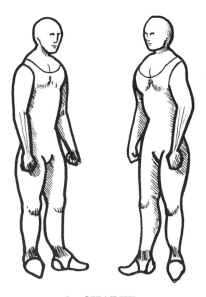

3. UPSTAGING

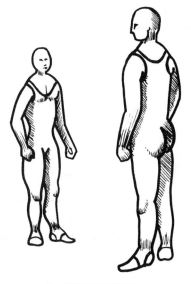

4. CHEATING

many occasions when the director will want this effect, it is bad practice to move upstage of one's partner without being so directed.

(4) *Cheating* means that the actor who has given the scene to his upstage partner cheats by bringing his body and/or face more nearly into profile. He still seems to be facing his partner, and if done within limits the audience cannot detect that he is cheating.

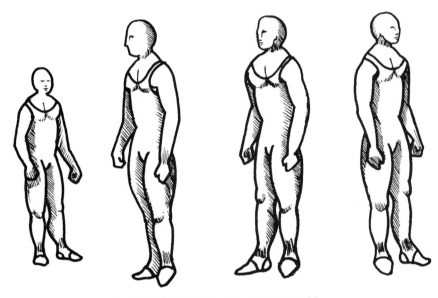

5. VARIATIONS OF CHEATING

(5) *Variations* of the foregoing positions are unlimited, depending upon the content of the scene. The relationships can be used seated, leaning, or lying down; actors can turn their backs toward each other one-quarter, profile or three-quarter; both can (if the play is nonrealistic) face full front. The body can be in one position and the head in another.

2. Through the *area* of the stage.

The chart pictured indicates the relative strength of areas of the stage. Other things being equal, a single actor is strongest when he is DC and weakest when he is UL. Stage right generally is considered stronger than stage left because of the conditioning of our eyes, which begin to read at the left side of the page (SR). Dean has confirmed this, observing that as

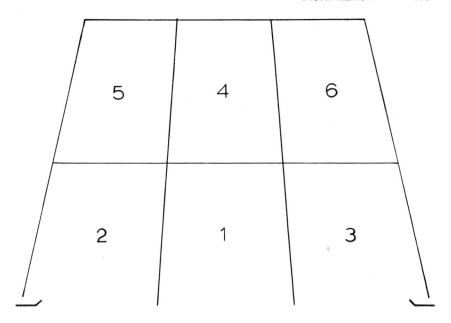

AREAS IN ORDER OF STRENGTH

the curtain goes up an audience can be seen to look first at its left (SR) and then toward its right (SL).[1] Note, however, these exceptions:

  a. When all the players in a scene are in the same area, this factor no longer applies as a means of giving emphasis.

  b. When a character downstage (areas 1, 2, or 3) must face a character upstage (areas 5, 4, or 6) the above strengths no longer apply; the downstage actor is "upstaged" and the audience sees less of him than the upstage actor. Therefore the actor farthest upstage in a group will usually take emphasis; this is also true when two actors sit on a sofa placed on a diagonal.

3. Through the use of *levels*.

Other things being equal, the actor on the highest level will be emphatic. To make full use of this principle, steps, risers and platforms are worked into stage settings wherever justifiable.

4. Through the use of *contrast*.

Other things being equal, the actor who is in some way different from the others will receive emphasis. For example:

a. If all but one are standing, the seated actor is emphatic.

1. Alexander Dean and Lawrence Carra, *Fundamentals of Play Directing*, rev. ed., (New York: Holt, Rinehart & Winston, Inc., 1965), pp. 105-106.

LYSISTRATA—LEVELS California State University, Long Beach. Directed by Alec Finalyson. Designed by Milton Howarth (Sets) and Herbert L. Camburn (Costumes).

THE DIARY OF ANNE FRANK—CONTRAST California State University, Long Beach. Directed by W. David Sievers. Designed by Milton Howarth.

     b. If all but one are facing out, the actor in profile or three-quarter position would be emphatic.

     c. If all but one are in a particular style or color of costume, the actor in a contrasting style or color will be emphatic.

5. Through the use of *isolation.*

     Other things being equal, the actor who is apart from a group —isolated in space—will be most emphatic. Newspaper advertising often uses this principle, surrounding the emphatic words

THE TIME OF YOUR LIFE—ISOLATION California State University, Long Beach. Directed by W. David Sievers. Designed by Harold Alexander.

with empty space. The old stock company adage expressed the same concept with the rule "to keep an arm's length from the star."

6. Through the use of *focus*.

When other actors focus on (i.e., look at) a particular actor, the audience tends to do the same. The eyes of the actor are

B   C   A   D   G   E F

THE HAPPY TIME—COUNTER FOCUS California State University, Long Beach. Directed by W. David Sievers. Designed by John H. Green.

therefore a very important means of directing audience attention. The actor should look at the speaking actor unless he has a definite motivation to look away or is asked to do so by the director.

    a. Looking elsewhere than at the emphatic actor is called *counter-focus.* If actor A in *The Happy Time* is the center of attention and B, C, D, G and F are listening to her, E need not focus on A, for example, but may counter-focus on F. If the audience's eye follows from E to F, it will then go where F is looking, which should be back to A. Note the counter-focus in *The Last Supper* by da Vinci.

    b. Counter-focus will be used by the director to add variety to the composition, to avoid overusing such a strong device as focus for emphasis, to reveal the character's reaction to what is being said, and to link various elements in the composition.

7. Through the use of *line.*

Lines, either straight or curved, lead the audience's eye like an arrow toward the emphatic figure, which may be at either end, depending upon the focus of the actors in the line.

    a. Lines can be supplied by the bodies of the actors, the height of their heads, arms, legs, or by costume elements, such as canes, swords, pikes, or rifles.

    b. To achieve variety, lines may be diagonal, straight, broken, curved, or the graceful S-curve. Straight lines are rarely formed in real life except in military situations, formal or public occasions; they must be used on the stage with caution, therefore, in realistic plays.

    c. *Repetition* can also be used for emphasis as a variation of line—a number of guards behind a king, a number of butlers behind a dowager, a number of secretaries behind a tycoon, etc. The more minor figures that are used repetitively, the stronger the emphasis upon the major figure. According to Arnheim[2] the eyes tend to move in the direction of diminishing intervals.

8. Through the use of *triangles.*

As an extension of the principle of line, the lines of a triangle tend to lead the eye of the viewer from either side toward

2. Rudolf Arnheim, *Art and Visual Perception* (Berkeley and Los Angeles: University of California Press, 1954), p. 23.

THE ADDING MACHINE—LINE California State University, Long Beach. Directed by Stanley Kahan. Designed by Ralph W. Duckwall (Sets), David Jager (Lights), Bert F. Ayers (Costumes) and Beala B. Neel (Makeup).

A MARRIAGE PROPOSAL—TRIANGLE California State University, Long Beach. Directed by W. David Sievers. Designed by Norma Thormodson.

the apex. Triangle compositions with the emphatic figure at the apex are therefore a standard form of theatrical grouping.

a. The apex normally is upstage if the emphatic figure is speaking to the others in the triangle.

b. The apex may be downstage if the emphatic figure has a motivation to face away from the others.

c. Equilateral triangles seem prearranged and should be avoided except in plays where symmetry is desired.

d. Triangles can become monotonous if overused and not varied. With eleven other means of obtaining emphasis, the director need not rely solely on triangles.

e. Triangles can be varied by irregular spacing of figures, by the use of counter-focus within the triangle, and by varying the head heights of the figures—some seated, some standing tall, some leaning, and taller actors not placed together.

9. Through *scenic reinforcement*.

Architectural elements in the setting can be used for emphasis; their placement is therefore of concern to the director as well as the designer.

LIBEL!—SCENIC REINFORCEMENT   Broadway production. Directed by Otto Preminger. Designed by Raymond Sovey.

a. An actor gains emphasis when framed in a doorway, arch or window.
b. An actor gains emphasis when related to strong elements such as columns, thrones, or masses.
c. An actor gains emphasis when standing where a strong scenic line terminates or where two scenic lines meet. A series of columns or arches may provide repetition to emphasize the actor.

10. Through *lighting.*
   Although the modern, realistic theatre has excluded the follow-spot which was conventional several generations ago, the control of light remains a very important means of giving emphasis. The director of a classic, nonrealistic or musical play may use this medium more freely.

A DREAM PLAY–LIGHTING   University of Illinois. Directed by Charles Shattuck.

a. Unless there are strong factors to counteract it, the most brightly lighted actor will receive the most emphasis.
b. The current popularity of multi-media lighting presents many emphatic possibilities.

11. Through *color.*
   Other things being equal, the actor who wears the brightest costume or most colorful makeup will have the most emphasis.

12. Through *movement* and *speech.*
   Although these are discussed in detail in Chapters 5 and 7, it

is important to note here that they are significant factors in creating emphasis. The more energized each becomes, the more emphatic each becomes.

Although a director seldom uses any of these twelve major factors of emphasis in isolation, he must remain constantly aware and certain of the shifting emphases while he experiments with combining the almost limitless possibilities of these factors.

III. <u>**The stage picture should have a meaningful, storytelling quality.**</u>

The second requirement of a good stage picture is that it should *tell the story,* or picturize the inner relationships in the scene. It should dramatize visually the inherent elements of action and clash at the moment. This is one of the most valuable purposes which picturization serves, and the one which makes the story meaningful to the "deaf old lady."

Picturization requires all of the director's conscious artistry, for in life people do not necessarily group themselves into meaningful pictures. Picturization is derived from nature, however, and requires only that the director select and arrange details to further his artistic purpose. Plays vary in their content to such an extent that picturization cannot be done by rule. To the experienced director creative and articulate stage pictures will come to mind easily as he studies the play. The beginning director should follow these steps:

A. Break the scene into *actions* and *beats* before picturizing.

If the director has completed his analysis of the play by action and beat during his interpretative study and marked the beginning of each new beat in the director's book, the composition of the stage picture will be facilitated. Before blocking the scene, the director should ask himself:

1. Who is the dominant figure in this particular beat?
2. What does he want or what is he trying to do in this beat?
   a. Physically.
   b. Psychologically.
3. Who else is in this particular beat, and what do they want?
4. What are the interpersonal relationships in the beat?
   a. Who is the opposition, if any, to the dominant figure?
   b. Toward whom does the dominant figure feel strongly— either strong affection or strong hostility.
   c. What do the others in the scene feel toward the dominant figure and toward each other? Whose side are they on? What are they doing?

B. Relate the characters to each other physically and emotionally in the stage picture.

    1. People tend to be near those they love, support, defend, protect, want to impress, or obtain a concession from.

    2. People tend to stay away from those they dislike, distrust, oppose, reject, or those who make them feel guilty.

    3. People approach those for whom they feel strong hostility, whom they want to threaten or prevent from doing something.

    4. People who are indifferent, afraid to identify themselves, busy with something else, or unrelated to the problem tend to remain apart and can be used to fill in the periphery of the stage picture.

    5. The family is a natural unit. Although its members may quarrel among themselves, they tend to stand together when threatened from the outside.

C. Select the area of the stage in which the particular beat can best be played.

    1. The relative strength of stage areas has already been discussed. The director will often deliberately choose a weak area in which to stage a certain scene (1) for contrast, (2) for variety, so as not to overuse any one area, (3) to make a later scene seem stronger, or (4) to soften the impact of sensational action such as the blinding of Gloucester in *King Lear*.

    2. Often it is preferable for the director through his use and arrangement of people and objects to create his own psychological weak and strong areas on stage.

D. Use the furniture in the scene to the fullest advantage in picturization.

Ideally the basic stage pictures desired by the director should be created prior to the planning of the ground plan. This is in order to be certain the furniture arrangement will be planned to enhance the pictures rather than dictate what they must be. In planning the ground plan, therefore, director and designer should have picturization in mind. Even within a given ground plan, however, a piece of furniture can be moved around or repositioned for a certain scene. In many plays the director is free to have various characters place furniture as needed for each scene.

    1. Associate certain furniture with certain characters when appropriate. Some examples:

        a. The dining table to which the family returns after each crisis in *You Can't Take It With You*.

b. The "dear, honored bookcase" which means so much to Gaev that he weeps over it in *The Cherry Orchard*.

c. In a production of *Summer and Smoke*, the young doctor never sat at his father's desk (though he leaned on it and put his foot on it) until his father's death brought him to maturity.

d. An Old Vic production of *Hamlet* used the same principle when Hamlet in a soliloquy sat upon his father's throne, an invasion of his stepfather's prerogative.

2. Use furniture to support the actors in moments of strong emotion. A table can be a buffer between two opponents; a chair can be a crutch in a moment of crisis; how a person feels about social conventions can be shown in the way he handles furniture.

3. People who want to ingratiate themselves or establish rapport usually select low and informal furniture to sit on such as hassocks, stools, a pillow on the floor.

E. Use the actors' bodies plastically to reveal the emotion that is going on within.

1. Dancers are familiar with the opposing principles of:
   a. Contraction-elevation.
   b. Tension-relaxation.
   c. Contact-rejection.

2. For the actor these principles can be applied:
   a. With the head—where it is focused or directed.
   b. With the body.
      Ambivalence or interruption of an activity can be picturized when the head is focused in one direction and the body in another. Leaning forward or backward may express interest or lack of it, reinforcing the visual line to the emphatic figure.
   c. With the arms.
      Reaching out, threatening, contacting others suggests extroversion; arms related only to self—folded across chest, hands in pockets, on face or in hair—suggests introversion.
   d. With the legs.
      The degree of formality or informality of the scene is often effectively expressed by actors' legs. The legs of actors seated on the floor may contribute to the line, sequence and unity of the composition. Alfred Lunt in *The Visit* provided a memorable example of legs as an expressive part of the body.

F. Try tentative stage pictures on the basis of the preceding five steps. Look at the picturization from out front, refining, modifying, and adjusting it for the purpose of:

1. Finding the most interesting and accurate way to picturize a given beat or scene, not merely the most "natural" or "normal." Be imaginative within the restrictions of the given scene. Where there is a choice, select the more theatrical or telling picture rather than an equally truthful but less theatrical one. Selection and arrangement make the difference between the artist and the copyist.
2. Avoiding the obvious.
3. Retaining a sense of truth, based on observation of real life and human character. Start with truth and if necessary enlarge it; do not start with the enlargement. Realistic drama requires that stage pictures should *seem* (not necessarily *be*) lifelike and natural.

IV. The third requirement of a good stage picture is that it should have balance.

Balance has been defined as "a state of equipoise, as between weights, different elements, or opposing forces; equilibrium." A well-balanced picture is aesthetically satisfying to the viewer, and an unbalanced one disturbing.

Balance in stage composition is achieved when the elements to the right of center equal those to the left of center. To analyze balance, it is necessary to draw an imaginary line bisecting the proscenium arch and dividing the stage picture into two equal halves. The two halves of the stage can be thought of as a see-saw, with a fulcrum at the center line (which is usually marked on the stage floor at the curtain line). The scene designer will normally provide a balanced set when empty of actors (except when a strong mass of actors is to play an entire scene in one position) and the director should use his actors to maintain this balance.

There are two types of balance, and the director may choose for each scene and each play which type is the more appropriate to use.

A. Symmetrical balance.

1. This is the simplest form of balance to achieve but also the least interesting. It exists when exactly the same number of actors and scenic elements are on the right side of the center line as are on the left, and with equal spacing, as though a picture of half the stage had been folded over and duplicated on the other half.
2. Because groups of people rarely divide themselves into equal

LE BOURGEOIS GENTILHOMME–SYMMETRICAL BALANCE Yale University. Directed by Halsted Welles. Designed by Donald Oenslager and Frank Bevan.

halves in real life, symmetrical balance seems artificial and calls attention to itself. There are times, however, when the director will find this desirable:

a. In plays of artificial style, or where there is symmetry in dialogue or content. *The Importance of Being Earnest, The Matchmaker.*

b. In plays set in periods when symmetry and order were characteristic in music, art, and architecture. Greek and Roman, seventeenth century, eighteenth century; operas of Mozart.

c. In scenes of royalty, great formality, state occasions, equal balance of opposing forces (such as the street fights in *Romeo and Juliet*), courtroom scenes where interest is shared equally by prosecution and defense, scenes involving the church and divine figures.

B. Asymmetrical balance (balance without symmetry).

Asymmetrical balance is not obtained by duplication of elements on right and left, but by more subtle, interesting and variable means. The net result, however, must be the *impression* that stage right is equal in weight to stage left. "Weight" in this context does not mean the literal weight, size, or number of actors, but rather their psychological, aesthetic, or emphatic weight. There are therefore no precise rules for arriving at asymmetrical balance; much depends upon the director's cultivating a sense of proportion and aesthetic sensitivity. Factors which affect weight for balance purposes include:

1. How much visual emphasis is placed upon the character. Each of the twelve means of obtaining emphasis can be used for balance. For example:

   a. One actor framed in an arch or against the sky will balance several against neutral backgrounds.
   b. One actor in a strong area or body position will balance several in weak areas or body positions.

ARMIDA ABANDONED BY RINALDO (by Tiepolo)—ASYMMETRICAL BALANCE

  c. One actor standing may balance several seated (or vice versa).

 2. How much psychological interest the character has for the audience.

  a. The authority of prestige of the character in the play. Policemen, judges, kings, and priests command more weight than average citizens. The same is true of "the boss," the most popular character, the most beloved, or most hated.

  b. Whether the character is speaking or not.
   As a rule, the speaker will command more weight than non-speaking actors.

  c. The significance of what is said or done.
   The suspense or amount of concern the audience feels for what is happening at the moment may add psychological weight to certain characters. A figure suggested impending action can balance several relaxed figures. In *Amahl and the Night Visitors,* a child taking a step without crutches is of sufficient interest to balance three kings, a page, and the mother.

AMAHL AND THE NIGHT VISITORS—PSYCHOLOGICAL INTEREST
California State University, Long Beach. Directed by W. David Sievers. Designed by John H. Green.

 3. How far characters are from the center line.
 This is the *principle of the see-saw.*

  a. A lighter figure will balance a heavier figure if the lighter one is proportionately farther from center. To balance actors or groups with different aesthetic weight, vary the distance from center, trying roughly to approximate the formula W x D = W' x D' — weight times distance from center equals weight on the opposite side times distance from center on the opposite side.

b. When a composition in which one actor balances two or three is thrown off balance by the entrance of a fourth who joins the group, the sole character must move farther from center to restore balance. If a fifth or sixth joins the group, however, he need not move again. There is an old saying that "The eye counts to five."

4. Whether minor figures remain individualized or become a *mass*.

a. More than three figures placed near each other tend to lose individuality and become a mass, with less weight than the same three individuals might have separately.

b. Figures overlapping or partially covering one another tend to be thought of as one for purposes of weight.

c. Mass can be made stronger with secondary centers of attention or counter-focus.

5. How much visual interest is added by scenery, furniture, costumes, and lighting.

a. Scenic elements or imposing furniture may add weight to an area of the stage.

b. Brighter colors tend to have more weight than subdued ones. White has more weight than black.

c. Warmer areas in lighting tend to have more weight than cold ones.

6. The principle of the "Golden Section."
Since ancient Greece, experiments in dividing a rectangle into its most pleasing proportions—or where the eye seems to be most comfortably at rest—have resulted in the *Golden Section*. This is a vertical line which may be computed as 38 percent (a little over one-third) of the distance from stage right and 62 percent of the distance from stage left. Many famous paintings have their center of attention approximately at the Golden Section, among them Rembrandt's "The Pilgrims at Emmaus," Van Dyke's "King Charles I," Monet's "Haystacks," and Manet's "Lunch on the Grass." The phenomenon of the Golden Section has the following implications for the stage:

a. The Golden Section is an area where the eyes of the spectators come comfortably to rest.

b. It is therefore an effective place for a center of attention.

c. The stage seems in balance when there is a center of attention at the Golden Section and a *lighter* weight balancing it stage left.

d. If the center of attention is stage left, it will take more weight stage right to balance it than if the picture were reversed.

e. Figures stage left seem to have more weight than they would stage right.

This curious fact has been observed by scholars in aesthetics.[3] The right side of a painting (stage left) seems *heavier* in weight (not importance) than the left side (stage right). Paintings which are well balanced with their center of attention at the Golden Section seem off balance when viewed in reverse. Try viewing Monet's "Haystacks" or Raphael's "Sistine Madonna" in reverse. "Haystacks" is printed in reverse on page 121, does it seem off balance? Very likely this phenomenon has to do with the cerebral dominance of persons conditioned to read from left to right. More tension of the eye muscles is required to look to the right (stage left), giving the psychological impression of added weight to figures stage left.

C. Use of imbalance.

The stage will not always be in balance, either symmetrically or asymmetrically. The uses of imbalance include:

1. Deliberate imbalance.

Times when the director may desire an unbalanced picture include:

a. When the director wants to create tension or a disturbing empathic response in the audience, as in *Angel Street* when the detective is down left and stage right is empty except for the door through which the sinister husband may return at any moment.

b. When the director wants to picturize the upset of forces or imbalance in the story, as in *King Lear* when Lear and the Fool are pitted against the ravages of the storm.

c. When only half of the stage is used for a scene. In a partial stage picture, the audience apparently is willing to ignore the unused half of the stage and concentrate on stage right or left alone, provided there is balance within that area.

3. Arnheim, *Art and Visual Perception;* Gaffron, Mercedes, "Right and Left in Pictures," *Art Quarterly,* XIII, 1950, pp. 312-331; Wolfflin, Heinrich, *Principles of Art History,* New York: Dover Publications, Inc., 1929.

HAYSTACKS IN SNOW (by Claude Monet)

MONET'S "HAYSTACKS" IN REVERSE

In this respect the stage is unlike the painting, where the artist almost always uses the entire space available on the canvas.

2. Unavoidable imbalance.

   Every moment in a production need not present a picture of perfect balance. The requirements of the story and the need for transitions between main pictures may result in frequent imbalance. These moments will be brief, and fortunately are not frozen for all time as in a painting; nor does the playgoer observe with the studiousness of a museum-goer. The stage picture is not static but ever-changing, making its impact unconsciously on the audience. Spectators seem willing to accept transitional moments of imbalance in exchange for a climactic moment of memorable visual impact.

V. The fourth requirement of a good stage picture is that it should have unity.

Unity is achieved when the parts of the composition are so interrelated that the whole picture is viewed as one thing. In a unified picturization there is no unimportant or unrelated part, and nothing can be taken away or added without affecting the harmony and completeness of the picture. The director's means of achieving unity include:

A. Controlling the center of attention.

   Unity is achieved when there is one dominant center of attention and, if desired, subordinate centers of interest which add variety without distracting from the primary center.

B. Providing "eye-path" or connecting links between figures, groups or centers of attention.

   Dean has called this element of composition *sequence;* aestheticians often speak of it as *glance-path.* Its purpose is to provide (1) an easy path so that the audience's eye will move from one actor or group to another, and (2) a compelling path which will not permit the audience to be diverted or distracted along the way. The director can accomplish this by:

   1. An actor placed as a linking or transitional figure between two groups.
   2. The focus of the actors.
   3. The line of arms, legs, and bodies.
   4. Line in the scene design.
   5. Furniture, properties, and even pictures on the wall.
   6. Not letting an actor get "pinned down" in a strong area during a scene in which he has no lines or significant reactions.

THE DANCE FOYER AT THE OPERA (by Edgar Degas)—UNITY

7. Rhythmic spacing of figures or groups. Where a regular interval is established between groups, other groups will seem unified within the whole if they are spaced at half or twice the distance. (If A and B are four feet apart, B and C might be effectively placed either two or eight feet apart.)

C. Tying down the edges of the picturization.

1. Figures placed at the down left or down right edges of the set serve the important purpose of directing the eyes of the audience back into the set. If they should focus out of the picture frame, the audience may find itself doing likewise.
2. A picturization with its edges tied down is said to have *stability*.
3. The larger the mass of actors upstage, the more figures that will be needed in the DR and DL corners to provide stability or up-and-downstage balance.

D. Using all the available space interestingly.

1. Related to C is the need to fill up the empty space, not only at the edges of the picturization but within the picture itself. Unless used for emphasis, empty stage space may interrupt eye-path and detract from unity.
2. In addition to working for unity, the director should sense the

challenge of using his stage space for maximum effect. If the designer has provided levels, steps, or interesting upstage areas, it would seem a waste to confine the actors to a shallow downstage plane. Utilizing stage space also permits greater variety in picturizations.

VI. **The fifth requirement of a good stage picture is that it should have variety.**

In addition to the four requirements mentioned previously, the most interesting staging of a given scene would be the one which provides maximum variety for the eye.

A. Except where the director wishes to call attention to style through repetition of positions, he should try to find as many different ways as possible, within the context of the scene, in which to group actors. Notice how da Vinci in *The Last Supper* has achieved variety by having no two of the disciples in exactly the same body position.

B. Some bad habits which young directors may unconsciously acquire and which detract from variety include:
1. Lining up actors in straight lines.
2. Forming a semicircle around a principal actor.
3. Having equal spacing among a group of actors.
4. Allowing actors to copy another actor's body position.
5. Facing actors full front to attract greater emphasis than the situation warrants.

VII. **The sixth and last requirement of a good stage picture is that it should be functional.**

In addition to aesthetically meaningful requirements, the picturization should meet the functional requirements of actors and director. It should:

A. Permit every actor to be visible (except in large crowd scenes where some will be partially covered or invisible from some seats).

B. Permit easy movement to the next stage picture. The director must consider "where he goes from here" in planning each picture, so that the next actor to speak or move will be in a suitable position.

C. Keep actors clear of a door just before a new character is to enter.

D. Make it easy for the actors to play the scene, helping them to feel comfortable and to find the proper emotion for the scene.

VIII. Special problems in picturization.

Keeping in mind that meaningful pictures and proper character relationships are most important, the director must sometimes deal with other problems.

A. Table scenes.

Scenes around a table present special sight-line difficulties, and the solution used by da Vinci in *The Last Supper* is too symmetrical and formal for a modern, realistic play. In realistic staging, as in everyday life, people would sit on all four sides of a table, and some would therefore turn their backs to the audience and cover their upstage partners. To improve visibility, here are some possible adjustments which can be made:

1. Use a round table, where appropriate, whether than a square one. Four figures can be placed on diagonals, with the two downstage ones cheating farther apart and the two upstage ones closer together. If a card table must be used, some cheating can still improve sight lines a little.
2. If a group of people must be seated at a long rectangular table, place it on a diagonal. The most emphatic positions are at the two ends, upstage being the stronger. When all seats are occupied, the downstage seats are potentially stronger (with cheating of the body) than the upstage seats.
3. The tallest actors might be seated upstage and the shortest (including children) downstage. Actors on the downstage side can help by leaning over the table.
4. The downstage seats should be reserved for characters who enter the scene late or leave early.
5. The actors on the downstage side should be motivated whenever possible to leave the table for some of their lines, or the upstage actors to rise for some of theirs.

B. Courtroom scenes.
1. The logical temptation to put the judge up center should be avoided if the attorneys have important discussions with him.
2. If the jury can be suggested or only partially shown, it will save space and decrease emphasis.
3. Traditionally the jury box is on the judge's left, with the witness stand between the judge and the jury.
4. The clerk, who is rarely important in the action, should be in a weak position.

C. Sofa scenes.
When two characters sit on a sofa placed diagonally, the actor far-

ther upstage might sit forward on the sofa and the actor who is downstage leans back.

D. Throne room scenes.

If persons addressing the king must share emphasis with him, the throne should not be on the upstage wall but preferably along the right or left side wall.

E. Crowd scenes.

It is often necessary to achieve separation of the crowd from the emphatic individual who addresses it. The old operatic solution of the crowd in a semicircle around the principal who faces front is no longer believable. Here are some better solutions to the problem:

1. Raise the principal actor on levels (even a table on which he might stand).
2. Isolate the principal figure from the crowd.
3. If the reaction of the crowd is important, the principal down left in a three-quarter position can address a crowd up right for brief scenes.
4. Avoid the same body position for numerous members of the crowd.
5. The illusion of a larger crowd can be given by:
   a. Keeping the majority of the crowd downstage with a few scattered upstage.
   b. Forming subunits within the crowd—family groups, clusters and pairs, with secondary emphasis upon those most involved.
   c. Having figures lean into the set from doorways and windows.
   d. Using shadows and sound effects to suggest more people.
6. In handling a large crowd it will be helpful to:
   a. Designate leaders for each subunit or cluster of people.
   b. Give members of the crowd specific things to do.
   c. Make sure each member of the crowd knows where to focus.
   d. Keep crowd members out of sight lines to the principal figure.

IX. Summary.

As he watches rehearsals from out front, the director should check his stage pictures to make sure that they meet the criteria of good picturization.

**THE COUNTY ELECTION (by George C. Bingham)—EFFECTIVE CROWD
SCENE**

A. A center of attention.
   1. Kinds of visual emphasis.
   2. Means of achieving emphasis.

B. A meaningful, storytelling quality.
   1. Breaking the scene into actions and beats before picturizing.
   2. Relating the characters to each other physically and emotionally.
   3. Selecting the area of the stage in which the beat can best be played.
   4. Using the furniture to the fullest advantage.
   5. Using the actors' bodies plastically to reveal emotion.
   6. Trying tentative stage pictures, refining and modifying them.

C. Balance.
   1. Symmetrical balance.
   2. Asymmetrical balance.
   3. Use of imbalance.

D. Unity.
1. Controlling the center of attention.
2. Providing "eye-path."
3. Tying down the edges of the picturization.
4. Using all the available space interestingly.

E. Variety.
1. Variety in body positions.
2. Bad habits to avoid.

F. Functional requirements.
1. Visibility of the actors.
2. Easy movement to the next picture.
3. Clearing doorways before entrances.
4. Making the actors comfortable in the scene.

G. Special problems.
1. Table scenes.
2. Courtroom scenes.
3. Sofa scenes.
4. Throne room scenes.
5. Crowd scenes.

Selective Bibliography

Albright, H. D.; Halstead, William P.; and Mitchell, Lee. *Principles of Theatre Art*. Boston: Houghton Mifflin Company, 1955.
Dean, Alexander and Carra, Lawrence. *Fundamentals of Play Directing*. Rev. ed. New York: Holt, Rinehart & Winston, Inc., 1965.
Dietrich, John E. *Play Direction*. New York: Prentice-Hall, Inc., 1953.
McMullan, Frank. *The Director's Handbook*. Hamden, Conn.: Shoe String Press, 1964.
Selden, Samuel. *The Stage in Action*. New York: F. S. Crofts, 1946.

THE BOY FRIEND California State University, Long Beach. Directed by Stanley Kahan. Designed by Marcia Fredericks (Sets), Herbert L. Camburn (Costumes) and John H. Green (Lights).

THE KING STAG California State University, Long Beach. Directed by Herbert L. Camburn. Designed by Ralph W. Duckwall (Sets), Carol Robinson (Costumes and Makeup) and John H. Green (Lights).

5 Movement

I. Introduction.

In the previous chapter blocking was analyzed as though the play consisted of a series of still pictures. In practice, however, the stage presents a moving picture, flowing from one telling moment to another. As the director begins in his pre-rehearsal blocking of the play to visualize how these major pictures will be composed, his next problem is how to get the actors where he needs them and at the proper time. This chapter will suggest some principles to help the director in making these decisions.

Although many of these principles are appropriate to directing in all of the various types of theatres, the concentration in this chapter is on proscenium staging. Special principles and techniques unique to arena, thrust, and other forms of non-proscenium theatre are emphasized in Chapter 6.

Movement can do more than merely connect the various stage pictures; the movement of an actor on stage may be in itself a powerful means of communicating meaning—intellectual or emotional—to an audience. Experience with audiences has yielded these traditional rules of movement:

A. A *moving figure attracts* the eye of the audience away from a static figure.

B. The actor therefore should *move only on his own lines*, with the following specific exceptions:

1. When the director *wants* the audience to look away from the speaker, as for example during a routine reading of a newspaper while surreptitious action goes on behind the reader's back.
2. When the movement itself is of sufficient interest to warrant a pause in the dialogue, as for example when all are watching to see what action a character will take, when no one is speaking, or between the sentences of another actor's speech.
3. When it is necessary to make a *"counter-cross"* or to *"dress stage."*
    Two or more characters are on stage and one character crosses in front of another; at the instant he is covered, the character who is crossed in front of "drops down" or counter-crosses to approximately the place vacated by the first person who crossed. The counter-cross must be done unobtrusively, casually, and motivated by the desire to see or hear better what the crossing actor is doing or saying. The purpose of the counter-cross is to restore the balance of the composition and improve the visibility of actors who would otherwise be covered. Actors should "dress stage" without being told.
4. When the director is dealing with very realistic ensemble acting which requires that the principal movement retains a strong center of interest but has constant peripheral movements of other characters in relationship to it.

C. The actor moving on his own lines should cross *below* others, so that part of the line spoken during the cross will not be lost behind another person. There are very few exceptions to this rule; an actor might cross *above* another when:

1. He is playing a servant or stealthy character.
2. The other person is seated, and the actor will be visible over his head.
3. He can get to a door more directly for an exit, and his partner does not need to face him during the exit dialogue.
4. He is counter-crossing.

D. A cross may be direct or indirect, broken up or continuous, curved or straight, depending upon the lines, the character and the situation.

1. A curved cross, in which the actor describes a concave arc, keeps him opened up to the audience longer than does a direct cross.

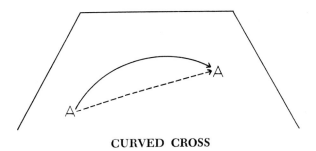

CURVED CROSS

2. An upstage cross can be broken up with pauses, pivots, turns and steals to keep from turning one's back to the audience. Inexperienced actors must be cautioned not to walk backwards or to sidle unless a very weak impression is desired; an actor can work his way upstage by a series of zig-zag movements—a motivated step to the right, a pivot, a step to the left, etc.

3. In a normal movement forward, the actor should shift his weight to his downstage leg and step off—a short step—with his upstage leg.

E. Turns should be made *toward* the audience unless the director indicates otherwise (when for example the actor is in the three-quarter position and an open turn would seem roundabout, or when the director wants a particularly weak or special movement). In making the turn toward the audience, the actor shifts his weight to his upstage foot and steps off with his downstage foot.

F. Every movement *must be motivated*, must have a purpose. Because it is sure to catch the eye of the audience, movement should not be random, aimless, or distracting. The inexperienced actor's most common fault is the tendency to make little, purposeless, repetitive movements because of nervousness or insecurity. The actor should use an economy of means, beginning a scene with a *tabula rasa*—a motionless, relaxed body—so that every movement will serve a purpose and convey some meaning. To reverse the familiar adage, the actor should be told, "Don't just do something—stand there." The purposes which movement can fulfill include the following, and one movement may serve more than one purpose simultaneously.

II. **The purposes of movement that stem from inner meaning.**

In this category are those movements which are chosen because they help the audience experience the inner content of the scene:

A. To give vent to a strong emotion. F) to establish mood

B. To tell the story G) line motivation

C) To underline interpersonal relationship

D) transition of beats.

E) to reveal character from to audience.

When a person is feeling a strong emotion, either happy or unhappy, his impulse is to express the emotion with bodily movement. Explosive lines, exclamations, and laments seem to impel the actor across stage space. If the director does not sense this, very often the actor will say, "I feel like moving here." Such a movement may serve the additional value, as we shall see under the technical purposes, of helping the actor achieve the emotional intensity required. *In this and following examples, movements supplied by the director are indicated in italics.*

Example: *Romeo and Juliet*, Act III, Scene 5. Lady Capulet and the Nurse are trying to restrain Capulet from his outburst at Juliet.

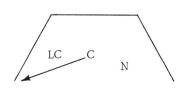

NURSE: May not one speak?

CAPULET: (*XLC to Nurse*) Peace, you mumbling fool! Utter your gravity o'er a gossip's bowl; For here we need it not.

LADY CAPULET: You are too hot.

CAPULET: God's bread! (*He shakes off* LADY C'S *restraining hand and XDR, pacing angrily.*) It makes me mad. Day, night, hour, tide, time, work, play. Alone, in company, still my care hath been to have her match'd;

B. To tell the story.

Whole stories can be told with movement alone, as in the dance theatre. Any story can be made more powerful if told through movement as well as pictures and words. Many memorable moments in the theatre are provided solely by movement, as in the last scenes of *The Visit* and *Tea and Sympathy*. Notice how a new development in the story is told through a movement in this scene from *Summer and Smoke*.

Example: DR. BUCHANAN: Be quiet, damn you. (JOHN *heads defiantly for door DL.*) Stay here! And listen to me. (JOHN *stops DLC.*) There is no room in the medical profession for wasters — drunkards — lechers!

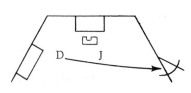

JOHN: (*A few steps towards his father.*) All right, then let me out of it!

DR. BUCHANAN: You were never in it. A medical diploma don't make you a doctor. No doctor fit to be called one would show that sort of criminal irresponsibility toward his—

JOHN: (Shouting) Then let me out of it!

DR. BUCHANAN: I've sent your things to the Alhambra Hotel. (*XDL past* JOHN *to door.*)

JOHN: Dad! I was with the old lady from seven till three in the morning. (*Sinks onto couch.* DR. *stops in doorway to listen.*) When she — lapsed into coma, I went out for some air. I saw the death of my mother, and ever since then I've had a dread of it that makes me unsuitable material for a doctor. I'm made for the science of medicine but not the practice of it.

DR. BUCHANAN: (Pause) (*X slowly to* JOHN *and puts hand on his shoulder.*) Pick up your things at the Alhambra Hotel and — bring them back to the house. I need you here.

JOHN: Yes, sir. (DR. *looks at his son a moment then turns and goes out.*)

C. To visualize interpersonal relationships as they change. In moments of stress, people move near those for whom they feel strong emotions—negative or positive—and remain farther apart from those to whom they are indifferent.

Example: *The Diary of Anne Frank,* Act II, Scene 3.

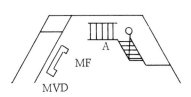

MRS. FRANK: (*X to* MRS. VAN DAAN *and forces the money into her hand.* MRS. VAN DAAN *moves away.*) Give this to Miep. She'll find you a place.

ANNE: (MRS. F. *starts back to put her purse away when* ANNE *comes* DLC *to intervene.*) Mother you're not putting Peter out. Peter hasn't done anything.

MRS. FRANK: He'll stay, of course. When I say the children, I mean Peter too.

PETER: (*Rises from steps.*) I'd have to go if Father goes.

MRS. FRANK: (*X past* ANNE *to* PETER.) He's no

father to you. . .that man! He doesn't know what it is to be a father.

PETER: I wouldn't feel right. I couldn't stay. (*He starts slowly up steps to his room.*)

MRS. FRANK: Very well, then, I'm sorry.

ANNE: (*Runs between her mother and* PETER, *and seizes* PETER'S *arm.*) No, Peter! No! (*Turns to her mother.*) I don't care about the food. They can have mine! I don't want it! Only don't send them away. It'll be daylight soon. They'll be caught. . .

D. To visualize transitions in thought or the beginning and end of beats. In this way movement can help the audience follow the development of the character's thoughts and emotions.

Example: *A Doll's House*, Act I.

MRS. LINDE: But dear Nora, what gentleman do you mean?

NORA: Dear, dear, can't you understand? There wasn't any old gentleman: it was only what I used to dream, and dream when I was at my wit's end for money. (*Rises from sofa, XURC.*) But it's all over now — the tiresome old creature may stay where he is for me; I care nothing for him

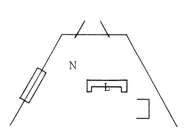

or his will; for now my troubles are over. (*Turns URC to face* MRS. LINDE.) Oh, Christina, how glorious it is to think of! Free from cares! Free, quite free. To be able to play and romp about with the children; (*Moves UR to window and adjusts drape femininely.*) to have things tasteful and pretty in the house, exactly as Torvald likes it! (*Looks out window.*) And then the spring is coming with the blue sky. Perhaps then we shall have a short holiday. Perhaps I shall see the sea again. (*Turns to face* MRS. LINDE.) Oh, what a wonderful thing it is to live and to be happy!

E. To reveal character to the audience.
People reveal themselves by the way they move, and especially by the way they walk.

Example: *Summer and Smoke,* Act I, Scene I.

ALMA: (*As* ALMA *sits on the bench and chatters,* JOHN *slowly circles above her, giving her a "once-over.*") The Gulf wind has failed us this year, disappointed us dreadfully this summer. We used to be able to rely on the Gulf wind to cool the nights off for us. but this season has been an exceptional season.

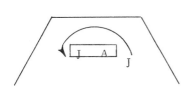

JOHN: (*Ends DR of bench, puts his foot up on it and scrutinizes* ALMA. *Slowly*). Are you — disturbed about something?

ALMA: (*Fidgeting nervously with her purse.*) That firecracker was a shock.

JOHN: You should be over that shock by now.

ALMA: (*Rises to get away from his gaze, and XDLC.*) I don't get over shocks quickly.

JOHN: I see you don't.

ALMA: You're planning to stay here and take over some of your father's medical practice?

JOHN: (*Sits, sprawling, legs wide apart on bench.*) I haven't made up my mind about anything yet.

F. To establish mood.
   1. A tragic mood is suggested by slow, direct, intense movements.
   2. A bright mood is suggested by short, quick, vivacious movements.
   3. High comedy is suggested by graceful, poised, curved crosses and movement.
   4. Melodrama is suggested by tense, fast, direct movements.
   5. Farce is suggested by sudden, jerky, incongruous, and rapid movements.

Example: *The Barretts of Wimpole Street,* Act I. One of the brothers has just announced that their father expects to go away for two weeks on business. (See ground plan, page 76.)

HENRIETTA: (*Flings arms around* GEORGE'S *neck and kisses him.*) Oh, George! How wonderful! How glorious! Do you polk, George?

GEORGE: Don't be childish!

HENRIETTA: Well, I polk. (*She dances the polka around the room, while humming "Little Brown*

Jug," all the brothers join in the humming. OC-
TAVIUS *claps his hands. The door opens quietly
and* EDWARD MOULTON-BARRETT *enters.*)

ELIZABETH: (*Breathlessly, as she sees him.*) Papa
— (*an awkward silence.* HENRIETTA *stops dead
in the middle of the room.*) Good evening, Papa.

BARRETT: (BARRETT *crosses in a deliberate slow,
long cross to fireplace ignoring them all. They
are breathless. He turns at the fireplace.*) (*Before
fireplace L, in a cold measured voice, looking
straight before him.*) I am most displeased.

THE BARRETTS OF WIMPOLE STREET—ENTRANCE OF FATHER
(with Miss Julie Haydon as guest artist) California State University, Long Beach.
Directed by W. David Sievers. Designed by John H. Green and Rosemary Stevens.

G. To provide motivation for another actor's next line.
Often two lines seem to follow each other without adequate motivation. Putting an appropriate movement between them may help
motivate what follows.

Example: *The Diary of Anne Frank*, Act I, Scene 3. Mr. Frank has
just agreed to make room for Mr. Dussel, at Kraler's
request. (See ground plan, page 85.)

MR. FRANK: Dussel! I think I know him.

MR. KRALER: I'll get him.

MR. FRANK: (MR. KRALER *goes down stairwell.* VAN
DAAN *smacks his hands behind his back and paces*

angrily DL. MR. FRANK *notices him.*) Forgive me. I spoke without consulting you. But I knew you'd feel as I do.

III. The purposes of movement that stem from technical or functional necessity.

In this category are those movements dictated by the nature of the theatre itself rather than the inner meaning of the play, and chosen by the director as he visualizes the play as it will look to the audience. Movement given to the actors for technical reasons must, however, *seem motivated* or justified from inner necessity rather than executed mechanically in obedience to the director's wishes. The director should therefore try to suggest to the actor a motivation for each technical movement as he gives it; when he does not have time to do this (and quite often he will not) the actor should try to find his own motivation. Among the technical purposes of movement are the following:

A. To link the important stage pictures and get the actors where they will need to be for succeeding lines or business (to "set up" the next picture).

Example: *The Diary of Anne Frank,* Act I, Scene 2.

MRS. FRANK: What did he mean, about the noise?

MR. FRANK: First (*He XDL to chair below stove. All proceed to take off garment after garment.*) let's take off some of these clothes.

MR. VAN DAAN: (*He XDR to* MRS. VAN DAAN *at sofa.*) It's a wonder we weren't arrested, walking along the streets...Petronella with a fur coat in July...and that cat of Peter's crying all the way.

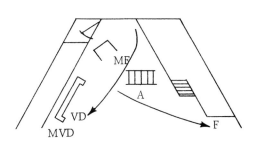

ANNE: (As she is removing a pair of panties.) A cat?

MRS. F R A N K: (Shocked) A n n e, please!

ANNE: It's all right. I've got on three more. (MRS. F. *sit UR chair.*)

MR. FRANK: Now. About the noise...

(*Through a series of technical moves, they are in a position for the picturization of "The Rules about Noise."*)

2) B. To keep the actors opened up for visibility and projection. (To control the center of attention and prevent upstaging on important lines.)

Example: *Blithe Spirit*, Act II, Scene 3. (See ground plan, page 223.)

RUTH: Is he highly strung, do you think?

DR. BRADMAN: Yes. (*XDLC and sets medical bag down.*) As a matter of fact I wanted to talk to you about that. I'm afraid he's been overworking lately.

RUTH: Overworking?

DR. BRADMAN: He's in rather a nervous condition — nothing serious, you understand —

RUTH: [*XDC to him. (Otherwise he is upstaged for important comedy lines to follow.)*] What makes you think so?

DR. BRADMAN: I know the symptoms. Of course the shock of his fall might have something to do with it, but I certainly should advise a complete rest for a couple of weeks.

3) C. To open up doorway areas prior to an entrance.

Example: *You Can't Take It With You.* Act I, Scene 2. (See ground plan, page 86.)

TONY: (*XUL to* PENNY'S *desk.*) My mother believes in spiritualism. That's just as bad as your mother writing plays, isn't it?

ALICE: It goes deeper. Tony. (*XDR, to below table.*) Your mother believes in spiritualism because it's fashionable, and your father raises orchids because he can afford to. (*Turns to him DR.*) My mother writes plays because eight years ago a typewriter was delivered here by mistake.

TONY: (*XDR to her.*) Darling what *of* it?

ALICE: And — (*X past him to RC,* GRANDPA'S *place at table.*) and look at Grandpa. Thirty-five years ago he just quit business one day. He started up to his office in the elevator and came right down again. He just stopped. He could have been a rich man, but he said it took too much time. So for thirty-five years, he's just collected snakes, and gone to circuses and commencements. It never occurs to any of them...

GRANDPA: (*Appears UL in doorway which requires the UL area to be cleared previously.*) Hello there, children!

4) D. To provide variety for the audience.

Many talky or static scenes require that the director add movement purely to relieve the visual monotony for the audience. Long speeches and soliloquies generally require breaking up with movement. The sheer physical necessity to look at another area of the stage will help hold the audience's attention.

Example: *The Importance of Being Earnest,* Act III.

JACK: I fear there can be no possible doubt about the m a t t e r. (*X haughtily DLC toward* ALGERNON.) This afternoon during my t e m p o r a r y absence in London on an important question of romance, he

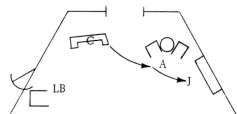

obtained admission to my house by means of the false pretense of being my brother. (*X past ALGERNON to fireplace DL*). Under an assumed name he drank, I've just been informed by my butler, an entire pint bottle of my Perrier-Jouet, Brut, '89; a wine I was specially reserving for myself. (*XURC toward* CECILY.) Continuing his disgraceful deception, he succeeded in the course of the afternoon in alienating the affections of my only ward. He subsequently stayed to tea, and devoured every single muffin. (*XDR to* LADY BRACKNELL.) And what makes his conduct all the more heartless is, that he was perfectly well aware from the first that I have no brother, not even of any kind. (*Turns to face ALGY DLC.*) I distinctly told him so myself yesterday afternoon.

5) E. To "dress stage," restore the balance, or otherwise improve the composition.

Example: *Romeo and Juliet,* Act III, Scene 3.
(Enter Nurse to Friar Laurence's cell)

NURSE: (*X to FRIAR.*) O holy Friar, O, tell me, holy friar, Where is my lady's lord, where's Romeo?

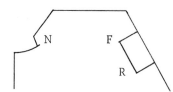

FRIAR: There on the ground, with his own tears made drunk.

NURSE: (*X past* FRIAR *to* ROMEO. FRIAR *counters* R *to watch what* NURSE *is going to do.*) O, he is even in my mistress' case, Just in her case!

F. To help the actor express his emotions.

It is important that *the actor feels comfortable in making the movement.* Particularly in scenes of strong emotion, the right movements may stimulate the actor to reach a depth of emotional intensity, and wrong movements may inhibit him and get in his way. The James-Lange theory of psychology may explain the observable fact that actors often are helped through physical autosuggestion to achieve emotional responses. A director who has been an actor himself will intuitively avoid asking his cast to play strong scenes seated or in confining parts of the stage. To achieve a large emotion, the actor needs bodily freedom to move. The movement may itself awaken the emotion. (For an example, refer back to the one given in II, A to which this purpose is closely related.)

G. To provide a rhythmic pattern through repetition (particularly in plays where nonrealistic style and pattern are desired). A movement or gesture remains in the audience's memory when reinforced by repetition until it becomes characteristic.

Example: *Dark of the Moon,* Act III, Scene 3.

JOHN: What's it to you to have Barbara's life?
FAIR WITCH: We ain't jest winnin her life. We bringin' you back. Bringin' you back to the moonlight and us.
JOHN: No, you ain't.
DARK WITCH: To the moonlight, and us.
JOHN: That ain't for me.
FAIR WITCH: Remember John boy, can't you remember? Remember those nights up there in the sky, you in my arms on the screamin' wind—how free we all was then. Can't you remember?
JOHN: But it's over. It's finished.
DARK WITCH: It's just the beinnin'. When you a witch again, you'll see things different.
JOHN: But I'll always remember, and I'll always love her.

FAIR WITCH: You'll change your mind. (Laughs and disappears)

DARK WITCH: We'll be a-waitin'. (Also laughs and disappears)

DARK OF THE MOON—RHYTHMIC PATTERN OF MOVEMENT Idyllwild Arts Foundation. Directed by W. David Sievers.

H. To get laughs.

Business, movement, and even "hokum" designed to get laughs can greatly enrich farce and comedy. Inventive directors and actors will find many ways to use movement for comic touches.

Example: *The Rivals*, Act III, Scene 4. Bob Acres has just writ-

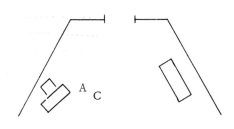

ten a challenge to Ensign Beverley, though he is mortally afraid of a duel. He asks his friend Captain Absolute to deliver the challenge, not knowing that Absolute and Beverley are the same person. As soon as Absolute takes the letter, Acres wishes he had it back.

ACRES: I want you to find him out for me, and give him this mortal defiance.

CAPTAIN ABSOLUTE: Well, give it to me, (*Taking letter*) and trust me he gets it.

ACRES: Thank you, my friend, my dear — (*Lunges to grab the letter back as soon as* ABSOLUTE *takes it.*) but it's giving you a great deal of trouble.

CAPTAIN ABSOLUTE: Not in the least. (*XDR, putting letter in R hand.*) I beg you won't mention it. No trouble in the world, I assure you.

ACRES: (*Follows DR to* ABSOLUTE'S *R, reaching for letter,* ABSOLUTE *transfers letter to L hand.*) You are very kind. What it is to have a friend! You couldn't be my second, could you, Jack?

CAPTAIN ABSOLUTE: Why no, Bob — not in this affair; it would not be quite so proper.

ACRES: Well, then, I must get my friend, Sir Lucius. (*Moves above* ABSOLUTE *to his L, reaching deftly for letter.* ABSOLUTE *eludes him, shifting letter to R hand.*) I shall have your good wishes, however, Jack?

CAPTAIN ABSOLUTE: Whenever he meets you, believe me. (ACRES *moves R above* ABSOLUTE *desperately reaching for letter.* ABSOLUTE *puts it neatly in his pocket.*) Well, my little hero, success attend you.

9) I. To heighten tension or build to climax.

Although movement is not the only means at the director's disposal for building a scene to a climax, it is one of the very effective ways of heightening dramatic intensity. Climax is covered in detail in Chapter 9.

Example: *The Crucible,* Act I, Scene 2.
(Proctor's wife has just been taken off to prison.)

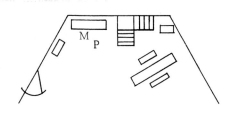

MARY: (*S l o w l y she XDRC and t a k e s* ELIZABETH'S *apron UR to fireplace.*) Mister Proctor, very likely they'll let her come h o m e once they're given proper evidence.

PROCTOR: (*Rises suddenly and XUR to her fiercely.*) You're coming to the court with me, Mary. You will tell it in the court.

MARY: (*Edges away from him DR.*) I cannot charge murder on Abigail.

PROCTOR: (*Follows her DR vehemently.*) You will tell the court how that poppet come here and who stuck the needle in.

MARY: (*Cornered, her back to wall, she blurts out in desperation.*) She'll kill me for sayin' that! Abby'll charge lechery on you, Mr. Proctor.

PROCTOR: (*Stops*)...She's told you!

MARY: I have known it, sir. She'll ruin you with it. I know she will.

PROCTOR: Good. Then her saintliness is done with. We will slide together into our pit. You will tell the court what you know.

MARY: (*X past him DLC.*) I cannot. They'll turn on me.

PROCTOR: My wife will never die for me. (*XDLC and grabs her.*) I will bring your guts into your mouth, but that goodness will not die for me.

MARY: I cannot do it. I cannot.

PROCTOR: Make your peace with it. Now Hell and Heaven grapple on our backs, and all our old pretense is ripped away. (*He flings her to the ground.*) Make your peace.

MARY: (*Sobs*) I cannot.

PROCTOR: Peace. It is a Providence and no great change. (*XR to door and opens door looking after* ELIZABETH.) We are what we always were, but naked now. Aye, naked, And the wind, God's icy wind, will blow.

CURTAIN

16) J. To reinforce or punctuate the dialogue through "pointing" and "throwing away" of lines.

This technical purpose of movement, which provides a means of emphasizing certain lines and subordinating others, is listed last not because it is less important, but only because it requires more detailed explanation. It is actually one of the most important techniques at the director's command; the effective integration of movement with dialogue makes blocking relatively simple and may at times give less experienced actors the appearance of professionals.

1. Movement before, during, or after a line.
   Extending the principle that the actor should move only on his own lines (with certain exceptions), it follows that there are logically only *four* possible times for him to move:

   a. Before he speaks.
   b. After he speaks.
   c. While he is speaking.
   d. Between phrases or words within his own speeches.
      Example: The following lines from *The Importance of Being Earnest* done each of the four ways will have different effects:
      a. JACK: (Kneels) Gwendolen, will you marry me?
      b. JACK: Gwendolen, will you marry me? (Kneels)
      c. JACK: (Kneeling as he speaks) Gwendolen, will you marry me?
      d. JACK: Gwendolen, (Kneels) will you marry me?
      a. ALGERNON: (Crosses to Cecily) But, seriously, Cecily, if my name was Algy, couldn't you love me?
      b. ALGERON: But, seriously, Cecily, if my name was Algy, couldn't you love me? (Crosses to Cecily)
      c. ALGERNON: (Crossing as he speaks) But, seriously, Cecily, if my name was Algy, couldn't you love me?
      d. ALGERNON: (Crossing as he says first part of line) But, seriously, Cecily, (Stops) if my name was Algy, couldn't you love me?

2. "Pointing" and "throwing away"

Experiment with the two foregoing examples will yield the following conclusions:

a. Movement or business *before* the line emphasizes or "points" the *line*. Therefore to point a line, put movement just before it.

b. Movement or business *after* the line emphasizes or "points" the movement. Therefore to point a piece of business or *movement* put an anticipatory line just before it.

c. Movement or business *during* the line emphasizes *neither* and hence tends to equalize both line and business. Therefore one way to underplay or "throw away" a line is to move while speaking it.

d. Movement or business *between* phrases within a speech points the part of the speech that comes after the movement. It is appropriate when a speech is part weak and part strong, and gives a cleaner separation of ideas than to move and speak together.

   (1) When the author repeats phrases for emphasis, the first can often be treated as weak and the second as strong. For example: (Pacing) "What could I have done? (Stops and turns) What could I have done?"

   (2) To point an exit line, move to the exit on the preceding weak line or phrase, turn and point the final line. To say the final line in the center of the stage gives the actor a long and usually weak cross to the door.

e. These rules are particularly useful in playing *comedy*. An actor can get a laugh either by pointing or throwing away a line.

   (1) If the line or part of it requires pointing to get a laugh, there should be no movement during it. Movement or business may be put just prior to the comic part. Brief, pointed gestures or business may also be used immediately *after* a comic line for punctuation. For example: fanning, flicking ashes from a cigarette, putting a hat on, sitting down.

   (2) A laugh can also be obtained by applying these rules in reverse, i.e., point for a big effect and give the audience a lesser one. For example: "Do you know what I am going to do about it? (Rises pompously) Nothing!"

f. One type of line which often takes a forward movement is a question or exclamation directed to a specific character. If the line ends in an emphatic point, it is well to come to a stop before those words.

3. Dividing the dialogue into strong and weak lines.
The director must be able to sense which lines are strong (to be pointed) and which are weak (to be thrown away).

   a. Weak or throw away lines are not necessarily poor or value-less lines. They are merely lines that can receive relatively less emphasis than strong ones for the sake of contrast. Weak lines still must be heard clearly by the audience (or if they serve no purpose they should be cut).

   b. Movement is not necessary on every weak line; many times vocal techniques alone are sufficient to set apart the strong and weak lines, as will be pointed out in Chapter 9.

   Example: Notice the value which these movements give in punctuating a speech from *Blithe Spirit.* (See ground plan on page 232)

   CHARLES: (*Rises, XR to RUTH.*) Once and for all, Ruth, I would like you to understand that (*Stops*) what happened last night had nothing to do with alcohol. (*Turns with shrug, and XDL.*) You've very adroitly rationalized the whole affair to your own satisfaction, but your deductions are bared on complete fallacy. (*Stops DL & faces R.*) I am willing to grant you that it was an aberration, (*XUL apologetically.*) some sort of odd psychic delusion brought on by suggestion or hypnosis. (*Turns to face RUTH, UL*) I was stone cold sober from first to last (*moves to UL chair.*) and extremely upset into the bargain. (*Sits vigorously.*)

IV. How to use movement in blocking a scene.

With the purposes, both internal and external, which movement can serve clearly in mind, the director is ready to proceed to the actual work of blocking the play in his director's book. As a result of his interpretative study of the play as suggested in Chapter 3, the director will have formed some ideas concerning the movement and flow of the play, as well as some basic images of the pictorial composition. On the basis of these concepts, he has discussed a possible ground plan with the designer, remembering that the ground plan should be developed to enhance the actions and pictures he foresees, not dictate or limit them *ex post facto.* They arrive at a final, specific, and detailed ground plan to scale. Only then, with a scale ground plan in front of him (sometimes with the aid of toy figures or twisted pipe cleaners) can the director block the play in detail, visualizing every movement and recording the result in his director's book. As he blocks the play, the director may find himself going through something like the following process. He must decide:

A. *Who* is to make the movement.

Analyzing each scene by beats and actions will reveal who takes the initiative or "whose scene it is." This character will most likely have the dominant movement in the beat, the other characters responding to him with reactions or compensating movement. When the beat changes and another character asserts himself, he will take over the dominant movement.

B. *Why* the movement is needed.

(On the basis of one or more of the purposes which have been listed.)

C. *What* kind of movement is needed.

   1. Types of movement.

      a. Changes in body position.

         (1) Facings and facial expression.
         (2) Changes of posture.
         (3) Gestures.
         (4) Turns.

      b. Movement in space.

         (1) Crosses.
         (2) Rises and seatings.
         (3) Contact with other actors—grabbing, pushing, restraining, embracing.
         (4) Contact with scenery or properties.
         (5) Changes of level—ascents and descents.

      c. Business.

         (1) With hand props.
         (2) With character props—fans, cigars, gloves, etc.
         (3) Pantomime.

   2. Emotional values of movement.

      a. Aggressive versus regressive.

         (1) Aggressive movements impel one actor toward another.
         (2) Regressive movements impel one actor away from another.

      b. Possessive versus rejecting.

         (1) Possessive movements impel one actor toward another.

(2) Rejecting movements impel one actor away from another.

c. Dominant versus passive.

(1) Movements which dominate others are strong.

(2) Movements which yield to others are weak.

d. Peacemaking or mediating.

e. Expected versus unexpected.

(1) Expected movements are often weak.

(2) Unexpected movements or those which go against the empathic desire of the audience are strong.

f. Completed versus incomplete.

(1) Completed movement is generally strong.

(2) Incomplete movement is generally weak.

(3) Interrupted movement may be either strong or weak. The actor must make the movement as though he expected to complete it if it were not interrupted by another actor.

3. Technical values of movement.

All movement can be categorized technically as either *strong* or *weak* in value. The strength or weakness of the movement should correspond to the strength or weakness of the dialogue with which it is associated unless deliberate incongruity is desired for comic effect.

a. Strong movements:

(1) To move from a weaker body position to a stronger one. (From three-quarter to profile or one-quarter, etc.)

(2) To move from a weaker stage area to a stronger one. (Cross from UL to DL, etc.)

(3) To rise.

(4) To step forward, onstage or downstage.

(5) To ascend steps or levels.

(6) To move out from behind furniture.

(7) To move in contrast to others.

(8) To move to scenic elements of strength—columns, thrones, arches, etc.

(9) To move to brighter areas in light.

(10) To move out from a group.

(11) To cross from stage left to stage right is stronger than from stage right to left. (Dean[1] concludes that this

1. Alexander Dean and Lawrence Carra, *Fundamentals of Play Directing*, rev. ed. (New York: Holt, Rinehart & Winston, Inc., 1965), pp. 194, 195.

results from the conditioning of our eyes to read from the left side of the page toward the right. Movement counter to this tendency sets up a resistance in the eye muscles which makes the movement seem more emphatic. An army going off to battle thus is most effective going from SL to SR, returning to defeat from SR to SL.)

b. Weak movements:

(1) To move from a stronger body position to a weaker one.
(2) To move from a stronger stage area to a weaker one.
(3) To sit (or if sitting to slouch or lie down).
(4) To step back, offstage or upstage.
(5) To descend in level (except that descending steps may be strong if it brings the actor to a strong downstage area).
(6) To move behind furniture.
(7) To move along with others.
(8) To move away from scenic elements of strength.
(9) To move to a darker area of the stage.
(10) To merge into a group.

4. Style of movement.

a. Realistic, literal movement.
b. Enlarged realistic movement.
c. Theatricalized movement, calling attention to itself.
d. Symbolic movement or selective partial movement representing the whole.

5. The amount of movement.
The type of the play or scenes will govern the amount of movement that is appropriate.

a. Tragic or serious scenes require relatively less movement.
b. Comic, farcical, and melodramatic scenes require more movement.
c. Talky, static scenes require more created movement for interest and variety.

6. The size of the movement.
Factors which affect the size of movement include:

a. The character making the movement—whether expansive or inhibited.
b. The size of the auditorium to which it must be projected.
c. The width and depth of the setting.

        d. The length of the lines which must be integrated with the movement.

    7. The tempo of the movement.
Movement must advance rather than impede the tempo of the scene. Factors which govern the tempo of movement will include:

        a. The intensity of the inner emotion which motivates the movement—how anxious the character is to further his beat by making the movement.
        b. Where the movement comes in relation to a climax.
As scenes build to climax movement becomes progressively faster or slower, depending on the nature of the scene.
        c. The interest which the movement will have for the audience—how long it will "hold."

D. *Where on the stage the actor should move.*
On the basis of the factors analyzed in Chapter 4, the director will decide where he wants to group his actors.

    1. The director should work from one main picture to another.
He visualizes a strong or climactic moment, noting on his ground plan in his director's book where each actor should be for the most effective picturization.
    2. He then *works backwards,* going back several lines or even pages in order to find an appropriate line on which to move each actor where he later needs him.

E. *When the actor should move.*
The selection of the actual line on which to move is done on the basis of the principles given on pages 146-48, which discuss movement in relation to dialogue.
It is better not to adhere to the stage directions of the acting edition; these movements were originally devised for other settings, ground plans, actors, theatres, and interpretations of the play.

    1. The director (or the actor himself at rehearsal) will find a line which seems appropriate to move on (i.e., a weak line, a question, exclamation, or anticipatory half of a strong line).
    2. It should be long enough to get the actor where he needs to go.
    3. It should not contribute to a repetitious pattern of movement. (See V following.)

F. *How the actor should move.*
The movement visualized by the director and performed by the actor must be done in character, naturally, and spontaneously. The movement should feel right to the actor, should be **properly**

integrated with the dialogue, and should be rehearsed until the actor can make the movement without looking where he is going or making it seem studied. Some traditional techniques for making movement appear motivated and keeping the actor opened up to the audience include these:

1. Gestures.
    a. Whenever there is a choice gestures are made with the upstage hand or arm. The most common exceptions are saluting and shaking hands, which traditionally are done with the right hand whether it is upstage or downstage.
    b. In handing a prop from one person to another, the actor may reach for it with his upstage hand, then change it to his downstage hand to pass it on, rather than crossing his body with the upstage arm (except in a comic characterization of an awkward person).
    c. Gestures that cover the face, particularly the mouth, should be carefully managed so as not to interfere with projection.

2. Sitting and rising.
    a. The actor should sit and rise in character. How the legs and feet rest while sitting is an important element in characterization. If the character is graceful and poised, he might sit with his upstage leg forward and his downstage leg drawn back.
    b. In approaching a chair, the actor can feel for it with the back of his leg rather than having to turn around and look before he sits.
    c. When a chair is placed facing partly upstage, the actor can still sit in it without being upstaged; he can cheat his body and sit sideways in the chair, bringing his face into profile for most of his lines.

3. Entering and exiting.
    a. The actor should always close a door after entering or exiting except when directed otherwise.
    b. If the door is on the side wall, it should be opened with the upstage hand and closed with the downstage hand. If the door is on the rear wall, it is opened with the arm nearest the hinges and closed with the arm which is toward center stage.
    c. The actor should anticipate an entrance cue in sufficient time to arrive in position on the word cue except when directed otherwise.

    d. When two characters enter together, the speaking one usually enters last.

    e. A butler stands on the upstage side of a door in announcing someone.

    f. Don't let the audience's first view of an actor be of his back, unless some special purpose is served thereby. The actor should try to avoid facing upstage on his entrance even if all the other actors are upstage of him.

    g. The actor should not anticipate where people or objects will be on stage. Unless the room is well-known to him, the actor should hesitate in the door area long enough to survey the room.

    h. At rehearsals the actors should pay particular attention to the outline of the set marked on the floor. They should enter where the door will actually be, pantomiming opening and closing it if necessary rather than drifting in and out or walking through walls.

    i. An effective exit is made by getting the actor near the door on the *speech prior to his last,* so that after his last line he can disappear promptly. It is usually quite weak to walk to an exit with no lines to say or after the exit speech is finished; the only exception to this would be when a character's decision to leave is of more significance than his lines. An actor would seldom have occasion to exit on someone else's lines.

4. Economy of movement.

The actor should learn to stand still, not rocking back and forth nor fidgeting from leg to leg. Meaningless movements, gestures or repetitive mannerisms soon begin to distract the audience. The actor should also guard against bobbing his head up and down while speaking or bending from the waist for emphasis.

5. Miscellaneous.

    a. When an actor looks out a window, he should establish the off-stage object in such a position that he does not have to remain with his back to the audience.

    b. In turning on and off lights, deliberate covering usually is necessary; the actor's body should cover the business, with the actor keeping his hand on the switch or lamp until the lights come up or down.

    c. In handling a telephone, the actor should keep it farther from his mouth than usual in order not to muffle his voice.

V. The pattern of movement.

As the individual movements fall into place in relation to dialogue, a pattern of movement begins to emerge. The pattern will need to be refined, clarified, and polished over a period of weeks, new points added for enrichment and awkward moments fixed. Except in highly theatricalized plays, the audience should not be conscious of pattern.

A. Means of achieving a varied and natural pattern of movement:
1. Actors should avoid repeating the same movement.
(One cross to window in the speech from *A Doll's House* on page 136 —would be effective. A second cross might be boring. Many ideas for movement in a scene will have to be rejected by the director simply because they have already been used in the same scene.)
2. Avoid spacing the movements too regularly.
(A pattern of turning away for two lines and then turning back on the third would soon become monotonous.)
3. Avoid a series of movements which are all equal in strength.
(As will be seen in the study of climax, a scene should either build toward climax or relax after it. Movement within a beat should therefore become progressively stronger or progressively weaker.)
4. Avoid two persons moving in exactly the same or exactly the opposite direction at the same time, unless a particular comic effect is desired. (In real life two people rarely move in parallel, and to use such movement on the stage gives a studied or prearranged impression.)

B. Means of achieving a theatricalized or self-conscious pattern:

1. In theatrical plays such as *The Importance of Being Earnest* or *The Matchmaker,* the foregoing four "things to avoid" can be done deliberately and with studied repetition. (Also many of the other principles and practices of movement discussed in this chapter can be reversed effectively.)

2. Pattern suggests conformity and as such can be used for telling effect, both comic and serious.
(For example, each of the sons in *Life with Father* enters for breakfast and kisses his mother. The youngest breaks the pattern by sliding down the bannister into the room. In *Tea and Sympathy* the boys habitually check the pay phone as they pass it, to see if a dime has been left in the return hopper— a delightful "touch" supplied by director Elia Kazan.

C. Movement in constricted space.

Confining sets present particular problems concerning the avoidance of monotony in the movement pattern.

The following scene from *Summer and Smoke*, Act I, was played in a constricted set which utilized only one third of the stage, in order that the park and the doctor's office could be simultaneously visible. Notice that the placing of the mother on a bench DL makes it possible for Alma to come at her from a variety of positions and keep herself visible. If the mother had been upstage, it would have weakened every one of Alma's emphatic moments.

Alma is speaking to her mother, who has the mentality of a child. Her mother has accused her of being in love with the boy next door (which happens to be true).

(1) XDC toward mother who sits on DL bench.

(2) stops DL.

(3) Alma XUC

(5) Moves wearily away toward DR.

(7) XDLC toward mother.

(9) Turns to face mother.

ALMA: "If ever I hear you say such a thing again, if ever you dare to repeat such a thing in my presence or anybody else's, then it will be the last straw! You understand me? Yes, you understand me! You act like a child, but you have the devil in you. And God will punish you — yes! I'll punish you too. I'll take your cigarettes from you and give you no more. I'll give you no more ice-cream either. Because I'm tired of your malice. Yes, I'm tired of your malice and your self-indulgence. People wonder why I'm tied down here! They pity me — think of me as an old maid already! I'm young. Still young! It's you — *it's you*, you've taken my youth away from me! I wouldn't say that — I'd try not even to think it —if you were just kind, just simple! But I could spread my life out like a rug for you to step on and you'd step on it, and not even say "Thank you, Alma!"

Closes door DR behind Nellie who has gone out, and wheels to face her mother.

(4) Comes DC a step to threaten her.

(6) Stops DR, turns to face mother.

(8) Ashamed of what she said, she turns away, DR.

(10) XURC.

(11) Wheels to face mother, URC.

Which is what you've done always — and now you dare to tell a disgusting lie about me — in front of that girl!

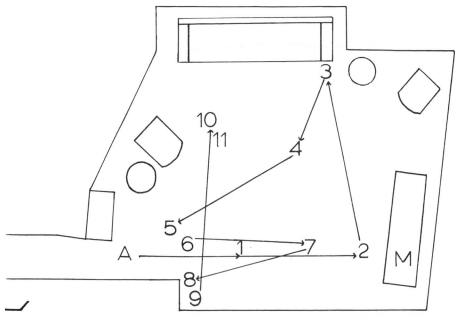

SUMMER AND SMOKE—MOVEMENT IN CONSTRICTED SPACE California State University, Long Beach. Directed by W. David Sievers. Designed by John Nicholson.

VI. Summary.

The neophyte who may feel overwhelmed by the intricacies of movement should be reassured that no matter how detailed the pre-block-
ing is, proper changes in blocking may grow organically over a period
of many rehearsals as a result of the creative interaction of actors
and director. No two directors will block a scene with exactly the
same movement, and no principles given in this chapter are to be
considered inviolable. The techniques of movement grow out of the
widely accepted concepts that: (1) a moving figure attracts the
eye of the audience away from a static figure; (2) with certain exceptions, actors should move only on their own lines; (3) the speaking actor should cross below other standing actors; (4) a curved
cross keeps an actor opened up longer than does a direct cross; (5)
turns should usually be made toward the audience; (6) every movement must be motivated.

A. The purposes of movement that stem from inner meaning.

    1. To give vent to a strong emotion.
    2. To tell the story.
    3. To visualize interpersonal relationships as they change.
    4. To visualize transitions in thought or the beginning and end
       of beats.
    5. To reveal character to the audience.
    6. To establish mood.
    7. To provide motivation for another actor's next line.

B. The purposes of movement that stem from technical or functional
necessity.

    1. To link the important stage pictures and get the actors where
       they will need to be for succeeding lines or business.
    2. To keep the actors opened up for visibility and projection.
    3. To open up doorway areas prior to an entrance.
    4. To provide variety for the audience.
    5. To "dress stage," restore the balance or otherwise improve the
       composition.
    6. To help the actor express his emotions.
    7. To provide a rhythmic pattern through repetition.
    8. To get laughs.
    9. To heighten tension or build to climax.
   10. To reinforce or punctuate the dialogue through "pointing" and
       "throwing away" of lines.

C. How to use movement in blocking a scene.

    1. Who is to make the movement.

2. Why the movement is needed.
3. What kind of movement is needed.
4. Where on the stage the actor should move.
5. When the actor should move.
6. How the actor should move.

D. The pattern of movement.

1. To achieve a varied and natural pattern of movement.
2. To achieve a theatricalized or self-conscious pattern.
3. Movement in constricted space.

Selective Bibliography

Albright, H. D.; Halstead, William P.; and Mitchell, Lee. *Principles of Theatre Art.* Boston: Houghton-Mifflin Co., 1955.

Battye, Marguerite. "Stage Movement" in *Acting and Stage Movement,* by White and Battye. New York: Arc Books, 1963.

Dean, Alexander and Carra, Lawrence. *Fundamentals of Play Directing.* Rev. ed. New York: Holt, Rinehart & Winston, Inc., 1965.

King, Nancy. *Theatre Movement: The Actor and His Space.* New York: Drama Book Specialists, 1971.

McMullan, Frank. *The Director's Handbook.* Hamden, Conn.: Shoe String Press, 1964.

Reinhardt, Paul D. "Movement in Period Plays," *Educational Theatre Journal,* XIV, 1, March, 1962.

Selden, Samuel. *The Stage in Action.* New York: F. S. Crofts & Co., 1946.

Strickland, F. Cowles. *The Technique of Acting.* New York: McGraw-Hill, 1956.

Thornton, Samuel. *Laban's Theory of Movement; A New Perspective.* Boston, Mass.: Plays, Inc., 1971.

MOTHER COURAGE   California State University, Long Beach. Directed by Mathias Reitz. Designed by Beala B. Neel (Sets), Warren Travis (Costumes) and John Davis (Lights).

6 Non-Proscenium Staging

I. Introduction.

Although proscenium staging is still the predominant form in our contemporary theatre, other types of staging have become increasingly popular. Central staging has made possible a renaissance in the community theatre movement since World War II. Open or thrust staging has increased in prominence in repertory and university theatres. Flexible staging has become the ideal for many experimental and modern theatre artists. Today, a theatre director can hardly afford to be unfamiliar with the techniques required by these essentially non-proscenium forms. If he knows the principles of good theatre as applied to the proscenium stage, he can easily adapt them to other forms. All that has been covered in most of the chapters in this book can be considered applicable to central, open, and flexible staging. It is primarily in picturization, some aspects of movement, and the handling of the technical elements of theatre that these forms most differ from proscenium staging. The director may find it frustrating to unlearn much he has been taught about proscenium staging, but he will find it easier to adapt than would a director trained in any of the other forms and adapting to proscenium staging.

II. Central Staging.

Central staging has been variously referred to as "theatre-in-the round," "circus theatre," "arena theatre" and "penthouse staging." No matter which label is used, its main aspect is that the audience is seated on all sides of the acting area which may in turn be square, rectangular, circular, oval, or elliptical in shape.

A. Advantages.

1. It can be done by a group which has no proscenium theatre. Lack of a home is no longer an insurmountable obstacle to a community or school group which wants to start a theatre. Stores, auto sales rooms, tents, ballrooms, gymnasiums, classrooms, museum and exhibit halls, and even forbiddingly large proscenium stages have been successfully converted to central staging.

2. It greatly reduces a group's budget for scenery. Volunteer man-hours necessary to build sets are also minimized, a considerable advantage to groups without stagecraft facilities and personnel.

3. It may represent a far more satisfactory solution for a director than to struggle against overwhelming odds on an oversized proscenium stage with obsolete lighting equipment, inadequate technical help and budget, in an auditorium in which projection is difficult and which is never filled for a dramatic presentation—and in which the director cannot get sufficient rehearsal time because other groups share the facilities.

4. Audiences like it. Aesthetically, it offers an intimacy and contact with the actors which many people prefer to the long distances between performers and spectators in the balcony of professional playhouses.

5. It stimulates the imaginations of audiences to provide their own environmental background for the production.

B. Disadvantages.

1. It is not equally well-suited to all types of plays, as the possibilities for spectacle are greatly reduced. Some of the visual magic of the theatre is missing. Most directors would concede that modern comedies and realistic dramas are the best choice for central staging, although other plays have been quite successfully center-staged. Many directors believe that plays in the following categories would offer a more fully satisfying theatrical experience on a proscenium or other form of stage:

   a. Plays which depend upon spectacle and background for localizing environment, creating mood and atmosphere, such as A *Midsummer Night's Dream, The Teahouse of the August Moon,* and *The Visit.*

b. Plays which because of their subject matter require aesthetic distance between audience and performer.

c. Plays which depend upon large crowd scenes.

d. Multi-set plays which require detailed realistic treatment, or which have complex properties that need shifting.

2. It requires a high degree of concentration on the part of the actors. Actors must play with a sense of truth and attention to detail, act with their whole bodies and always remain in character, oblivious to the faces they can recognize in the audience.

3. Costumes, make-up, and properties must be carefully prepared and authentic, as they are subject to scutiny from all sides.

4. Entrances and exits are often less effective than on the proscenium stage.

5. Illusion is frequently more difficult to achieve and maintain, and certain stage effects present knotty but not insoluble problems—shootings and killings, disappearances, playing musical instruments, for example.

6. Changes of setting, particularly quick changes between scenes, are difficult to manage.

7. Good lighting may require more instruments and more careful planning than on proscenium stages.

8. There is less likelihood that a young person will be convincing in an older role, and central staging therefore may impose some limitations on casting.

C. Problems of Blocking.

1. Picturization.

The director accustomed to one stage picture in the proscenium theatre will have to get accustomed to planning each scene for the benefit of all four sections of his theatre. There are no strong and weak areas of the stage and there should be no preferred seating for the audience. The director should spend part of every rehearsal in each section of his auditorium.

a. Emphasis.
In central staging the non-compositional factors of emphasis become more important than the compositional ones. Of the twelve means of obtaining emphasis discussed in Chapter 4, the only ones practicable in central staging are:

(1) Level—of limited value because (a) it is hard to motivate the use of levels in the average interior set, (b) the elevation on which the actor stands may itself

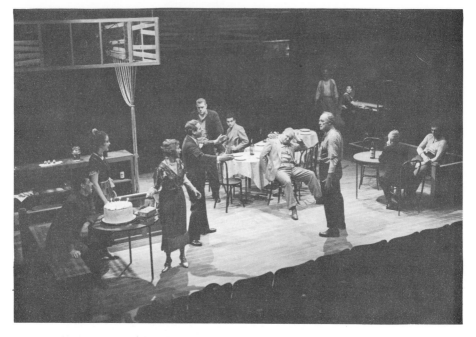

THE ICEMAN COMETH   Arena Stage, Washington D.C. Directed by F. Cowles Strickland. Designed by Curtis Cowan.

block visibility of part of the stage for some in front row seats, and (c) the elevated actor must still turn his back on at least a quarter of the audience. When feasible, however, levels can increase emphasis on the actor.

(2) Focus of the actors.

(3) Contrast, particularly between standing and sitting. Whenever possible actors with few lines should be seated and those with the majority of the lines should be standing.

(4) The speaking actor will not always be the center of attention for all parts of the auditorium. *Reaction* of other actors to what is being said therefore becomes more important than in proscenium staging—for it is all some spectators may be able to see at the moment.

(5) Lighting.

(6) Color.

(7) Movement.

b. Visibility.

Problems of emphasis in proscenium staging become in central staging simply problems of making actors visible.

Each section of the auditorium should be able to see at least one actor's face most of the time.

(1) Scenes with two people:
    (a) Walden Boyle emphasizes the value of an actor's working with his back to an aisle in order to give the best visibility to the largest number of spectators.[1]
    (b) Both actors should not face the same direction at the same time.
    (c) Playing with space between two actors makes better visibility than when they are close together. Keep the actors as far apart as can be justified, and find ways to pull them apart once they have closed in.
    (d) Except when playing with back to an aisle, actors should avoid facing each other directly when possible. One or both of the actors should step sideways and open up, facing his partner with a one-quarter position rather than full-front—what Kelly Yeaton calls "twisting the pairs,"[2] so that part of the audience sees each actor over the other's shoulder.
    (e) Scenes between two people on a sofa present special problems. A sofa forces both people to face the same direction, turning their backs on the same section of the audience. The director must find ways to overcome this by having one actor sit on an arm of the sofa, put his feet up and sit sideways, swivel his body around, etc.

(2) Scenes with three people:
Such scenes are easier to handle than twosomes. An open triangle works well, providing each part of the auditorium with a view of at least one actor's face.

(3) Group scenes:
    (a) Keep as many minor characters seated around the periphery as possible, to motivate the principal character's moving to direct speeches to them.
    (b) Eliminate or combine minor characters to reduce

---

1. Walden P. Boyle, *Central and Flexible Staging* (Los Angeles and Berkeley: University of California Press, 1956).

2. Kelly Yeaton, "Arena Production," in *Producing the Play*, ed. John Gassner, (New York: The Dryden Press, 1953). Also section on "Simplified Staging" in same volume.

the number on stage, as each person adds to the problem of keeping the principals visible.

(c) Where large crowds are required (as in *An Enemy of the People*) use level to make the speaker visible—letting him stand on a bench, table, or prop rock.

(d) Minor figures who can appropriately sit or lie on the floor aid in visibility.

(e) Minor figures may stand in the aisles, or even, as in a New York arena staging of *Julius Caesar*, behind the spectators.

(f) Avoid groupings with all backs turned outward.

2. Movement.

All of the purposes of movement given in Chapter 5 which stem from inner meaning apply equally well to central staging, and all of the purposes which stem from technical or functional necessity apply with the exception of preventing upstaging and dressing stage or restoring balance. The primary purpose for which the director must use movement in central staging, however, is to vary the picturization so that each section of the audience sees each principal actor's face for part of every beat, scene, or long speech.

a. The "pig on a spit" theory.
While the actor must face each section of the auditorium during a scene, he must not do this mechanically or rotate from one section to the next in sequence like a pig on a spit.

b. A better way of thinking of the actor's movement is suggested by the term coined by Margo Jones,[3] "making the rounds." During a long speech—a telephone conversation for example—the actor must find motivation for turning his body in all directions.

c. Movement in central staging must, as in proscenium staging, be motivated from within the character. As more movement is required, more inventiveness on the part of the actor in creating justified movement is necessary. It is especially important to find motivation to move away from other people even while talking to them (based on the principle of strong and weak lines).

d. A stage picture cannot be held for as long as it might be in proscenium staging. Kelly Yeaton has said that "No group-

3. Margo Jones, *Theatre-in-the-Round* (New York: Rinehart and Co., 1951).

ing is bad if it doesn't last long," and further declares that "A useful concept for the movement of arena groups is that of a net of human tensions connecting all of the characters involved in the action. . . . The movement of any person in the net should involve changes in each of the others, and often corresponding readjustments of position or attention."[4]

e. Furniture needs to be placed toward the outer edges but not necessarily on the periphery of the acting area in order to motivate movement centrifugally from center toward the perimeter. It is helpful for actors to be able to move around the furniture units.

f. Entrances and exits.
Entrances and exits will unavoidably be less pointed than in proscenium staging. Except for buildings designed especially for central staging, it is rarely possible for the actor to disappear promptly from a lighted area. Some suggested ways of dealing with the problem include:

(1) To treat the aisles through which the actors enter and exit as a convention, keeping them dark and assuming that the character is offstage as soon as he is within an aisle, so that the other characters are free to resume the dialogue without waiting for him to disappear.

(2) To treat the aisles as a playing area, letting the actors speak as they walk up and down the aisles. Disadvantages of this technique are that light is then required in the aisles, part of the audience needs to swivel their bodies around into an awkward position to see the actors, and the entire audience becomes more conscious of other spectators than is desirable during these exits and entrances.

(3) To use the doors to the auditorium for the actors.

(4) To rewrite some of the entrance and exit speeches so that a pointed entrance line is preceded by several throw-away lines, and a pointed exit speech is followed by several weak lines, permitting the actor to continue his movement up or down the aisle without sacrificing significant lines.

(5) To have the actors get up and down the aisles as quickly as possible, minimizing the awkward movements when

4. Yeaton, *Arena Production.*

they must brush past spectators and jeopardize the illusion.

g. Blocking and recording the movement.

There is no fixed nomenclature for dividing the central stage into areas. Some directors use directions based on:

(1) The compass—cross North, cross Southeast, etc.
(2) The clock—cross to nine o'clock, four o'clock, etc.
(3) The sections of the auditorium, as designated on tickets —cross to B section, D section, etc.
(4) Location of furniture and objects of actors' attention— cross to the sofa, cross away from Robert, into the group, etc.
(5) Arbitrary numbering of specific action or stage property areas.

Examples of blocking for central staging: (the same speech for which a suggested proscenium blocking was given in Chapter 5, page 141.) A symbol such as ⊖ should be used to show which way a character is facing.

In the proscenium composition, Lady Bracknell could be standing, for emphasis. In central staging, she and Gwendolen would most likely be seated, and Algernon and Cecily, whose arms are around each other, standing with their backs to an aisle. The scene, in the morning room of the house, could just as effectively be played in the garden set of the previous act. Jack begins with back to the aisle between Sec. A and B.

1. X to C facing Lady Bracknell.	JACK: ↓ It pains me very much to have to speak frankly to you, Lady Bracknell, about your nephew, but the fact is that I do not approve at all
Turns to glare at Algy.	of his moral character. ↓ I suspect him of being untruthful.

LADY BRACKNELL: Untruthful! My nephew Algernon? Impossible! He is an Oxonian.

	JACK: I fear there can be no possible
2. X toward Algy.	doubt about the matter. ↓ This afternoon, during my temporary absence in London on an important question of romance, he obtained

3. X past Algy to between D and C sections, facing aisle.

admission to my house by means of the false pretense of being my brother. ⬆ Under an assumed name he drank, I've just been informed by my butler, an entire pint bottle of my Perrier-Jouet, Brut, '89; a wine I was specially reserving for

Turns to Cecily.

myself. ⬆ Continuing his disgraceful deception, he succeeded in the course of the afternoon in alienat-

4. Moves to tea cart and picks up empty muffin dish.

ing the affections of my only ward. ⬆ He subsequently stayed to tea, and devoured every single

5. X center near chair at Sec. B facing Sec. A.

muffin. ⬆ And what makes his conduct all the more heartless is, that he was perfectly well aware from the first that I have no brother, that I never had a brother, and that I don't intend to

6. Sits in chair, Sec. B (toward Sec. A).

have a brother, not even of any kind. ⬆ I distinctly told him so myself yesterday afternoon.

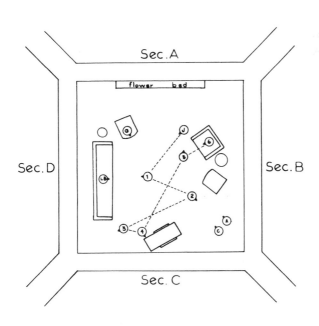

THE IMPORTANCE OF BEING EARNEST, Act III

3. Voice.

Although less vocal projection is required in central staging than in a large proscenium theatre, it may be surprising to discover that *more* projection is needed in central staging than in a comparable size room used for proscenium staging. The reason is apparent: the actor's back is to part of his audience at all times, and the consonants, particularly the all-important final consonants that make for understandability, may easily be lost when the spectator neither sees accompanying facial expression nor hears the speech directly.

D. Central staging technical problems.

1. Scenery.

a. Some designers for central staging have found ingenious ways of using skeletal scenery or a wall of their auditorium or an aisle between sections of the audience for bits of scenery necessary in the action—a porch on which the flower pot drops, for example, in *The Seven Year Itch* or a wall on which a painting can hang in *The Glass Menagerie*.

THE PURSUIT OF HAPPINESS California State University, Long Beach. Directed by W. David Sievers. Designed by Herbert L. Camburn.

   b. Doors and windows can be established by:

      (1) Pantomime.
      (2) Placing them at the heads of aisles.
      (3) Utilizing actual entrances to the arena.
      (4) Very thin skeletal outlines of the doors and windows created with 1" x 1" lumber or aluminum tubing.
      (5) Half-doors and windows, no more than 2' high.

   c. Mirrors and pictures on walls can be convincingly pantomimed if the actor is truthful and consistent, or they can be reduced to table size.

   d. Changes of setting can be accomplished by:

      (1) Having actors in the cast who play butlers, maids or lackeys shift the furniture and properties in view of the audience at intermission. The shifts must be carefully rehearsed, performed in character and without haste.
      (2) Having members of the technical crew, dressed in clean and appropriate work clothes do the shifts in view of the audience at intermission.
      (3) Having crew members or actors make the shifts in the dark during blackouts between scenes. They must be dressed in black, must carefully rehearse each move, and should have music to cover the noise of shifting. Complicated shifts should not be attempted in the dark, for the audience may soon grow either embarrassed or bored.
      (4) Use of simultaneous settings and a change in light. The stage area can be divided into two or more areas, separated by very low wainscoting, hedges, fences or outlines of walls.

2. Properties.

In central staging, furniture and properties take over many of the functions of scenery—setting the locale, creating atmosphere, reinforcing the emphasis on the actor. Ideally they should be specially designed.

   a. All furniture *must* be low—never higher than eye-level of spectators in the first row, preferably even lower. Overstuffed armchairs with wing-backs are ruled out, as are upright pianos, fireplaces, and cupboards. (Sometimes such items may be placed against a small bit of wall between sections of the auditorium.)

b. The back of the furniture must be as much in character as the front.

c. Complete authenticity in hand props is necessary. A card game would require prestacking the deck; newspapers, mixing drinks and eating scenes are given close scutiny by the audience and leave little room for faking.[5]

d. When props are pantomimed, there should be a consistency and unity within the style of the production.

e. Rugs, grass mats or planters can be used to demark the borders of acting areas.

f. Tall lamps, vases, and trim props should not be used.

3. Costumes.

Much of the pictorial color and style of period plays must be supplied by costume. Like properties, they must bear scrutiny at close range, front and back. Modern costumes require frequent cleaning, and removal of make-up from around collars.

4. Make-up.

Heavy character make-ups are often unconvincing in central staging. This is a serious problem for young people playing older roles. Directors in central staging tend to cast to type and rely very little upon make-up.

5. Lighting.

The time and money invested in scenery on the proscenium stage should be spent on painstaking lighting in central staging, which makes a major contribution in the creation of mood and emphasis.

a. Lighting instruments should be so placed that bounce or spill of light on the spectators is eliminated or minimized.

b. The actor's face needs to be well-lighted from all sides.

c. The switchboard needs to be so placed that the lighting crew has a view of the stage area.

d. Fluorescent paint should be used to mark aisles and any places actors need to find in the dark.

e. Blackouts or dimouts become the equivalent of the curtain.

f. Closing a drape or pulling down a shade may be suggested by the actor's pantomime accompanied by a well-timed dim-down in light. Kelly Yeaton's article in *Producing the Play* is a valuable analysis of lighting problems in central staging.

5. For ingenious solutions to property problems, see Yeaton, *Arena Production*.

6. Music.

Together with lighting, music serves as a substitute for a curtain in swelling a scene to climax and punctuating it with finality. The use of music has become standard in central staging, as it drowns out the noise of actors making their entrances in the dark and props being shifted. Stereophonic, multi-speaker sound systems should be used if possible.

7. Sound effects.

Authentic sound may also form a valuable substitute for the missing visual elements of spectacle. What would in proscenium theatre be only an "off-stage sound" may in central staging become a significant part of the total impact, surrounding the spectators and heightening their feeling that they are participating with the actors in the situation.

III. Open or Thrust Staging.

This recent emphasis in theatre architecture permits the audience to sit on three sides of a platform or thrust which projects into the auditorium, thus providing the possibility for actors to be in a close relationship with the spectators. Usually there is no proscenium arch and a curtain may or may not be used. Most directors agree that if a person has a firm grasp of both proscenium and central staging conventions, he will have little difficulty adapting to open staging. Essentially, it is a matter of selecting appropriate techniques from both forms and being constantly aware that while many picturization principles retain value, all blocking must be conceived in terms of the sight lines of an audience seated on three sides of an acting area. Picturization and movement must therefore be plastically dimensional in this sense and especially avoid favoring the conventionally thought of front of the audience. Although arena blocking principles are valuable (with one less side of the audience with which to be concerned), usually less movement is necessary than in central staging.

A. Based on concepts of the Greek and Elizabethan theatre, it was pioneered in modern times by Frederic McConnell at the Euclid-77th Street Theatre of the Cleveland Playhouse, and found to be adaptable to a wide variety of styles and types of plays, and to permit considerable use of pictorial scenic elements. Developments of this type of theatre at Stratford, Ontario, and Minneapolis incorporate a much deeper thrust, use no curtain, and few scenic elements.

THE THREE SISTERS At the Tyrone Guthrie Theatre, Minneapolis. Directed by Tyrone Guthrie. Designed by Tanya Moiseiwitsch.

B. The Tyrone Guthrie Theatre at Minneapolis, shown in photograph, has been used with realistic props and furniture as in *The Three Sisters*, but it has worked equally well for an almost totally prop-less and furniture-less production of *Death of a Salesman*. It is ideally suited to the staging of classics written in pre-proscenium periods. The problem of entrances has been alleviated by the use of tunnels leading out from the platform underneath the spectators.

C. The Repertory Theatre of Lincoln Center in New York utilized a similar platform in its temporary quarters, although the new Vivian Beaumont Theatre incorporates both a proscenium with great depth and a thrust platform. From his experience in directing in its temporary ANTA Washington Square Theatre, José

Quintero wrote of the new demands which the platform stage makes upon the actor, who is forced to a "deeper kind of reality" in his playing:

> In directing a play for the open stage, what must be avoided is blocking the view of some portion of the audience. One must be inventive to keep the play mobile, almost as if it were a "figure eight," without the movement being unmotivated or capricious. Certain areas in view of the entire audience assume varying values, such as the farthest section. One makes the initial statement back there and then breaks it down into its components down center.[6]

D. The Mark Taper Forum of the Music Center of Los Angeles features a thrust stage and a semi-circular arrangement of its 750 seats. The special lighting equipment is set into the ceiling, and the backstage area houses a moving ramp and a large cyclorama

THE MARK TAPER FORUM   The Music Center, Los Angeles.

6. Barry Hyams, "A Theatre: Heart and Mind," in *Theatre: The Annual of the Repertory Theater of Lincoln Center. Vol. I.* (New York: A Repertory Theater Publication in association with Playbill, Inc., 1964.)

screen. There have been a wide variety of types of plays and musicals staged in the Mark Taper Forum, all using scenery or scenic elements, often quite elaborate and each setting designed for a specific production. Scene shifting is normally limited to the moving ramp at the rear, with some overhead flying mechanisms in full view. Occasionally additional mechanical devices are added to the stage floor when the production demands.

IV. Flexible Staging.

Audience acceptance of various forms of staging has opened up many exciting possibilities for flexible theatres in which placement of stage and audience is tailored to the requirements of each production. From the directorial standpoint, this presents the ideal situation for he can reshape the theatre to best accommodate his concept and approach to each particular play. Depending on the form he selects, the director then uses those directing principles and conventions which are appropriate to the planned physical situation. Open staging, central staging, L-shaped staging, proscenium staging, tennis court staging, or mixtures of these and others are all possibilities, depending upon the flexibility. All that is essentially necessary is ample free floor space and movable risers and platforms. Walden Boyle[7] describes some of these variations which movable risers for the audience made possible at the University of California at Los Angeles.

A. The University of Miami Ring Theatre was built as a flexible theatre to accommodate any kind of play. It can be changed into almost any form from proscenium to a 100′ stage with the audience seated on two sides.

B. The "Dramatic Laboratory Teaching Station" is proving to be a workable answer to the problem of finding a home for the theatre arts in high schools without adequate auditoriums. Developed by Horace Robinson, such a room would include both a small stage with an adjustable proscenium opening and a space for arena staging. End-staging, central staging, and horseshoe staging are all possible in this room, with the intimacy and flexibility that are desirable for young players.[8]

C. California State University, Long Beach has developed a new Studio Theatre in which both the stage floor and audience seat-

7. Boyle, *Central and Flexible Staging.*

8. Jack Morrison, "A Dramatic Laboratory Teaching Station for High Schools," *Secondary School Theatre Conference News,* **II,** 3, Summer, 1964.

ing are adjustable. By means of mechanical lifts and use of specialized seating, the floor of a conventional proscenium stage can be extended forward in four foot increments to form a variable sized thrust stage. In turn, the first four modules of the full thirty-six foot thrust will adjust upward to complete the risers for audience seating around a perfectly balanced arena stage. Finally, by removing seating on two sides of the arena, a tennis court stage flanked by formal risers at each end is available. Optimum lighting circuits and instruments are structurally oriented to each of these stage forms. In a theatre with this flexibility, tailoring the stage form to the requirements of each production becomes most feasible.

CALIFORNIA STATE UNIVERSITY, LONG BEACH—STUDIO THEATRE

V. Summary.

All the principles of good theatre apply to non-proscenium staging except for special treatment of picturization, movement, and technical elements so that each section of the audience sees part of every beat, long speech, or scene and at least one actor's face is visible to each section most of the time.

A. Central staging.
   1. Advantages.
   2. Disadvantages.
   3. Problems of blocking.
      a. Picturization.
      b. Movement.
      c. Voice.
   4. Central staging technical problems.
      a. Scenery.
      b. Properties.
      c. Costumes.
      d. Make-up.
      e. Lighting.
      f. Music.
      g. Sound effects.
B. Open or thrust staging.
   1. The Cleveland Playhouse.
   2. The Tyrone Guthrie Theatre.
   3. The Repertory Theatre of Lincoln Center.
   4. The Mark Taper Forum.
C. Flexible staging.
   1. The University of Miami Ring Theatre.
   2. The Dramatic Laboratory Teaching Station.
   3. California State University, Long Beach Studio Theatre.

Selective Bibliography

Albright, H. D.; Halstead, William P.; and Mitchell, Lee. *Principles of Theatre Art.* Boston: Houghton Mifflin Company, 1955.

Boyle, Walden P. *Central and Flexible Staging.* Berkeley and Los Angeles: University of California Press, 1956.

Dietrich, John E. *Play Direction.* New York: Prentice-Hall, Inc., 1953.

Goodman, Randolph. *Arena Theatre—1957: A Bibliography.* New York: American National Theatre and Academy, Service Pamphlet, August, 1957.

Hughes, Glenn. *The Penthouse Theatre.* New York: Samuel French, 1942.

Hyams, Barry, ed. *Theatre: The Annual of the Repertory Theatre of Lincoln Center,* vol. I. New York: Playbill, Inc., 1964.

Jones, Margo. *Theatre-in-the-Round.* New York: Rinehart and Co., 1951.

McConnell, Frederic. "Using the Open Stage: A Ten Year Experiment at the Cleveland Playhouse," *The Theatre Annual,* vol. 17, 1960.

Meyer, Richard and Nancy. "Lincoln Center's Bargain Theatre," Players Magazine, vol. 40, no. 7, April, 1964.

Morrison, Jack. "A Dramatic Laboratory Teaching Station for High Schools," *Secondary School Theatre Conference News,* II, 3, Summer, 1964.
Southern, Richard. *The Open Stage.* New York: Theatre Arts Books, 1959.
Joseph, Stephen. *New Theater Forms.* New York: Theatre Arts Books, 1959.
Williams, Dallas S. "A Bibliography for Arena Theatre," *Educational Theatre Journal,* vol. 10, no. 3, October, 1958.
Yeaton, Kelly. "Arena Production," in *Producing the Play.* Ed. John Gassner. New York: The Dryden Press, 1953. Also section on "Simplified Staging" in same volume.

INHERIT THE WIND   California State University, Long Beach. Directed by
Stanley Kahan. Designed by Ralph W. Duckwall (Sets), Herbert L. Camburn (Costumes) and Fred C. Allen, Jr. (Lights).

7 Vocal Interpretation

I. Introduction.

Just as the director composes visual pictures that are meaningful and aesthetically satisfying, so he must also compose oral patterns, using as his means the voices of the actors. Chapters 5 and 6 were designed to train the director's eyes. This chapter is concerned with training his ears and heightening his ability to hear how his play should sound. It is by now a commonplace to say that American actors do not spend enough time working on voice. Anyone who has heard European actors knows that their voices are usually more flexible and useful as a means of expression. Much of this is due to the importance given to this aspect of actor training in the European theatre. Whether he likes it or not the director in the American theatre will find he is frequently a voice coach, among his many other duties.

He and his actors should take as their goals to make the voice an instrument for conveying:

A. Audibility

B. Intelligibility

C. Emotional impact
   No matter how much an actor feels his part, the audience will be moved only to the extent that he succeeds in communicating his feelings, and his voice is one of his principal means of doing this.

He will not move or delight an audience either, unless he can be heard and understood. The vocal techniques presented in this chapter should be thought of not as substitutes for the actor's emotional truth, but rather as a means by which the director can help his actors express the meaning of the play and their own true emotions.

II. Interpretation of lines.

Included among the techniques which the director uses in coaching actors in the interpretation of lines are those which help the actor (1) express the meaning of the lines, (2) express the serious or humorous emotional content of the lines, (3) build the scene to climax, and (4) achieve variety. It must first be assumed that the actor understands clearly his beat or action—what he is trying to do psychologically that motivates him to say the particular lines at the given moment. He must also know to whom the lines are said, what they mean, and how he feels about the things he is saying. If the actor understands all these in theory and still is unable to interpret the line effectively in practice, the director may help him by reference to one or more of these technical devices for oral communication:

A. Emphasis.

    1. The word which when emphasized unlocks the meaning of a phrase is called the *key word*. Every phrase or thought-group of words should have a key word, just as every speech should have a key sentence and every scene a key speech.

    2. The actor should underline key words and sentences in his script with one, two or three lines to indicate the amount of emphasis. A key word generally is emphasized by a rise in pitch, an increase in volume and/or elongation of the vowels. Notice how meaning can be altered by shifting emphasis within a sentence.

        a. *I* don't think there is much likelihood, Jack, of you and Miss Fairfax being united (but others apparently do think so).

        b. I don't *think* there is much likelihood, Jack, of you and Miss Fairfax being united (but I may be wrong).

        c. I don't think there is *much* likelihood, Jack, of you and Miss Fairfax being united (but there is a faint chance).

        d. I don't think there is much likelihood, Jack, of *you* and Miss Fairfax being united (but she may marry someone else).

e. I don't think there is much likelihood, Jack, of you and *Miss Fairfax* being united (when you are engaged to someone else).

f. I don't think there is much likelihood, Jack, of you and Miss Fairfax being *united* (but it needn't stop your loving each other).

g. I don't think there is much *likelihood,* Jack, of you and Miss Fairfax being united (its entirely problematic).

Can you think of additional possibilities to add to the above examples which might suggest other shades of meaning?

Stanislavski once suggested that his actors underline all the emphatic words of a scene in their scripts and then play an improvisation in which they speak only the words they had underlined.

3. Pointing.

Even a routine reading of prose requires emphasis on key words for understandability of meaning. In dramatic dialogue, however, it is necessary to give even greater weight to particular words or phrases for emotional impact or for humor. This is called "pointing" the word or phrase. Pointing may employ any combination of the following techniques:

a. A rise in pitch or a fall in pitch.
b. A rise in volume or a fall in volume accompanied by increased intensity.
c. A slowing down in tempo.
d. A pause before the word or sentence.
e. Movement or gesture before the word or sentence.
f. Elongation of the vowel sounds.

4. Throwing away. (Subordination)

The reverse of "pointing" is "throwing away" and it is an equally valuable technique, for without it there would be no contrast, no black to offset white. (The principle of strong and weak lines was discussed in connection with movement, Chapter 5.)

a. "Throwing away" means to minimize the importance of a phrase or sentence through a casual, flippant or disinterested reading of the line. It does *not* mean to mumble the line so that it cannot be understood. It is merely a way of telling the audience that the line is relatively less important than other lines in the speech. Means of throwing away a line include these five possibilities:

(1) A level pitch.
(2) More rapid tempo.
(3) Moving during the line.
(4) Reduction in volume.
(5) Less emphasis or intensity.

    b. The change from throwing away to pointing need not occur at the ends of sentences, but wherever the thought changes. Several weak sentences can be phrased together or joined with a weak introductory phrase in a strong sentence for greater contrast and naturalness.

B. Inflection.

Inflection is a change in pitch within a word itself. The pitch may glide upward or downward during a vowel tone, or step upward or downward between syllables.

1. The possible inflections are:
    a. Rising
    b. Falling
    c. Circumflex—rising and falling within the word.
    d. Inverted circumflex—falling and rising within the word.

2. Some possible interpretations derived from inflection include the following:

    a. A rising inflection creates suspense for the words yet to come; it implies incompletion, uncertainty, or interruption: "Oh?" "Today . . ." "Who?" "I believe . . ."

    b. A falling inflection implies finality, completion, certainty. "Well!" "Sure!" "Yes." "I see!"

    c. A circumflex inflection gives melody and added emphasis to certain words: "Tomorrow" "Unforgettable" "Well!"

3. A *pitch pattern* results when any one inflection is used repetitively. One of the most common faults of inexperienced actors is the use of a rising or falling inflection at the end of every line. Such a pitch pattern results in deadly monotony, and must be broken up by attention to the meaning of the phrases in relation to each other. It causes a severe lack of variety and markedly detracts from the actor's interpretation of his role.

C. Oral punctuation and phrasing.

The actor should become aware that the punctuation marks required in written English do not always correspond to phrasing of thought units in oral communication. When reading lines for meaning charged with the character's personal emotion, the actor will discover:

1. Every period does not necessarily require a falling inflection or a pause. A rising inflection should be used at the end of a sentence which is one of a group of ideas that make up a unit or which build to a pointed line.

   Example: LADY BRACKNELL:

   I hope not, Algernon.

   It would put my table completely out. ⟶

   Your uncle would have to dine upstairs:

   Fortunately he is accustomed to that.

2. Within a long sentence, a rising inflection may be used when the actor needs to pause to take a new breath or when he is pausing for emphasis.
3. A question mark is not always indicated by rising inflection.
4. A comma sometimes but not always indicates a pause; if it is so used, it usually is preceded by rising inflection.
5. A colon or semicolon generally suggests more to follow, hence takes a rising inflection.
6. An exclamation point usually takes a falling inflection.
7. Dashes or dots usually take a rising inflection, indicating broken sentences or incomplete thoughts.
8. In Shakespeare or poetic dialogue, the end of a line does not necessarily mean the end of a thought; the run-on line requires either a level or rising inflection so as not to suggest finality.
9. The number of words which the actor should phrase together depends upon:
   a. The thought unit itself.
   b. The emotional state of the character.
   c. The relative importance of the words in relation to the whole speech.
   d. The breath control of the actor.
   e. The tempo of the scene.

D. The use of the pause.
   There is no more effective single technique in acting than the full use of the pause. Charles Macklin, the famous eighteenth century English actor, is supposed to have described his three kinds of pauses as, "the pause, the long pause, and the grand pause." In

a noted production of *Mary Stuart,* the distinguished actress, Eva
Le Gallienne, used what seemed to be the longest example of a
"grand pause" on record as she looked Mortimer up and down
wondering if he could be trusted. Yet every moment of it seemed
charged with the tension of Elizabeth's probing eyes.

1. In using the pause, the actor should keep in mind:
    a. A pause will hold as long as the situation and the actor can
       justify it.
    b. A pause points the line or movement which comes imme-
       diately after it.
    c. A pause implies suspense if the audience cares what comes
       next.
    d. A pause is usually more effective when preceded by a rising
       inflection.
    e. A pause is more effective, as a general rule, *within* an
       actor's speech than *between* two actors' speeches. In the
       latter case, it may seem that the second actor is merely
       slow in picking up his cue.

2. An actor may enrich a pause with the little "musical" sounds
    which are natural to everyday speech but which the play-
    wright often fails to indicate in words: chuckles, grunts,
    hmmmm, sighs, etc. A frequent error is to pause at the end
    of the printed line in verse dialogue, rather than at the end
    of the idea. This is a common tendency which should be care-
    fully avoided.

3. An actor should pause at the end of a line in poetic dialogue
    only when the thought is complete or when he can create sus-
    pense thereby.

E. Connectives between phrases.
    To help achieve variety and to interrelate the lines with the emo-
    tions motivating them, it is often helpful for the young actor to
    think to himself the connective phrases that the author might
    have put between sentences. Sometimes the relationship between
    lines can be clarified by the mental use of such connectives. Some
    examples might include the following:

    1. "On the other hand."
    2. "And by the way."
    3. "As a matter of fact."
    4. "Now wait a minute."
    5. "To prove what I just said."
    6. "And so here's what I've decided."

       7. "And to top it all."
       8. "You won't believe this."
       9. "I've got a new idea!"

F. "Topping" and "Undercutting" in building to climax.

In constructing the dynamics of a scene so that it seems "to go somewhere" and doesn't become monotonous, the director will want to pay particular attention to the surge and ebb, the rise and fall of emphasis, both within the individual actor's speeches and between actors' speeches (also see **Chapter 9**). Successful ensemble acting is based on the true give-and-take that makes possible topping and undercutting.

1. Topping.

   When one actor's line is given with a certain emphasis or force, the next line should be given with somewhat more emphasis or force in order to "top" the previous one. This may be done by:

   1. A rise in pitch.
   2. An increase in tempo.
   3. An increase in volume.
   4. An increase in intensity.

2. In a progression or build-up to climax, it is important for each actor to sense just how much force is necessary to top the previous line or actor. Too little will be monotonous, and too much will cause the build-up to reach its high point too soon, leaving no place to go with the remaining lines. The importance of careful rehearsal in the use of *topping* is obvious, and should be precisely planned by the actors and director.

3. Undercutting.

   Equally valuable in dynamics is a deliberate drop under the level of the previous line. It may be done as gradually as topping, or the actor may undercut abruptly so that a new build-up to climax can begin. It is also a useful technique for comic effect by understatement. Undercutting can be accomplished by:

   1. A fall in pitch.
   2. An increase in tempo.
   3. A decrease in volume.
   4. A decrease in intensity.

4. Repeated words.

   A particular case where topping or undercutting is almost obligatory is a line of dialogue in which the same word or phrase is repeated several times: "Stop, stop, stop," or "I won't . . . I won't . . . I won't." It would be fatal to deliver all three words or phrases with exactly the same emphasis. The director or the actor must decide to build them up or down.

G. Variety.

The human voice is one of the most beautiful of musical instruments, capable of almost unlimited adjustment. Yet monotonous reading of lines is one of the director's most persistent problems. The actor should be helped constantly to find new shades of meaning and vocal values in order to avoid monotony. If he has just done a particular thing vocally, that is sufficient reason for not doing it again soon. Achieving vocal variety requires practice largely in ear training.

Monotony has two causes: (a) the actor's failure to see or feel the moment-by-moment changes in his character's thoughts, motives, and emotions, and (b) inability to use fully the technical means for reflecting these changes to the audience. There are technically only four elements that can be varied, corresponding to the four physical properties of sound. These are:

1. Pitch
2. Volume
3. Tempo
4. Quality

1. Pitch.

Generated by the larynx and controlled by the ear, pitch changes are the most significant means of increasing the actor's expressive range. Low pitches generally are associated with deeply felt emotion, sincerity, authority, depression. High pitches are associated with excitement, anxiety, flippancy, and hysteria. Great dynamics of pitch change are associated with volatile, emotional, giddy, and superficial people. Less variety in pitch is associated with stable, laconic or repressed individuals.

a. It is important for the actor not to try to *force* his pitch down unnaturally in hopes of securing a so-called richer voice, for this can create an undesirable strain and a voice with an artificial quality.

b. He may, however, increase his overall pitch range (1) by relaxation, (2) by working at a piano, and (3) by breaking up his script—marking places where pitch should change by either:

    (a) A glide (inflection) upward or downward during a sound.

    (b) A step upward or downward between sounds.

2. Volume.

The principle of *crescendo* and *diminuendo* gives music much of its climactic effect. In drama too, within the permissible range required for projection, volume changes are a significant means of achieving dynamic and emphatic performance. They must be accomplished with corresponding increase in breath support.

3. Tempo.

Although it is a commonplace to say that a fast tempo is used in comedy and a slow one in tragedy, the fact is that both comedy and tragedy require a considerable variety of tempi in order to hold the audience's attention. Dynamics of tempo are useful chiefly as a means of communicating shades of meaning and signalling to the audience which ideas are more important and which less important. Nervousness on the part of the actor frequently leads to the increase of tempo as he tends to rush through his lines.

    a. *We tend to slow down on emphatic or important lines.* This is one way of "pointing" a line.

    b. *We tend to speed up on less important or casual lines.* This is called "throwing away" a line (also see Chapter 5).

4. Quality.

The fourth variable, quality, depends upon the particular resonance used. Quality is a reflection of characterization perhaps more than the other three, and is equally a mirror of inner emotional states. The way the actor holds tension in his lips, cheeks, and jaws will influence quality, as do tone placement in mouth, head, or chest, and the physical dimensions of the actor's skull, neck, mouth, and thorax.

Although there are many variations of quality possible in reflecting changing emotional states within a basic characterization, some of the most familiar vocal qualities have been classified as follows:

    a. Aspirate or breathy.

    b. Gutteral or throaty.

    c. Pectoral or chesty.

    d. Nasal.

    e. Orotund or "with a round mouth."

    f. Pharyngeal, back of throat and neck.

    g. Strident.

      h. Quavering.
      i. Falsetto.

H. Rhythm.
Added variety and interest can be given to speech by rhythm, which is the *regular recurrence* or ebb and flow of intensity.

1. Inner rhythm.
Stanislavski defines inner rhythm as ". . . the acceleration or diminishing of the *inner intensity*—the desire to realize the problem and to execute the inner or outer physical action."[1]

The inner rhythm of a speech will grow out of the playwright's construction of the scene, its language, its emotional content, and the emotional rhythm of the characters who play the scene.

2. Outer rhythm.
To capture the inner rhythm of the scene, the director and actor should be conscious of external keys to rhythm:

a. The spacing and frequency of key words and stress.
b. The distribution of long and short syllables.
c. The spacing and frequency of pauses.
d. The spacing and frequency of climaxes and diminuendos.
e. The meter of the speech, if in poetry.

3. Meter.

In poetic drama the actor must be aware of the additional problem posed by meter, which is the regular spacing of accented and unaccented syllables. The actor should read the lines with an awareness of and a rhythmic response to the meter, but *should never let meter take priority over meaning.*

a. The most frequently used meter, especially in Shakespeare, is iambic pentameter [five feet to a line, with a foot consisting of a short, (˘) then a long (´) syllable].

The clóck | strŭck níne | whĕn í | dĭd sénd | thĕ núrse.

b. Occasionally in reading Shakespeare it is necessary for the sake of meter (provided meaning is not obscured for the listener) to make an extra syllable in a word ending in "ed" when normal usage would contract it.

Ĭ múst | ŭpfíll | thĭs ó | siĕr cáge | ŏf ours
With bále | fŭl wéeds | aňd prͤe | ciŏus-júic | ed flow'rs.

1. Nikolai M. Gorchakov, *Stanislavski Directs* (New York: Funk and Wagnalls Co., 1954), p. 323.

c. Shakespeare felt free to vary his meter, substituting other meters where sense demanded, and the modern actor should likewise feel free from a slavish metronome-like fidelity to meter while attempting to capture the full beauty of Shakespeare's musical lines.[2]

I. Playing comedy.

1. The actor should *point* his comedy lines. This involves a combination of subtle techniques which telegraph the audience exactly when to laugh.

   a. By opening up more in body or facial position for the comic line.
   b. By getting to the punch line quickly once the joke begins to be caught.
   c. By giving special emphasis and particularly clear articulation to the last few words of the sentence which contains the humor.
   d. By preceding the word or words that contain the humor with a pause or piece of business.
   e. By moving on a preceding line and standing still on the comic line.

2. The others in a scene must help the actor get his laughs by:

   a. Feeding the straight lines rapidly, clearly, and with a serious, interested expression.
   b. Not moving, gesturing or reacting during the comic line, so as not to distract the audience. After the line is said, the other actors may help crystallize the laugh by punctuating it with reactions of their own.

3. The actors should *hold for laughs.*
   Holding for a laugh means to pause while the audience is laughing and unable to hear the next line. A well-timed laugh breaks suddenly and the welcome sound of laughter crests quickly, then subsides gradually.

   a. The actor should never deliver a line through a laugh. He may continue his movements or pantomime, or he may simply wait, remaining in character and in the scene. It is a theatrical convention that the cast waits while the audience laughs as long as it chooses.
   b. When the laugh has almost *but not quite* died out, the

---

2. For an excellent analysis of meter and rhythm in speaking Shakespeare, see Dorothy Birch, *Training for The Stage* (London: Sir Isaac Pitman & Sons, Ltd., 1952).

actor resumes his lines, repeating if necessary any words lost during the laugh.

III. Mechanics of Voice and Speech.

The techniques of interpretation previously noted presuppose that the actor will bring to rehearsal a relatively well-controlled vocal mechanism. All too often this is not the case, however, and the director may have to give the actor basic drills to work on outside of rehearsal and as a warm-up before a performance. It is important for the director in the nonprofessional theatre to understand the mechanics of voice and speech, the essentials of which are given on the following pages, together with exercises for the actor's drill and practice.

A. Relaxation.

Because so many of the actor's vocal problems come from tensions and misplaced strains, it is important to begin vocal drills with exercises for relaxation. The anxieties and heightened tensions associated with acting before an audience tend to inhibit the natural processes upon which voice is based, and it is in voice that a tense actor will first betray himself.

The following examples may be useful in the development of the actor's relaxation.

1. For general relaxation:
    a. Adding tension gradually, beginning with right foot, until entire body is as tense as possible. Then release all tension suddenly.
    b. Bouncing like a rag doll, letting arms and head flop loosely.
    c. Concentrating upon an object such as a pattern in another actor's clothes, an off-stage sound, a remembered piece of music, or a memorable film.
    d. Running a mental check list through the body, noticing if muscles are relaxed.

2. For specific relaxation of the mechanisms of voice:
    a. Yawning.
    b. Rolling the head in a circular movement as far forward, right, back, and left as possible.
    c. Contracting all the muscles of the neck and then releasing the tension suddenly; repeat with face muscles, then abdomen.

B. Breath control.

It is essential for the actor to realize that the impulse to speak and the strength of voice originate in the breathing mechanism and *not in the throat,* nor even in the lungs themselves, which are passive and must be activated by the muscles surrounding them.

1. Inasmuch as sitting, slouching, having a pile of books on one's lap or wearing tight garments inhibits deep breathing, the actor should begin the study of breathing in a relaxed but standing position.

2. The actor should locate the diaphragm, which is a membrane of muscle and sinew separating the chest cavity from the abdominal cavity. It lies horizontally, is somewhat dome-shaped when relaxed and is attached to the sternum in front, the lowest ribs at the sides, and the spinal column in the back. Place your hands at the base of the ribs and notice the action of the area around the waist during these four processes:

   a. Normal inhalation.
      To take in air, a larger area must be created in the chest cavity into which the air can go. To accomplish this, the diaphragm tenses, pushing down on the abdominal cavity and outward on the base of the rib cage, while muscles lift and expand the rib cage. Air will rush into the lungs to fill the vacuum created by the expanding of the area around and below the lungs. Normal inhalation is effortless and slow, taking about the same length of time as normal exhalation.

   b. Normal exhalation.
      When the diaphragm relaxes, the pressure from the abdominal viscera forces it upward. At the same time the muscles expanding the rib cage relax and the weight of the rib cage forces it to fall slightly by gravity. The result is that air is forced from the lungs. Normal exhalation is a relaxation.

   c. Inhalation for stage speech.
      Inhalation for speech must be done more actively and rapidly than normal. There is greater movement outward and downward with the diaphragm, and the rib cage expands at the sides and front. If the actor is hunched over, he is more limited in the amount of air he can inhale than if he is standing erect on his spine. In continuous speech, inhalation is much more rapid than exhalation, and is there-

fore done as a rule through the open mouth rather than the nose.

d. Exhalation for stage speech.

All speech in English (except an audible gasp) is done on the exhalation of the breath stream. To accomplish this, a steady, controlled pressure is exerted on the diaphragm by the abdominal muscles, and other muscles contract the rib cage. All the muscular movements are greater than in quiet breathing. They must *continue to sustain an even pressure* on the lungs until the sentence or phrase is complete. The following technical devices may be useful as a means of strengthening muscular control of the breathing mechanism:

Inhale and exhale normally and easily without speech. Place one hand in front and one at the side at the base of the ribs. Notice the movement of the hands, which should be outward on inhalation and inward on exhalation. Now place the right hand on the clavicle (collarbone) and leave the left hand at the diaphragm. As you perform these exercises make sure the left hand moves but not the right.

Inhale a good supply of air for speech and exhale it evenly on a sound such as "Ah" or "s. s. s."

Inhale as much air as possible, making sure the hand on the diaphragm moves outward. Exhale as you count from one in a steady, controlled tone. As you practice, the number to which you can count on one breath should be increased. Stop when the tone begins to waver.

Lie on the floor and place several heavy books on the diaphragm. As you lift the books on inhalation, the diaphragm will be strengthened.

Practice panting like a dog (for brief periods only, or the increased oxygen will make you dizzy).

Do a controlled laugh, with a new impulse from the diaphragm on each "ha."

Begin with a soft "Hey" and grow louder, supporting each sound with a fresh supply of air.

In none of these exercises should there be visible movement of or tension in the shoulders or clavicular area.

It was an old tradition with actors that the great curse speech from Bulwer Lytton's *Richelieu* should be said on one breath, as Edwin Booth was reputed to be able to do. Try it without a pause for inhalation:

"Mark, where she stands!—around her form I draw
The awful circle of our solemn church!
Set but a foot within that holy ground,
And on thy head—yea, though it wore a crown—
I launch the curse of Rome!"

C. Phonation.

The purpose of the controlled air stream described is to set in vibration the vocal cords, located in the larynx. As most of the muscular adjustments of the larynx are autonomic rather than conscious, it is sufficient for the actor to be aware of the following general concepts:

1. Pitch is generated by the vibrations of the vocal folds.
2. The vocal folds are lengthened when they are relaxed and shortened when they are tense. As in a piano, longer strings give lower pitches than shorter strings.
3. The size and thickness of the vocal folds also contribute to the pitch of a voice. Compare the thickness of the strings on any stringed instrument, such as a violin or guitar, and note how the thickness of the strings varies with pitch.
4. Tension in the throat and neck muscles is the principal obstacle to optimum pitch production. There is little the actor can do at will with his larynx, except to insure a relaxed and tension-free set of muscles surrounding the vocal folds.
5. Hoarseness is the result of strain in the vocal folds, produced either by too much tension in the neck or too little breath support when loud volumes are attempted.
6. Pitch variation is controlled largely by the ear. An actor's variety in pitch can be increased primarily by ear training. It is not necessary to be able to sing on key in order to recognize intervals in pitch and reproduce them.

   Some examples which may be useful as a means of increasing variety in pitch level:

   At a piano, sing up and down the scale to find the range of tones that can be sung. The individual's useful speaking level is approximately one-quarter of the distance up from the lowest note to the highest (including falsetto) sung notes.

   For those who do not find it easy to sing on pitch, count using a rise in pitch for each number. Each number should rise only one easy interval rather than a big jump. Descend in pitch the same way.

D. Resonance.

The sound generated at the larynx consists of a fundamental pitch and its overtones. The latter are weak in volume, however, and re-quire reinforcement which is supplied by resonating chambers which amplify the sounds. The sounding board of a piano, violin, or the tube of a clarinet gives the distinctive sounds to these instruments that permit us to identify them even when playing the same fundamental pitch. In the human voice, the resonators which give its distinctive quality are:

1. The pharynx (the back of the throat behind the tongue and the uvula) which is a conical tube extending from the larynx to the nasal cavities. With an elaborate set of muscles, the pharynx can modify its size and shape in a great number of combinations in order to provide the best shaped resonator for the various pitches produced by the larynx. The walls of the pharynx are lined with mucous membranes, which when relaxed and lubricated with saliva provide a rich tone, and when tense and dry cause a harsh or strident tone.

2. The mouth, which has both hard and soft reflecting surfaces. Its size can be varied by action of the lower jaw and by the variations of tongue positions. The hard palate (the roof of the mouth at the front) is the best sounding board off which to reflect sounds for carrying power or projection. The instruction to "bring the sound forward in the mouth" refers to this noticeably superior projection when tones are resonated in the front of the mouth as opposed to those resonated in the back. The larger the mouth cavity, the lower the pitches that can be resonated. A tight jaw therefore inhibits both resonance and projection.

3. The nasal cavities, unlike the mouth and pharynx, are not vari-able. Only three sounds in English, m, n, and ng, are resonated in the nose, although some actors, have noticeable nasal resonance on other sounds.

4. The sinuses, which like the nose are not adjustable, add only a small amount of head resonance. However, we are all aware of how a cold may affect the sinuses and hence resonation. Frequently one responds to such a speaker by noting, "Do you have a cold?"

5. The chest, particularly the bronchial tubes and trachea, act to reinforce lower pitches.

   The following examples may be useful in increasing flexibility of resonance:

   With good breath support, sing the sound of "ah" first with the mouth normally open, then gradually wider and wider until it is almost a yawn. Notice the enrichment of the tone.

   Resonate the same tone of "ah" in the mouth, the sinuses and the chest. This is often called mask, head, and chest resonance. Practice the vowel combinations, oo, oh, ah, ai, ee (u, o, a, e, i) until you find your optimum placement and most pleasing resonance. Relaxation, yawning and breathing exercises are helpful here. Add to these vowels the consonants *p* and *b*, which, because they are plosives, seem momentarily to increase the pressure in the pharynx and to inflate sagging passages: oop, ope, ahp, ape, eep, etc.

Notice the change in a well-resonated tone when you (a) close off the nose, (b) press your hand on your throat, (c) pat your chest vigorously, (d) strengthen or weaken the breath support, (e) make the same sound forward in the mouth and at the back of the throat, and (f) make the same sound with the neck and pharyngeal muscles contracted and then relaxed. For character parts, it is helpful to moderate resonances which are deviations from the norm: breathy, throaty, nasal, tight-jawed, wavering from the lack of breath, gravelly, gutteral. To avoid hoarseness, be sure to use no more extra tension than necessary, and to support the tones with greater breath than usual.

E. Articulation (enunciation).

The tones produced by the larynx and reinforced by resonance are vowel tones until the articulatory mechanism produces the consonants which are needed to form words. Because some of the consonant sounds are very high in frequency, they do not have as much carrying power for projection as do vowels. Many times when a spectator says, "I couldn't hear the actors," it would be more accurate to say that he heard vowel sounds but not the consonants, particularly the final consonants necessary for understandability of the words. Lip laziness is the most serious cause of poor projection, and the actor must acquire greater than normal vigor and precision of his articulatory mechanism, which is made up of:

1. The tongue.

This extraordinarily complex and sensitive bundle of muscles is capable of rapid, subtle, and infinitely variable adjustment. Although the movements are governed primarily by the ear, the actor needs to be conscious of tongue placement and to guard against letting the tongue hump up at the back of the throat and obstruct the projection of tones.

2. The teeth.

Loss of teeth or the acquisition of dentures requires the actor to relearn his tongue placement to make sounds against the teeth.

3. The lips.

Like any other muscles, those activating the lips can be strengthened, made more responsive and precise through exercise and practice. The actor trained on the stage may find he must reduce his lip activity slightly when appearing before the TV or motion picture camera, but the actor trained in the understated articulation of these media may be at a disadvantage on the stage.

4. The soft palate.

A kind of curtain at the back of the throat, the soft palate controls admission of sounds into the nasal cavities. A sluggish soft palate will create nasal speech or may blur the two sounds produced by contact of the soft palate and the back of the tongue, K and G.

F. Projection.

Voice in the theatre must be enlarged beyond the requirements of everyday conversation. Yet it must seem natural and conversational even while achieving audibility in the farthest seats of the theatre.

Mere shouting should not be confused with projection. Projection is required for both loud and soft tones, including stage whispers. Instead of saying "Louder," the director may help the actor to project better if he works with him to achieve:

1. A stronger and more intense emotional reinforcement for the line—not merely to want to say something but to want to communicate it urgently and forcefully. The best motivation for projection is from *within.*
2. Stronger support of the tone through breath control.
3. Placement of the voice forward in the mouth, reflecting tone off the hard palate and upper teeth.
4. Wider opening of the mouth to let the sound out rather than keeping it dammed up.
5. More vigorous action of the lips and tongue in forming consonants, particularly final consonants.
6. An opened-up body position (at least one-quarter position) so that the actor's voice stream is directed toward the auditorium.
7. Even greater articulatory emphasis for intimate or whispered tones. Much greater force of breath is necessary to sustain the aspirate quality.

IV. Problems of pronunciation.

A. Standards of pronunciation.

Correct pronunciation involves the choice of which vowels and consonants to use and which syllable to accent. Pronunciation makes a decided impression upon the listener, and generally identifies the speaker as to:

Educational and social background
Regional background
National background

For this reason the actor must choose an appropriate speech pattern as part of each characterization.

1. Standard "stage speech."
   During the nineteenth and early twentieth centuries the American stage was dominated by British influence, and standard speech for the American actor was British diction. The folk playwriting of Eugene O'Neill, Clifford Odets, Paul Green, and others, however, made native American dialects necessary on the Broadway stage.

2. General American pronunciation.
   There are today three general categories of American speech: Eastern, Southern, and general American. Unless performing a dialect play, actors should use the best speech of their own geographic region which is:
   a. Free of local idiosyncracy.
   b. Understandable to the audience.
   c. Not affected so as to call attention to itself.
   d. Consistent with the rest of the cast.

3. Further refinements within the three categories, i.e., New England, New York and variations of Southern, are necessary only when plays are localized in a particular area. The sound of R is perhaps the most characteristic identification of the region of the speaker.

4. Uncouth or crude speech.
   When the character being portrayed lacks education or refinement, the actor's speech should reflect this. Otherwise, however, mistakes in pronunciation grate on the ear and are inexcusable in a classic play. Some of the most familiar errors in pronunciation include:
   a. "Git" and "jist" for "get" and "just."
   b. Leaving off final "ng" in words like "going" and "doing."
   c. The "e" sound in "friend" (not "frind") and "gentleman" (not "gintleman").
   d. Corruptions such as "gonna" and "wanna," "whatcha," "awright."
   e. Elisions of the final consonant of one word to the beginning of the next. "Long Gisland."

f. Commonly mispronounced words such as "toward" (not "to-ward"), "athlete" (not "athalete"), "poor" (not "pore"), and, heaven forbid, "the-ator" for "theatre."

5. Pedantic speech.
It is equally incorrect, however, to overarticulate such unemphatic words as "the" and "a," which are correctly pronounced "thuh" and "uh" in connected speech. To do otherwise makes the speaker sound pedantic. Unless the character being portrayed is affected or speech conscious, the actor should not emphasize all words equally or give weak words and syllables too much weight.

B. Dialects.

1. Many of the most important twentieth century plays are written in a dialect. Where a director can find actors who can manage the dialect, it will enrich the performance and add authenticity. Included in this category are such plays as *Juno and the Paycock, Desire Under the Elms, The Field God, Summer and Smoke, Golden Boy, The Corn is Green, The Happy Time.*

2. It is always better to use too little dialect than too much. Never let dialect get in the way of understandability, nor use it if the entire cast cannot achieve a uniform and consistent dialect. Do *not* use a foreign dialect if the play is a translation from a foreign language.

3. Mastery of dialect is largely ear training. It can be accomplished best by listening to the speech of natives of the region or country and, where feasible, tape recording it. When this is not possible, authentic recordings of the dialect (made by natives, not simulated by actors) should be studied. In listening to dialects, the ear should be trained to concentrate on:

   a. Sound substitutions (which can be identified much more easily if the actor and director know phoentics).
   b. Variations in pronunciation and accent.
   c. Melody and inflection patterns.

V. Summary.

The actor's voice is one of his most powerful means of communication with an audience. It must serve the three purposes of audibility, intelligibility, and emotional impact. The director must have a highly attuned ear that is sensitive to voice and speech, and must know the techniques that can help the actor express the meaning of the play and his own truthful emotions, building scenes to climax and achieving vocal variety.

Vocal techniques which the director can use to help the actor include the following:

A. Interpretation of Lines.
  1. Emphasis
  2. Inflection
  3. Oral punctuation and phrasing
  4. The pause
  5. Connectives between phrases
  6. Topping and undercutting in building to climax
  7. Variety
  8. Rhythm
  9. Playing comedy

B. Mechanics of Voice and Speech.
  1. Relaxation
  2. Breath control
  3. Phonation
  4. Resonance
  5. Articulation
  6. Projection

C. Problems of Pronunciation.
  1. Standards of pronunciation
  2. Dialects

Selective Bibliography

Aggertt, Otis J. and Bowen, Elbert R. *Communicative Reading*. New York: Macmillan Co., 1956.

Anderson, Virgil A. *Training the Speaking Voice*. New York: Oxford University Press, 1942.

Coffin, L. Charteris. *Stage Speech*. London: Herbert Jenkins, 1963.

Herman, Lewis H. and Marguerite S. *American Dialects: A Manual for Actors, Directors and Writers*. New York: Theatre Arts Books, 1959.

———. *Foreign Dialects: A Manual for Actors, Directors, and Writers*. New York: Theatre Arts Books, 1958.

Kahan, Stanley. *Introduction to Acting*. New York: Harcourt, Brace and World, Inc., 1962.

Lee, Charlotte I. *Oral Interpretation*. Boston: Houghton Mifflin Co., 1952.

Lessac, Arthur. *The Use and Training of the Human Voice*. Privately published, 1961.

THE NIGHT THOREAU SPENT IN JAIL California State University, Long Beach. Directed by Harry E. Stiver. Designed by Ralph W. Duckwall (Sets), William French (Costumes) and Patrick Hadlock (Lights).

8 Characterization

I. Introduction.

Helping the actors to build effective characterizations is one of the director's major responsibilities. The criticism most frequently heard from the average playgoer is that an actor is or is not "convincing" in his part. Although the director's work in this realm will be made much easier if he casts skillfully, "type-casting" in the theatre is not always desirable even if it were always possible.

In the days of the old stock companies, it usually was simple enough to divide all the roles of a play into the standard categories: lead, ingénue, juvenile, (the "straight" parts), and character man, character woman, heavy, comic, and general utility (the "character" parts). Today, however, playwriting and acting have changed in keeping with the great advances in our knowledge of psychology, and in most contemporary drama all the parts are "character" parts—there are few "straight" roles. One of the indispensable tools of the director in the theatre today is an insight into human behavior, whether intuitive or acquired through study. In fact, the applied psychology learned as a derivative from an acting or directing experience is one of the strongest justifications for the theatre as an educational focus, recreation in community theatre, or as a meaningful and stimulating profession.

Helping the actors in characterization usually involves the director in the following steps: (1) finding the right conception of the character, and (2) finding ways to project this conception to the audience.

II. The conception of character.

The director's initial concept of the characters in the play should be a part of his interpretative study as described in Chapter 3. His concept of each role will have a strong bearing upon his discussions with the costume designer, his description of the parts at tryouts, and his selection of the cast. When the cast is complete and assembled for the first round-table readings, the director should discuss the characters in detail, clarifying his concepts, referring to lines in the play, and (where applicable) showing the cast the costume sketches. At this first phase of characterization, the director's emphasis should be upon the psychological factors, the inner aspects which will contribute to the actor's understanding of the character. The following psychological factors may be pertinent:

A. The character's major drive or goal in life and in the play (his "spine").

Some modern directors such as Elia Kazan and Harold Clurman find it helpful to begin with the central motivational force that impels the character through the action of the play. While some plays lend themselves better than others to this scheme of analysis, it would always be valuable to consider first the dynamic rather than the static aspects of character—the *verbs* rather than the *adjectives* that relate to the character and which answer questions such as these:

1. What does he *want* most, what are his needs and drives, what is he *doing* in the play? Hedda Gabler states her own spine quite specifically when she exclaims, "I want for once in my life to have power to mold a human destiny."

2. What is he willing or able to do to get what he wants? How conscious is he of his own true motives in doing what he does? How badly does he want his objectives and how vigorously does he pursue them?

In choosing verbs to answer these questions, it should be kept in mind that:

a. The verbs relate to the character as if he were in life rather than serving a dramatic purpose. The actor should try to get inside the character, rather than looking at him objectively as the playwright may have. The author's purpose may have been to show how corrupt a man is or to reveal information to the audience; this is not the character's own purpose, however.

b. *The choice of verbs is in itself characterization.* Insight into the character is revealed by the choice of the most appropriate and specific actions and beats. If, for example, the actress playing Juliet's nurse chooses as her action in Act II, Scene 5, "to tell Juliet what Romeo said," it will be much harder to make the scene come alive than if she chooses a more *characteristic* action: "to tease little Lady-bird about her first boyfriend." Again, it would be more helpful for the actress playing Amanda in *The Glass Menagerie* to choose the beat "to pretty up for a Southern gentle-man caller," rather than to think of the scene in terms of "to get ready for a dinner party." The first is specific in terms of Amanda's character, the second is general. A specific beat is invariably stronger and actually *easier* to play than a general beat and provides much richer characteri-zation.

B. The character's background.

Although in many plays the author has no time nor need to de-velop each character fully, the actor should consider the follow-ing factors which influence personality:

1. The character's family.

    a. Father and mother: what influence did each have on him?
    b. His brothers and sisters, if any, and his relationship to them.
    c. The type of discipline he was subjected to as a child.
    d. Affection, overprotection or rejection in childhood.
    e. The economic status of the family.
    f. Religious attitudes of the family.
    g. Any special situations in the family such as divorce, drink-ing, illness.

2. The character's innate intelligence.
3. The character's educational background.

    a. Level achieved.
       Education is most clearly revealed on the stage by patterns of speech, grammar, and pronunciation.
    b. Adjustment to school and peers.
    c. Interests and activities.

4. The character's political and sociological environment. The effect which war, occupation, pioneering, disillusionment, travel or the political temper of the times may have had upon him.

C. The character's adjustments to his background and the forces that moulded him.

1. Social adjustments.

   a. His manners.
   b. The kind of friends he has.
   c. Participation in social activities and organizations.
   d. The role he plays in a group.
   e. Feelings about his minority group status, if applicable.
   f. Dating, courtship, and attitudes on sex.
   g. His home and how he lives.
      (Even the kind of car a person drives is, in our society, a comment upon his personality.)
   h. Hobbies and interests.
   i. His ideals, beliefs, and political opinions.
      (1) His heroes.
      (2) His hates.

2. The character's marriage, if applicable.

   a. His choice of mate.
   b. His success in marital adjustment.
   c. His children and their relationship to him.

3. The character's vocation and career.

   a. The kind of work he does.
   b. How he feels about his work.
   c. How he got where he did.
   d. Whether he spends most of his time indoors or outdoors.

4. The character's emotional adjustments.
   Reactions to stress or conflict; the kinds of outlets utilized when under pressure, and the amount of pressure tolerable (often called the "frustration-tolerance level").[1]

ADJUSTMENT	EXAMPLES OF A CHARACTER WITH THIS ADJUSTMENT
a. Immature adjustments	
(1) Adjustments by defense mechanisms:	
Compensation	Melody, *A Touch of the Poet*
Rationalization	Chris, *Anna Christie*
Aggression	Joe Bonaparte, *Golden Boy*
Self-righteousness	McLeod, *Detective Story*
Masochism	Ephraim, *Desire Under the Elms*

1. This personality inventory adapted from George F. J. Lehner, *Explorations in Personal Adjustment* (New York: Prentice-Hall, 1949).

ADJUSTMENT	EXAMPLES OF A CHARACTER WITH THIS ADJUSTMENT
Sadism	Leo, *The Little Foxes*
Alcoholism	Doc, *Come Back, Little Sheba*
Narcotics	Mary, *Long Day's Journey Into Night*

(2) Adjustments by withdrawal:

Negativism	Larry, *The Iceman Cometh*
Fantasy	Laura, *The Glass Menagerie*
Regression	Blanche, *A Streetcar Named Desire*
Suspicion and hostility	Queeg, *Caine Mutiny Court-Martial*

(3) Adjustments by repression:

Anxiety	Rosemary, *Picnic*
Phobias	Evelyn, *Guest in the House*
Compulsions	Biff, *Death of a Salesman*

(4) Adjustments by physical symptoms:

Psychosomatic illness	Coney, *Home of The Brave*
Hysteria	Alma, *Summer and Smoke*

b. Mature adjustments:

(1) Dealing successfully with one's emotions	Rev. Harmston, *The Climate of Eden*
(2) Awareness of self	Papa, *The Happy Time*
(3) Sense of humor	Jacobowsky, *Jacobowsky and the Colonel*

The following techniques are frequently helpful for the actor in conceiving his character.

1. The director can ask the actor to write an imaginary biography of his character in the play, supplying all the details necessary for a full life story consistent with the information given by the playwright.

2. The director can suggest improvisations in which the actor plays his character in situations not in the play. If the actor fully understands his character and his spine, he should be able to sustain it in situations totally extraneous to the play. Try these juxtapositions in improvisation:

   a. Othello faced with Hamlet's dilemma in avenging his father.

b. Macbeth married to Ophelia.
c. Hedda Gabler married to Torvald Helmer.
d. Stanley Kowalski trying to find a man for his sister, Laura.

III. The projection of character.

Important as the foregoing psychological factors are in helping the actor to understand his character, it is only through physical factors— those so-called "externals" which an audience can see or hear—that an actor can project his character. The director should therefore discuss with the cast the physical aspects of character, not only as an outgrowth or expression of inner psychological needs and wants but also as an influence which affects the inner psychological state. (Laura's limp, for example, in *The Glass Menagerie,* is a physical factor which has strongly influenced her feelings of inferiority and wish to escape through fantasy; every person has some feelings about his physical health and appearance.) The psychological and physical aspects of character are thus mutually interrelated and interdependent; neither aspect alone can lead the actor to a complete characterization. The director should call the actor's attention to the following physical aspects of character:

A. The character's age.
   Occasionally the inexperienced actor places too much emphasis on the matter of age. For the young actor particularly it is often sufficient to fix the character's age within a ten or fifteen year span. Young actors all too often characterize anyone over forty with all the quavering and palsied qualities of senility. There is no substitute for detailed observation of people at various ages.

B. The character's bodily appearance.

   1. His health.
   2. His facial expression.

      a. Use of the eyes.
      b. Muscular set, particularly around the mouth.
      c. Make-up as an expression of character.

         (1) Complexion.
         (2) How the strains of life are reflected in lines and shadows.
         (3) Beards or whiskers, if any.
         (4) Street make-up, if a woman.
         (5) Moulding of the features and bone contour.

   3. His sight and height.

MORRIS CARNOVSKY AS KING LEAR

4. His hair and hair styling.
5. His clothing.

   a. How he wears it.
   b. How he handles it.
   c. Style and quality of clothing.

6. His posture, as an expression of age, health, and inner feeling.

C. The character's movements.

Using the body interestingly to depict character includes consideration of the following:

1. His walk.

   This is one of the most revealing aspects of character. Finding and using a character walk is not only revealing to the audience but also helpful to the actor in getting into character.

2. His gestures.

   A gesture which is used so often that it becomes identified with the character is called a "master gesture" or as Michael Chekhov termed it, "psychological gesture" or (PG).[2]

   Gestures may be either:

   a. Completed or left incomplete.
   b. Vigorous or weak.
   c. Compulsive or controlled.

---

2. Michael Chekhov, *To The Actor: On the Technique of Acting* (New York: Harper and Brothers, 1953), Chapter 5.

3. His use of "character props."

A property chosen by the actor or director because it helps establish character is called a "character prop." Included in this category are pipes, fans, canes, purses, gloves, watch chains, cigars, etc.

4. His energy level or vitality.

D. The character's voice.

1. As we noted in Chapter 7, the vocal means by which the actor can characterize include:

a. Pitch.
b. Volume.
c. Tempo.
d. Resonance or quality.

2. His speech.

a. Articulation—careless or precise.
b. Pronunciation—standard or colloquial.
c. Dialect, if applicable.

E. The character's rhythm.

The way in which movement, voice, and gesture are integrated and repeated produces a characteristic rhythm. Some rhythmic possibilities include:

1. Jerky or smooth (staccato or legato).
2. Volatile or even-tempered.
3. Impulsive or deliberate.
4. Ponderous or light.
5. Broken or continuous.

Directors and actors as well as students of make-up will find it very useful to collect candid photographs of people's faces, such as those that appear in *Time, Newsweek,* and newspapers, using only firsthand sources, not posed models, sketches or pictures of actors in character. In building a character, it is frequently helpful to find a photograph of a face which has qualities of the character as the actor and director visualize him.

A character may be developed and sustained by the use of improvisations based upon one specific physical element. One may use a facial expression from a painting, photograph, or actual person. There are numerous physical aspects which may be developed in such improvisations. They might include:

1. A facial expression.

2. A walk.
3. A gesture.
4. A prop.
5. A vocal or speech mannerism.
6. A dialect.
7. An idiosyncrisy of manner.

It is also helpful to select qualities of an inanimate or animate object which contain certain elements which suggest human qualities. A character may be built around these elements and developed in an improvisation. (The notable actor, Hume Cronyn, who played the title role in *The Miser,* for example, built his character around the movement of a crab.)

IV. Helping the actor find his character.

After the round-table readings in which characters are discussed from both psychological and physical aspects, the director begins blocking rehearsals, and for a brief period physical position on the stage and movement take priority over characterization. Even at this early phase, however, the director should keep in mind that blocking is *character in action;* helping the actor to choose the right physical actions, beats, and accompanying movement may go a long way toward helping him find his character. *Give him movement that is in character and he will begin to be the character.*

After the blocking is set, the director is free to concentrate on characterization. He may find the actor at a loss as to where to begin selecting usable elements from the long list of psychological and physical aspects of his character. Fortunately, however, there are some reliable guideposts so that the director and actor need not lose too much time groping for the character. The following considerations all tend to narrow down the possibilities and make the choice easier:

A. What the playwright reveals about the character.
   The playwright's intent is the final authority in all questions of interpretation. Playwrights vary widely, however, in the depth of their psychological insight, and their intent is not always transparent. Some acting editions include a two or three line description of each character which is often on a superficial level: "She is a typical college student, cute, vivacious." Such descriptions, particularly when they include the word "typical," are of course of little value; if the playwright has not given this college student cute and vivacious things to say and do, the actress will have

a hard time making her cute and vivacious. Of much more value in analyzing the playwright's intent are the following:

1. What the character *does* in the play.

   Capulet in *Romeo and Juliet,* for example, loses his temper not only at Montague but also at Tybalt, the Nurse, and violently at Juliet. He tells Paris that he wants his daughter to wait two more years before marrying, but the next day he agrees to her marriage in three days and then advances it to a day earlier. These actions reveal more about Capulet's character than if Shakespeare had written in the *Dramatis Personae,* "Capulet—a hot-tempered, impulsive father."

2. What the character *says* about himself.

   Although a character's own evaluation of himself may not be the way the author intends the audience to see him, there often are valuable clues in what a person says about himself. In *The Glass Menagerie,* for example, the gentleman caller analyzes himself with these words:

   > . . . I believe in the future of television! I wish to be ready to go up right along with it. Therefore I'm planning to get in on the ground floor. In fact I've already made the right connections and all that remains is for the industry itself to get under way! Full steam—(*His eyes are starry*). Knowledge—Zzzzzp! Money—Zzzzzp!—Power! That's the cycle democracy is built on! . . . I guess you think I think a lot of myself!

3. What *other characters* say about him and how they react to him. It is often of great value for the actor to see his character through the eyes of the others in the play, and a playwright sometimes puts his most penetrating observations of character into the mouths of others. It is Biff, for example, who gives the final appraisal of his father in *Death of a Salesman:* "He had the wrong dreams. All, all, wrong."

Because of the importance of clues such as these—often said when the character himself is offstage, the director must caution his actors against the all-too-common tendency not to read or listen to those scenes they are not in. Such an actor might, for example, miss the graphic picture of himself which Blanche gives of Stanley when he is offstage in *A Streetcar Named Desire:*

> He eats like an animal, has an animal's habits! Eats like one, moves like one, talks like one! There's even something—sub-human—something not quite to the stage of

humanity yet! Yes, something—apelike about him, like one of those pictures I've seen in—anthropological studies!

4. What the *playwright says* about the character in stage directions, prefaces, articles, and other published works.

   From brief stage directions to the lengthy character analyses in the prefaces of Bernard Shaw, the words of the playwright provide one of the best keys to the character. It is only when the playwright is ambiguous, sketchy or noncommittal that the director and actor must fill in the gaps from other sources. An actor playing General Burgoyne in Shaw's *The Devil's Disciple* could hardly complain of a lack of information after reading Shaw's seven-page character analysis, complete with documentation and such Shavian sentences as this:

   > . . . but his peculiar critical temperament and talent, artistic, satirical, rather histrionic, and his fastidious delicacy of sentiment, his fine spirit and humanity, were just the qualities to make him disliked by stupid people because of their dread of ironic criticism.

B. The growth of the character during the play.

   1. The question of whether characters "grow" or develop during the course of the play or whether they are the same at the fall of the curtain as they were at the rise is an old one in dramaturgy. Kenneth Macgowan[3] suggests a list of characters that are no different at the end than they were in the beginning: Hamlet, Willy Loman, Liliom, Cyrano, Candida, Captain Boyle.
   2. On the other hand, many characters develop during the play, both physically and psychologically: King Lear, Anne Frank, Liza Doolittle, Blanche Dubois, Juliet, Nora.
   3. Macgowan suggests that the development of character may be like a photographic negative which can be "developed" to bring out what was originally latent. This is more in keeping with modern psychology than some of the sentimental dramas with their too-easy conversions of character.
   4. In other plays, particularly mysteries, the character does not change but merely reveals more of himself to the audience, which may change in its reaction to the character.
   5. The director and actor should analyze the play from the standpoint of character growth in order to determine how much development can be made convincing and consistent, and at what

---

3. Kenneth Macgowan, *A Primer of Playwriting* (New York: Random House, 1951), p. 78.

stage of his growth the character is during each scene of the play. If, for example, the actress playing Nora in *A Doll's House* does not establish the doll-like, fragile qualities in Act I, she will have nothing to rise above in the last act.

C. The style of the production.

The director must find a way to harmonize the style of the characterizations with the style of the settings and costumes so as to achieve unity. The same character would be portrayed quite differently within a realistic setting than, for example, in expressionism or theatricalism. A classic play proscenium-staged with historical authenticity would require different styles in characterization than the same play done on the thrust stage or in suggestive, skeletonized sets. The same character would appear quite differently if treated by Chekhov, Shaw, Williams, or Albee. The differences growing out of style may include:

1. The amount of detail that is necessary or desirable.

   Anouilh's Antigone takes time, for example, to admire the golden, feminine curls of her sister, Ismene; Sophocles' Antigone does not.

2. The broadness or subtlety of the characterization.

   The Restoration character, Millamant for example, is characterized somewhat more subtly than her modern counterpart, Auntie Mame.

3. The size of gesture, movement and other elements of characterization.

   Actors feel more like making expanded gestures the moment they change their street clothes for period costumes (which free them from the necessity to reproduce literal reality). Period and stylized productions require a heightening of emotion and an enlarging of gesture and other elements of characterization. Maurice Evans' modern-dress G. I. *Hamlet,* for example, required smaller, more naturalistic characterization than his prior period-costume production.

4. The extent to which hand props and character props can appropriately be used.

   The fussy lawyers and notaries in Molière, for example, can legitimately develop broad character business with inkwells, quills, and scrolls which would seem entirely overdone for a lawyer in a modern play.

D. What the actor must supply for himself.

When the director has helped the actor to narrow down the possibilities and define fairly clearly what he is looking for in characterization, much of what remains must be done by the actor himself. The director can guide him to at least three possible sources of aid:

1. *Observation* as a basis for building a character.

    The actor need not "go out and live" in order to find his character, but rather "go out and *look*." There is source material everywhere around the actor if he will but look for it—on the bus, on the campus, in the park. Ideas for characterization may come from the actor's own experiences, from his friends, from pictures, stories, or simple everyday incidents.

    a. When the actor finds someone who suggests his character to him, he should try to do more than imitate the individual. He should watch the individual long enough to *empathize* with him—to begin to feel as he does. He should then bring the details back to rehearsal and try them.

    b. The actor may find a walk from one individual, a voice from another, a facial mannerism from a third, and fit them all into a composite characterization.

    c. The actor should avoid observation of other actors. This is secondhand; he should go directly to the source, which is in life. Actors should be discouraged particularly from going to the movie version of a play which they are rehearsing.

    d. Clichés and stereotypes should be avoided whenever possible. All college students and policemen are not identical nor do they react to certain situations in the same manner. All Italians do not gesticulate wildly, nor do all blue-collar workers act and talk like Archie Bunker.

    e. The actor should work to achieve a wide *variety* within the framework of his character. He should show as many facets and moods of his character as possible. To escape the charge made by one critic that an actor ". . . ran the gamut of emotions from A to B," he should work for both technical and emotional variety to hold the audience's interest.

2. Research.

    Where applicable in the case of historical or actual characters, the actor can help himself to identify with the character through research. The best sources are:

    a. Biography.
    b. History.
    c. Paintings.

    (These are particularly valuable for costume, facial expression, stance and gesture. Even when the character is fictional, paint-

PORTRAIT OF A MAN (by El Greco) Metropolitan Museum of Art, New York.

ings can help the actor steep himself in the period and perhaps find a portrait that suggests his character.)

3. Intuitive identification with the role.

In the final analysis, whatever the playwright fails to supply
and the actor's observation and research fail to uncover, the
actor must invent for himself.

a. The actor should turn to his intuition and imagination to
fill in all the gaps left by the playwright, who quite often
will not mention where a character has just come from
when he enters, what he does between scenes, or essential
information about minor characters.

b. The actor should create such a full inner life for his character that by opening night he knows the character even better than the director (or possibly the playwright). As this identification or empathy between the actor and his character grows deep, the director should respect it and not ask the actor to do anything which he feels his character would not do unless it is consistent with the total concept or style of the production.

   c. The actor's imagination is more intuitive than intellectual. He may know how Caesar or Lear feels, not because he clearly imagines life in ancient Rome or prehistoric Britain, but because he has felt or feels the same way himself. When he identifies himself with his character, he will have no trouble getting into character and playing the part.

V. Helping the actor get into character.

When the actor has a clear concept of the character and has done the necessary observation, research, and imagination to give him a specific idea of how to project the character through external elements, there comes a time—usually after the blocking is set—when he must try to get into character and play the part. All too little is known about this psychological process of assuming someone else's personality (called "introjection" in psychology), but it is usually apparent to the spectator and should be quite obvious to the director when the actor is deeply "in character" and when he is not.

At this stage of the rehearsals, getting into character is not so much an intellectual process as an emotional one of identification with his character. An unconscious element is undoubtedly involved to such an extent that it might be compared with autosuggestion or hypnosis. The actor should not at this point try to review consciously biographical detail such as "I am thirty-six years old and had an unhappy childhood . . ." but should rather put himself figuratively in the character's shoes, acting and reacting as he knows his character would. The director can give the actor considerable help in this process:

A. By creating a favorable rehearsal environment which fosters *experimentation*. Effective characterization often grows spontaneously out of a period of *trial and error*, in which the actor deliberately "tries on for size" the various facets of his character. The director must give the actor sufficient freedom so that he feels like daring and experimenting. The director can, for example:

   1. Encourage the actor to explore, create for himself, bring new ideas to rehearsal. The director should respect these contribu-

tions of the actor and integrate them into the whole where possible.

The finest recent statement of how an actor explores within himself at rehearsal until he finds something usable is in Sir Laurence Olivier's discussion of his approach to *Othello,* which should be required reading for every student of acting. On this point Sir Laurence says:

> During rehearsals I try things out very extravagantly— ways of using my hands, my eyes, my body. It's a kind of self-flagellation that I've given myself practically all of my life—early grasping this nettle of making a fool of myself. . . . Often an accident happens, often a turn of pose and a gesture and a stance and a position, an attitude—suddenly you say "Well, that's the man: I feel it is. That's him."[4]

2. Discover the aptitudes, resources, and personalities of the actors as individuals. Search for a spark within the actor that can be brought out and strengthened. (Remember that if the actor cannot give what the director wants, the director must adapt his conception of the role to something the actor *can* give.)

3. Help the actor to build a little bit at a time, finding things that work and growing from small moments of truth to larger moments.

4. When an actor hits upon a moment in the rehearsal that is just right, single it out after the rehearsal for praise and later reference. "Remember how you played the speech about the farm? —that was just right. Use that same quality in the last scene."

5. Keep a concentrated and disciplined rehearsal so that actors can remain in character during a scene. *Try to stop them as infrequently as possible* during the rehearsals when they are groping for a character.

6. Speak to the actors during rehearsal by the names of their characters.

7. Encourage improvisation and trial-and-error. Often an actor can hit upon a character through an improvisation or a bit of spontaneous invention. Anne Bancroft used an Irish accent in *The Miracle Worker* not for authenticity but because she discovered it helped her overcome her own New York dialect.

8. Make use of improvisations which help to identify the character's beats and actions. The outcome and all the cues are known ahead of time in a rehearsed play; it is therefore helpful for actors to improvise scenes in which one of the char-

4. Sir Laurence Olivier, "The Great Sir Laurence," *Life,* vol. 56, May 1, 1964, p. 88.

acters is given a changed beat or circumstance unknown to the rest of the cast. The other characters must listen and respond *in character* and with consistency and adjust appropriately to the new stimuli.

B. By getting the actor into the character or the character into the actor.

The director should realize that the actor may approach his character in one of two ways—working from the inside out or from the outside in; the actor can bring the character down to himself, or he can bring himself up to the character. The best method is the one that works for the individual actor.

1. Working inside out.

No matter how extreme a "character part" he is playing, an actor puts a good part of himself into every role he plays. A mild-mannered actor who is successful in playing sadistic villains must have a streak of sadism in him somewhere. Although critics may glibly say that "He wasn't acting Iago, he *was* Iago," the fact is that the actor can use only his own emotions to play a part. Iago's emotions do not exist in actuality, and become real only to the extent that the actor can arouse in himself the same (or analogous) emotions that the fictional Iago is supposed to have felt. An actor therefore will find it difficult to create a role successfully that is wholly outside his capacity to empathize with or to comprehend.

2. Working outside in.

Other actors find it easier to start outside with a clear image of the character and work inward, consciously selecting a voice, a walk, or gestures just as they select their color of grease paint and crepe hair to portray their character. In *Building a Character,* Stanislavski has noted:

> . . . external characterization can be achieved intuitively and also by means of purely technical, mechanical, simple external tricks. . . . The only proviso is that while he is making this external research he must not lose his inner self.[5]

Although Stanislavski most likely was not familiar with the psychological theory of James and Lange, many of his experiences as an actor confirm the principle that the emotions can be awakened by physical activity, i.e., if an actor assumes a

5. Constantin Stanislavski, *Building a Character* (New York: Theatre Arts Books: Robert M. MacGregor, 1949), p. 7.

sagging posture and a tired old man's voice, he will soon feel tired and spent inside; if he stands with legs wide apart and chest erect he will feel cocksure, probably more quickly than if he waits for these feelings to grow from within and alter his external stance. In other words, both Stanislavski and James-Lange imply that the actor should take advantage of *autosuggestion* in getting into character.

C. Other ways for the director to help the actor get into character.

   1. By making sure the actor gets into character before his entrance and sustains it until well past the exit.

      Although some experienced actors pride themselves on their ability to joke with the stage crew until a moment before an entrance cue and then walk on in character, most actors need a quiet period backstage at rehearsal as well as performance in which to get into character through pacing back and forth with the character's walk, thinking the character's thoughts, bringing to mind the image of the character or a moment in his life.

   2. By letting the actors use parts of a costume or a prop at rehearsal to help them get into character.

      Often the psychological act of wearing or using something pertaining to the character will help the actor feel his part at rehearsal. Although it is an unfair burden on the costume staff to expect a whole cast to be in costume before dress rehearsal, there are many times when it would be extremely helpful if the actors could work with shawls, cloaks, high heels, floor-length rehearsal skirts, canes, hats, swords, purses, gloves, etc., long before dress rehearsal.

VI. The character in the play.

The actor's search for a character has led him into introspection and a highly personalized center of attention. If he stops here, however, he will be playing in a vacuum, isolated from the others in the scene. The director's final step in characterization, therefore, is to integrate the individual characters, and the actor's final step is to redirect his concentration away from himself and onto the centers of attention that his character would have—the things that are said and done by the others in the scene.

A. Responding spontaneously and in character.

   After the actor's characterization has been crystallized and "set," he will find a new freedom to listen, to concentrate, to respond to the stimuli of the scene not as himself but in character. He will discover that some of the other actors have also built effective characterizations to which he can respond. He will discover new implications in the dialogue and new ideas for business. He will find himself reacting in ways that he had not planned or premeditated. It is then that the scenes begin to come to life, to "play." Stanislavski thus explained this exciting experience in the life of an actor:

> Thus a characterization is the mask which hides the actor-individual. Protected by it he can lay bare his soul down to the last intimate detail.[6]

B. Sustaining and modifying the character.

In the final phase of rehearsals, the director's attention will be on tempo and climax, on tightening the play and polishing its form. The actor must be prepared for this, and must know his character so well that he can sustain it through rehearsals that are primarily technical. If he is fully in character, a request to pick up cues faster, to increase the tempo or to top his partner should be a simple matter to justify from within; it should present no threat to his character. There may even be occasions when the director must ask him to modify his characterization for the sake of contrast with other characters, to create a better sense of integration (as for example when minor figures become too attention-catching), or to step the whole play up to a performance level big enough to project to the back row of the theatre.

VII. Summary.

One of the director's major responsibilities is to guide the actors in building effective characterizations. The two steps in this process are: (1) finding the right conception of the character, and (2) finding ways to project this conception to the audience.

A. The conception of character.
1. The character's major drive or goal in life and in the play (his "spine").
2. The character's background.
3. The character's adjustments to his background and the forces that moulded him.

B. The projection of character.
1. The character's age.
2. The character's bodily appearance.
3. The character's movements.

6. Stanislavski, *Building a Character*, p. 28.

        4. The character's voice.

        5. The character's rhythm.

   C. Helping the actor find his character.

        1. What the playwright reveals about his character.

        2. The growth of the character during the play.

        3. What the actor must supply for himself.

        4. The style of the production.

   D. Helping the actor to get into character.

        1. By creating a favorable rehearsal environment which fosters experimentation.

        2. By getting the actor into the character or the character into the actor.

        3. Other ways for the director to help the actor get into character.

   E. The character in the play.

        1. Responding spontaneously and in character.

        2. Sustaining and modifying the character.

Selective Bibliography

Albright, H. D. *Working up a Part*, 2nd ed. Boston: Houghton Mifflin Company, 1959.

Blunt, Jerry. *The Composite Art of Acting*. New York: Macmillan, 1966.

Boleslavsky, Richard. *Acting: The First Six Lessons*. New York: Theatre Arts Books, 1933.

Chekhov, Michael. *To the Actor: On the Technique of Acting*. New York: Harper & Row, Publishers, 1953.

Cole, Toby and Chinoy, Helen K., eds. *Actors on Acting*. New York: Crown Publishers, Inc., 1949.

Funke, Lewis and Booth, John E. *Actors Talk about Acting*. New York: Random House, Inc., 1961.

Kahan, Stanley. *Introduction to Acting*. New York: Harcourt, Brace and World, Inc., 1962.

McGaw, Charles J. *Acting is Believing*, 2nd ed. New York: Holt, Rinehart & Winston, Inc., 1966.

Stanislavski, Constantin. *An Actor Prepares*. Translated by Elizabeth Reynolds Hapgood. New York: Theatre Arts Books, 1936.

———. *Building a Character*. Translated by Elizabeth Reynolds Hapgood. New York: Theatre Arts Books, 1949.

———. *Creating a Role*. Translated by Elizabeth Reynolds Hapgood. New York: Theatre Arts Books, 1961.

THE ADDING MACHINE California State University, Long Beach. Directed by Stanley Kahan. Designed by Ralph W. Duckwall (Sets), David Jager (Lights) and Bert F. Ayers (Costumes).

THE IMPORTANCE OF BEING EARNEST California State University, Long
Beach. Directed by W. David Sievers. Designed by Ralph W. Duckwall (Sets) and
Herbert L. Camburn (Costumes).

9 Tempo and Climax

I. Introduction.

The necessity for structuring the tempo and climax of a performance arises from the nature of the theatre itself. In real life, events may happen tediously, repetitiously or over extended periods of time. To hold the attention of an audience in the theatre, however, there must be an intensification and condensation of reality. Moreover, our restless age of playgoers, conditioned by the trigger-happy tempo of television, come to the theatre in a more impatient mood than playgoers of Shakespeare's day or even Shaw's. Some aspects of tempo and climax have been referred to in the chapters on picturization, movement, and vocal interpretation. Although the director plans his tempo and climaxes during his preliminary interpretative study of the play, his actual work with the cast to achieve performance tempo and climax is one of the last phases prior to dress rehearsal—after the blocking, movement, characterization, and inner truth are well established.

II. Tempo.

Tempo may be defined as the speed at which new impressions or ideas *seem* to occur for the audience's benefit. The word *seem* is essential, because pure speed is by no means the same thing as what John Dietrich has called "the impression of speed."[1] The test of good

1. John E. Dietrich, *Play Direction* (New York: Prentice-Hall, Inc,. 1953), p. 176.

tempo in the theatre is whether the audience is continually interested (they manage to let the director know by coughing and rustling when they are not). The impact of the author's ideas and his skill in arranging them will determine how rapidly the director must present these ideas in order to hold the attention of the particular audience for whom he is directing the production. When, for example, the final curtain falls on Arthur Miller's *The Crucible* at 11:45 P.M. and audiences are surprised at the time because it had not seemed like a long play, the director has done his work well.

A. Ways to speed up the tempo of a play.

To convey the impression of speed, the director can use one or a combination of the following methods:

1. To decrease the time between new impressions.

    a. By cutting. (Refer to Chapter 3, Sec. II, G.)
    b. By getting to the next new impression more quickly.

2. To add more impressions.

    a. By creating interest in moments that might have been glossed over.
    b. By variety in movement, picturization, and individual actors' performances.

3. To intensify the impressions.

    a. By heightening the climaxes; climax thus becomes a means of achieving tempo just as tempo becomes a means of building to climax.
    b. By having the actors do what they do more fully, want their objectives more keenly, and make their emotional reactions, either serious or comic, more intense.

B. Inner factors which affect tempo:

1. The frequency of new beats, new impressions, new stage pictures, the entrance of new characters, or new complications in the plot. When a beat is played out, it is time to begin a new one. The director should attempt to gauge the frequency of the new impressions during his interpretative study of the play; if the playwright has not timed the progression of new impressions effectively for a contemporary audience, judicious cutting should be done at that time—before the actors learn their lines.
2. The rhythm and speed of responses of the characters.
3. The intensity of the individual beats or scenes themselves.

4. The content and significance of the play itself.
   Ideas that are trivial or superficial should be hurried briskly over rather than dwelt upon, so that the audience does not have time to react with "So what?" or "Who cares?"
5. The form and style of the play.
   Realism offers the director less opportunity to use contrived tempi than do some other styles. Plays with a strong plot or built-in suspense can afford to move very deliberately, whereas talky plays need to be kept on the move. Tragedy and serious drama have a slow tempo that grows out of the inner development of the action, whereas farce usually acquires momentum and ends up at breakneck speed (lest the joke wear thin).
6. The frequency of major and minor climaxes and their progressive or cumulative effect, growing from weaker to stronger as the play progresses.
7. The vigor and animation of the actors themselves.
   A vigorous actor can pick up a scene merely by walking on stage.

C. External factors which affect tempo:

1. Picking up cues promptly.
   a. The normal response to a cue is for the actor to inhale his breath and be ready emotionally so that he can begin to talk the instant the last word of the cue line is spoken. If the actor waits until he hears the cue word before getting ready to respond, there will be an undesirable pause which when multiplied throughout the play will noticeably affect tempo.
   b. The jumped or overlapped cue.
      There may be times when it is desirable for one actor to begin speaking before the previous one has finished, sacrificing the understandability of a few words for the cumulative emotional impact.
   c. The broken line.
      When one character is to interrupt another, the first actor should use rising inflections, and the second actor should break in promptly so as not to make necessary the adding of additional words.

   Example: *The Late Christopher Bean,* Act. II.
         (Ada, who has gone to Abbie's room to try and steal her portrait, returns while Susan is on the phone.)

THE LATE CHRISTOPHER BEAN California State University, Long Beach. Directed by W. David Sievers. Designed by Anne McFadden.

Prompt pick-up of cue at places marked with *

SUSAN: (Into phone) Just a minute. I'll call him.

MRS. HAGGETT: (Turns to Ada) (*) Did you get it?

ADA: (Gasping, her hand on her heart) (*) No!

DR. HAGGETT: (*) She didn't catch you?

SUSAN: (*) Pa!

Jumped cue. (Ada answers DR.'s question without waiting for SUSAN'S line.)

ADA: No. But if the biscuits hadn't been burning she would have caught me. I was just lifting it off the hook when I looked over my shoulder and there she stood with her head in the oven.

SUSAN: (*) Pa!

Jumped cue.

MRS. HAGGETT: We'll just have to try again. We'll eat dinner quiet as if nothing happened. I'll send her out on an errand. Come on, Ada. We'll finish setting the table.

SUSAN: (*) When you're done plotting and whispering over there, New York's calling Pa.

MRS. HAGGETT: (*) New York — *again?*

SUSAN: (*) I can't get the name. It sounds to me like Knoedler & Company.

DR. HAGGETT: (*) I won't speak to him! I won't speak to no more from New York!

Broken line. SUSAN must interrupt DR. promptly, or may jump cue slightly.	Tell him I'm out! Tell him I've gone away! Tell him — SUSAN: ⌐ You can tell your *own* lies, Pa! DR. HAGGETT: (*) All right, I will. (Takes phone)

2. Finding more key words to emphasize.

Inexperienced actors often hurry through a speech when, if they would slow down and emphasize key words for their full significance, they could in effect convey the impression of speeding up, i.e., there would be more points of interest for the audience.

Example: *The Importance of Being Earnest,* Act II. Read this speech first rapidly and without special emphasis:

GWENDOLEN: Well, to speak with perfect candor, Cecily, I wish that you were fully forty-two, and more than usually plain for your age. Ernest has a strong upright nature. He is the very soul of truth and honor. Disloyalty would be as impossible to him as deception. But even men of the noblest possible moral character are extremely susceptible to the influence of the physical charms of others. Modern, no less than Ancient History, supplies us with many most painful examples of what I refer to. If it were not so, indeed, History would be quite unreadable.

Now read the speech giving emphasis to the key words indicated:

GWENDOLEN: Well, to speak with perfect *candor*, Cecily, I wish that you were fully *forty-two*, and more than usually *plain* for your *age*. *Ernest* has a *strong upright* nature. He is the very *soul* of truth and *honor*. *Disloyalty* would be as *impossible* to him as *deception*. But even men of the noblest possible *moral* character are extremely *susceptible* to the influence of the *physical charms* of *others*. *Modern,* no less than *Ancient History,* supplies us with *many* most *painful* examples of what I *refer* to. If it were not *so,* indeed, *History* would be quite *unreadable.*

3. Pointing and throwing away lines.

As was demonstrated in Chapter 7, the pointing and throwing

away of lines is a most valuable technique not only for variety but for the tempo of the play. Unemphatic or trivial lines can be "thrown away" by speeding up the delivery, and emphatic lines can be "pointed" by slowing down.

Example: *The Importance of Being Earnest*, Act. I.

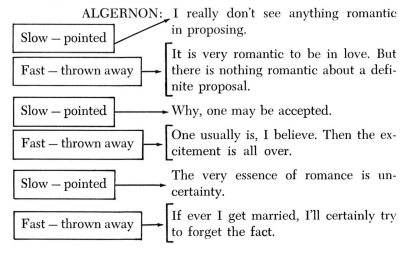

ALGERNON: I really don't see anything romantic in proposing.

Slow — pointed

Fast — thrown away → It is very romantic to be in love. But there is nothing romantic about a definite proposal.

Slow — pointed → Why, one may be accepted.

Fast — thrown away → One usually is, I believe. Then the excitement is all over.

Slow — pointed → The very essence of romance is uncertainty.

Fast — thrown away → If ever I get married, I'll certainly try to forget the fact.

4. Using pauses effectively.

    a. The pause must be filled with meaning, revealed through facial expression, gesture or movement; otherwise it should come out.

    b. The pause is more effective *within* one actor's speech than *between* actors' speeches. By beginning to speak, the actor shifts the audience's attention to him and he may then pause for full effect. If he pauses before he speaks, the audience may not be sure what is happening or whether someone has forgotten a line.

Example: *The Importance of Being Earnest*, Act. I.

WRONG: LADY BRACKNELL: Do you smoke?
            JACK: (Pause) Well, yes, I must admit I smoke.

RIGHT: LADY BRACKNELL: Do you smoke?
          JACK: Well . . (Pause) yes, I must admit I smoke.

    c. Exceptions to the foregoing:
        (1) Cases where a group is focused on one character whose reactions are of such interest to the other characters and to the audience that the pause before he speaks will "hold"—St. Joan in the trial scene, for example.

(2) Direct questions to an individual, who precedes his answer with a movement or piece of business designed to heighten the audience's interest in his answer.

5. Avoiding delays to entrances and exits.

   a. Actors should anticipate entrance cues so as to be in positions and ready to speak on the word cue.

   b. Actors should cross to doorways before their last line, delivering their last line in the doorway so as to avoid an uninteresting pause while they exit.

Examples: *The Importance of Being Earnest*, Act. I.

ENTRANCE:

> LADY BRACKNELL begins to move from the wings toward the open doorway, so as to see them, react and be ready to speak on the cue.

GWENDOLEN: (To Jack who is kneeling before her) What wonderfully blue eyes you have, Ernest! They are quite, quite blue. ⬆ I hope you will always look at me just like that, especially when there are other people present. (*Enter LADY BRACKNELL*)

LADY BRACKNELL: Mr. Worthing! Rise, sir, from this semi-recumbent posture. It is most indecorous.

EXIT:

JACK: I can produce the hand-bag at any moment. It is in my dressing-room at home. I really think that should satisfy you, Lady Bracknell.

> She X to doorway.

> Turns at doorway to face Jack.

LADY BRACKNELL: Me, sir! What has it to do with me? ⬆ You can hardly imagine that I and Lord Bracknell would dream of allowing our only daughter — a girl brought up with the utmost care —➘to marry into a cloakroom, and form an alliance with a parcel? Good morning, Mr. Worthing! (LADY BRACKNELL sweeps out in majestic indignation.)

6. Using movement to heighten the tension of a scene.
   In addition to the value of movement in punctuating, pointing, and throwing away lines, movement that is restless, agitated, or rapid can help to sustain the tempo of a scene that might otherwise be talky or tedious.

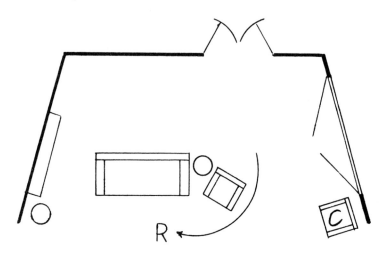

Example: *Blithe Spirit*, Act II, Scene 1.

XDC in perplexed meditation.	RUTH: Did you feel quite well yesterday — during the day, I mean?
	CHARLES: Of course I did.
Turning to face him.	RUTH: What did you have for lunch?
	CHARLES: You ought to know, you had it with me.
Paces DR.	RUTH: Let me see now, there was lemon sole and that cheese thing.
	CHARLES: Why should having a cheese thing for lunch make me see my deceased wife after dinner?
	RUTH: You never know. It was rather rich.
	CHARLES: Why didn't you see your dead husband then? You had just as much of it as I did.
XUR above sofa.	RUTH: This is not getting us anywhere at all.
	CHARLES: Of course it isn't; and it won't as long as you insist on ascribing supernatural phenomena to colonic irritation.
	RUTH: Supernatural grandmother.
	CHARLES: I admit she'd have been much less agitating.
XUC a few steps.	RUTH: Perhaps you ought to see a nerve specialist.
Rise indignantly.	CHARLES: I am not in the least neurotic and never have been.

XULC toward him.	RUTH: ↑ A psychoanalyst, then.
	CHARLES: ↑ I refuse to endure months of expensive humiliation only to be told at the
XDC past her.	end of it that at the age of four I was in love with my rocking-horse.
	RUTH: What do you suggest?
Sits DC.	CHARLES: ↑ I don't suggest anything, I'm profoundly uneasy.
XC to above his chair and feels his head.	RUTH: ↑ Perhaps there's something pressing on your brain.
	CHARLES: If there were something pressing on my brain I should have violent headaches, shouldn't I?
	RUTH: Not necessarily. An uncle of mine had a lump the size of a cricket ball pressing on his brain for years and he never felt a thing.
Springs up and XDR to fireplace.	CHARLES: ↑ I know I should know if I had anything like that.

7. Finding a *variety* of tempi within the play and taking every opportunity suggested by the text to change the tempo.

   a. Make sure that the first ten minutes of the play, when audiences are adjusting their eyes and ears to the stage, do not move too rapidly. If valuable expository points are lost, later scenes may lack significance; if the first scene moves too fast, later scenes may seem to drag by contrast.

   b. Avoid a "let down" after a particularly fast or effective scene by pacing the succeeding scene faster than might otherwise be necessary.

   c. Suspense can be created by a deliberately slower tempo than the audience would expect of the characters under given circumstances.

   d. The director should help the actor decide in each scene whether he is to pick up the tempo of the others or whether the rhythm of his character requires him to play at a different tempo than the rest in the scene.

   e. Sudden changes in speed can be used to good effect in creating variety and sustaining an audience's interest.

   Example: *The Late Christopher Bean*, Act II. (No pauses except where ‖ indicated.

SUSAN plays at a deliberately slower tempo than DR. H.	SUSAN: (Comes downstairs, frightened.) ↑ What is it, Pa? What do you want?
	DR. HAGGETT: Have you seen any old pictures of Chris Bean's lying around?

SUSAN: (Relieved) Oh, is that all?

| Fast, building to a shout. |

DR. HAGGETT: ↑ "Is that all? Is that *all?*" Don't talk like a fool!

SUSAN: Pa, what's come over you, hollering this way?

DR. HAGGETT: Answer my question.

SUSAN: Yes, of course I have.

| Simultaneously |

MRS. HAGGETT: *What!*

DR. HAGGETT: *Where?*

SUSAN: Last time I seen 'em they was in the barn.

| He is fast, hurrying her. She can build suspense by using a slower tempo. |

DR. HAGGETT: In the *barn?*

SUSAN: Yes, Pa.

DR. HAGGETT: How many?

SUSAN: I don't know rightly. || Eight or ten, I guess.

DR. HAGGETT: *Eight* or *ten!*

SUSAN: Yes, they was in the old box stall.

DR. HAGGETT: I'm in and out of that barn all day long. Taking the Ford out and putting it up again. *I* ain't seen no pictures! || When did you see 'em last?

SUSAN: It couldn't have been so long ago. || I remember showing 'em to Warren Creamer.

| Angry now, SUSAN picks up faster tempo and each tops the other. |

DR. HAGGETT: Aha! Then that's what's become of 'em. Warren Creamer's stole 'em.

SUSAN. He *ain't.* He *wouldn't.*

DR. HAGGETT: They was in the barn. You showed 'em to Warren. They ain't there now and I'd have seen 'em. Warren *must* have stole 'em.

SUSAN: No!

DR. HAGGETT: You get Warren over here this minute. No! Here! I'll get him. (Crosses to telephone at desk.)

SUSAN: Pa! Please — (He snatches up the phone.)

| Topping both of them. |

MRS. HAGGETT: ↑(Suffocating) *It ain't no use,* Milton.

DR. HAGGETT: Why ain't it?

MRS. HAGGETT: || Warren didn't steal 'em.

DR. HAGGETT: How do you know he didn't?

MRS. HAGGETT: I || burnt 'em.

DR. HAGGETT: || You *what?*

MRS. HAGGETT: || I put 'em on the bonfire and burnt 'em.

DR. HAGGETT: || All eight or ten?

MRS. HAGGETT: || I'd have thought there was more.

Sudden change to slow tempo for climax and variety.

D. Planning for tempo and achieving it in rehearsal:

1. Keep in mind the desired tempo when planning the blocking and movement of the play.

   a. It will be difficult later to speed up a scene which has been blocked with deliberate or long movements.

   b. Inner factors which affect tempo should be a part of the director's original interpretation and planning of the production.

2. Wait until near the end of the rehearsal period to put pressure on actors to pick up cues and achieve external tempo.

   a. Working for speed too soon may force actors to hurry artificially and overlook necessary motivations and responses.

   b. When the foundations are well laid and performances are truthful and well motivated, it will be relatively simple to tighten up the pickup of cues and take out unnecessary pauses.

   c. Remember that a fast tempo requires the actors to articulate more precisely than does a slow tempo.

3. A revision or final tightening of the tempo may be necessary after the director has observed audience reaction at the preview or first performance.

   a. Where restlessness or coughing is noted, the tempo may need to be speeded up.

   b. Where points are missed by the audience, the tempo may need to be slowed down.

   c. Holding for laughs will greatly affect the actual speed of the performance: though seeming to move rapidly, many minutes will be added to the playing time of a successful comedy.

III. Climax.

Climax and tempo are closely interrelated and generally occupy the director's attention at the same time in the rehearsal period. It is the surge and fall of intensity in the drama that creates in the audience the impression of a fast tempo, and it is often through the dynamics of tempo that a build-up to climax is achieved.

A. Definition of climax.

Climax can be defined as a moment of high dramatic interest. The term comes from the Greek for "ladder," and suggests that there are various rungs or steps by which the actor progressively ascends to and descends from a high point. Minor climaxes are the highest moments of individual beats or scenes, act climaxes are the moments of greatest impact in each act, and the major climax of the play is the highest point in the action of the entire play.

1. Climax is a relative device and would not be meaningful to an audience without contrasting moments of falling intensity. As "anticlimax" has become a derogatory term, it is better to borrow from music and call a contrasting moment of subsiding intensity a "diminuendo." This will be analyzed more fully under the principle of subordination later in the chapter.

2. *Climax* should be distinguished from *crisis,* for the terms are not interchangeable. Crisis is a term in dramaturgy which refers to the *turning point* in the lives or destiny of the characters. This moment is not necessarily climactic in its theatrical effect, but as the audience reflects back on it, it was a time when the die was cast for the ultimate denouement—perhaps a moment of quiet or even casual decision such as Hamlet's fateful, "No, Up, sword, and know thou a more horrid hent." (Act III, Scene 3.)

B. Finding climaxes in the script.

1. Before attempting to block a play, the director should select and mark in his director's book those moments of highest dramatic intensity.

2. Climaxes may grow out of either:

   a. Calculated and conscious decision.
   "Till then, I banish thee on pain of death. . . ." (*King Henry IV, Part 2*)

   b. Uncontrolled or unpremeditated emotional outbursts.
   "Yea, noise? Then I'll be brief. O happy dagger! This is thy sheath; there rest, and let me die." (*Romeo and Juliet*)

3. Make sure that at least one climax is selected for:

    a. Each long speech or soliloquy.
    b. Each beat.
    c. Each scene. ⎞   (The larger units should contain sev-
    d. Each act. ⎬   eral minor climaxes and a major climax
    e. The play itself. ⎠   arranged in cumulative order.)

4. The director must know how strong each climax should be in relation to earlier and later climaxes, in other words, where a particular climax fits in the over-all pattern of surges and falls. Boleslavsky likened this to an awareness of the floors at which the elevator stops in its ascent to the top.[2]

5. Where the author has failed to provide a climax for each beat, scene or act, the director and actors will have to superimpose and motivate a build-up to climax; otherwise the beat or scene will not "get anywhere."

C. Inner factors which can create a climax.

1. The emotional progression of the actors. The actors grow in their emotional involvement in the situation, giving vent to more and more intense emotions until the most powerful level is reached at the moment in the play selected as the climax by the director. The actors need to hold some of their emotional strength in reserve for this moment, rather than reaching their climax too soon and creating an anticlimax or a plateau. If actors had sufficient inner resources and perfectly expressive voices and bodies, they would need little help from the technical elements listed following. Most often in the educational theatre, however, the director will need to use external techniques to help the actors bring out with the necessary intensity the emotions which they feel.

2. A moment of insight, discovery, or recognition which comes to the character, and which can create a climax without necessarily requiring a forceful emotional intensity, provided there is complete understanding of the implications of the moment and the actor permits himself to be deeply affected by them. Such moments are often most telling when they drop quietly under the previous build-up.

2. Richard Boleslavsky, *Acting: The First Six Lessons* (New York: Theatre Arts, Inc., 1933), 6th lesson.

OUR TOWN

MR. WEBB:
> *Off stage.*

Where's my girl? Where's my birthday girl?

EMILY:
> *In a loud voice to the stage manager.*

| She is sobsing. |

I can't. I can't go on. It goes so fast. We don't have time to look at one another.

| She looks up, almost with surprise as the realization comes to her. |

> *She breaks down sobbing. The lights dim on the left half of the stage.* MRS. WEBB *disappears.*

I didn't realize. So all that was going on and we never noticed.

| Quiet but firm. |

Take me back—up the hill—to my grave. But first: Wait! One more look.

| Emotion beginning to well up. |

| Starting to build. |

| With simple affection. |

Good-by, Good-by, world. Good-by, Grover's Corners . . . Mama and Papa. Good-by to clocks ticking . . . and Mama's sunflowers. And food and coffee.

| Slowly builds as each memory awakens a stronger emotion. |

And new-ironed dresses and hot baths . . . and sleeping and waking up. Oh, earth, you're too wonderful for anybody to realize you.

| Climax — drops under in loudness but with intense and deeply felt awareness. |

> *She looks toward the stage manager and asks abruptly, through her tears:*

| Softer, with the wisdom born of suffering. |

Do any human beings ever realize life while they live it?—every, every minute?

STAGE MANAGER:
No.

> *Pause.*

The saints and poets, maybe— they do some.

EMILY:
I'm ready to go back.

> *She returns to her chair beside Mrs. Gibbs.*
> *Pause.*

D. External techniques which can create a climax.

    1. Picturization (Refer back to Chapter 4.)

        a. By using the strongest possible emphasis or center of attention. The strongest body position of the emphatic character(s), the most powerful area of the stage, levels, focus, line, etc., can all contribute to a visual stage picture of climatic power. The element of contrast is vital, making it necessary to save these strong elements for the climax and deliberately use weaker body positions, areas, levels, etc., for scenes preceding the climax.

        b. By saving the most telling picturization to dramatize the strong emotions within the characters at the moment of climax. For example, a climax was achieved through picturization in Act III of O'Neill's *A Moon for the Misbegotten* in the California State University at Long Beach production when the drunken Tyrone tries crudely to drag Josie toward her bedroom after she has already offered him her love; she shakes him loose so forcefully that he falls back down the steps. The actor playing Tyrone landed on his hands and knees, and stayed on the ground like an animal during the next two speeches, crawling on all fours toward the porch to grovel for the whiskey bottle.

        c. By disturbing the balance of a well-balanced composition, or by restoring the balance after it has been upset. The father's entrance in Act I of *The Barretts of Wimpole Street*, for example, upsets a balanced composition and thereby adds to the climactic effect of his entrance. In the last scene of *Romeo and Juliet*, to illustrate the opposite, the unbalanced composition is restored to symmetry as Capulet and Montague clasp hands in reconciliation over the dead bodies of their children.

        d. By adding more characters to the picture so that their reactions can reinforce the climax. Shakespeare was intuitively aware of this principle of the director's art, and provided lines in *Romeo and Juliet* to motivate the addition of as many townspeople as the director has room and budget for during the street scene after the death of Tybalt, for which Romeo is banished.

    2. Movement. (Refer back to Chapter 5.)

        a. By making a strong movement or series of strong movements just before the climactic line, such as crossing from a weak area to a strong area, or opening up from a weak body position to a strong one. (See list of strong movements given in Chapter 5, page 150.

b. By increasing the size, duration or vigor of a movement as the scene builds to climax.

c. By increasing the speed of movement as the scene progresses.

In the example from *The Late Christopher Bean* given on page 234. Dr. Haggett's cross to the telephone at the climax of the scene would be much more rapid than his cross to Susan at the beginning of the scene.

d. By decreasing the speed of movement for contrast.

Danny in *Night Must Fall,* for example, bustles briskly about the stage getting Mrs. Bramson things she wishes—books, candy, etc. In the climactic moment when he picks up the pillow to smother her, he moves with deliberate, extremely slow rhythm.

e. By increasing the number of people moving.

The shipwreck scene, for example, in Act I of *The Tempest,* can be built to climax by having more and more people—sailors and passengers—run across stage in alarm.

f. By suddenly stopping all movement.

The entrance of the father in the midst of an impromptu polka in *The Barretts of Wimpole Street* illustrates the effectiveness of this technique.

g. By gesture.

Just as with the other techniques used in building to climax, gesture must be utilized sparingly, so that the actor does not reach the largest extension of his arms too soon but saves it for the climactic moment. The repetition of a gesture weakens its climactic effect. Thus in the example on page 238 from *Our Town,* if Emily plans to extend her arms in a large gesture on "Oh, earth," she must use a smaller gesture on "Goodbye, world!"

3. Voice. (Refer back to Chapter 7.)

There is a natural tendency to use the four variable properties of voice together—i.e., pitch tends to rise and tempo to decrease when volume increases. However, each can contribute to climax separately and the actor can use one or more of the following in different parts of a speech that must build to climax:

a. By changes in volume.

A progressive increase in volume is one of the most frequently used techniques for building to climax. Again the actor must guard against using his loudest volume too soon and being unable to top himself at the climax. In a long speech that must build to climax by means of volume, the actor should try to find places to drop back—growing momentarily softer—and begin the build anew. A sudden decrease from loud to low, intense delivery can also be climactic in effect.

Example: *A Midsummer Night's Dream,* Act III, Scene 1. Trying to maintain pitch, tempo and quality constant, the speech may be read as indicated to build to climax with volume alone.

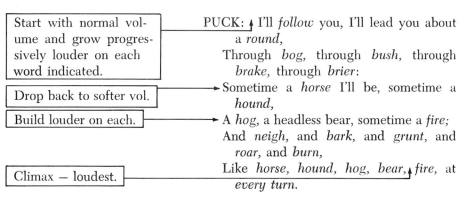

Start with normal volume and grow progressively louder on each word indicated.

Drop back to softer vol.

Build louder on each.

Climax — loudest.

PUCK: I'll *follow* you, I'll lead you about a *round*,
Through *bog*, through *bush*, through *brake*, through *brier*:
Sometime a *horse* I'll be, sometime a *hound*,
A *hog*, a headless bear, sometime a *fire*;
And *neigh*, and *bark*, and *grunt*, and *roar*, and *burn*,
Like *horse, hound, hog, bear, fire*, at *every turn.*

   b. By changes in pitch.
A rising pitch usually accompanies a surge in anger or joy and a loss of emotional control; a falling pitch usually accompanies a climactic moment based on suppression of emotion, threat or decision. Too much rise in pitch, particularly in women's voices, may cause shrillness, and hence pitch is limited in its usefulness in building to climax.

Example: Puck's speech from *A Midsummer Night's Dream* may be read trying to maintain volume, tempo and quality constant and using a progressively higher pitch on each word indicated.

   c. By changes of quality.
Quality is the most variable of the four properties of voice, and the one that most closely mirrors inner content. In moments of climax, the voice may reflect an authoritative, exultant, or explosive quality reinforced with chest or full-mouth resonance, or it may reflect a strained, tense or desperate quality with strident, aspirate or throaty resonances.

Example: Puck's speech from *A Midsummer Night's Dream* may be read trying to maintain constant volume,

pitch, and tempo, and using a different quality
descriptive of the content and progressively
more mischievously exultant on each word indicated.

d. By changes of tempo.
The cumulative effect of a progressively increasing tempo
is also widely used for climax when motivated by emotional pressure, haste, or anticipation. When the climax is
motivated by authority, emphasis, or deeply felt decision,
the tempo would progressively decrease or slow down suddenly.

Example: Puck's speech from *A Midsummer Night's Dream*
may be read trying to maintain volume, pitch
and quality constant and growing progressively
faster in tempo.

e. By topping in vocal intensity.
Topping and undercutting as techniques in building to and
from climax have already been covered in Chapter 7. When
two or more actors have a give-and-take of lines which
must build to climax, topping is essential; it can happen
only when there are teamwork and interplay between the
actors building the scene. In a long speech or soliloquy,
the individual actor can use the same principle in topping
himself.

Example: Puck's speech from *A Midsummer Night's Dream*
may be read trying to make each key word in a
sequence top those that precede it.

f. By the use of the pause.
As we have seen, the pause is a highly effective way of
pointing the line or business which comes immediately
after it. Falstaff's climactic "By the Lord, I knew ye as
well as he that made ye," after he has been caught lying
about the Gadshill robbery in *King Henry IV* can be made
more effective if the actor takes full advantage of a pause
after "By the Lord," while the audience is held in suspense watching the keen-witted old man as his shrewd
mind invents an outrageous lie to top them all. A pause
can also contribute to a climax when there is much ani-
mated talking and noise which is suddenly stopped cold
at the climax, as for example, in the famous entrance of
the Kirbys in *You Can't Take It With You*, in which they

surprise the madcap family in a variety of outlandish activities.

4. Reinforcement from other theatrical elements.

Although any of the theatrical elements can contribute to or reinforce a climax—scenery, for example, in *No Exit* when the bricked-up window is revealed, or costume in the return of the bloody, soaking-wet Shadow in *Winterset*—the elements most frequently used to heighten a climactic moment are:

a. Lighting.

When the form or style of the play permits, a climax can be made visually powerful by a stronger accent of light on the emphatic character(s) and a dimming down of the other areas of the stage. Some plays can also take advantage of special lighting effects at climactic moments— the colorful dawn in the last act of O'Neill's *A Moon for the Misbegotten,* the whirling nightmare of lights in *The Adding Machine,* and the flashes of lightning in the storm scenes of *King Lear.*

b. Sound effects.

The storm scene of *King Lear* receives additional reinforce-

A MOON FOR THE MISBEGOTTEN—LIGHTING California State University, Long Beach. Directed by W. David Sievers. Designed by Milton Howarth. Lighting by John H. Green.

ment from the thunder and wind, and there are many other plays in which sound effects can be used to heighten climaxes. The final, unforgettable climax in *The Diary of Anne Frank* is accomplished almost entirely by sound effects—the screeching brakes of the secret police, the heavy boots ascending the stairs, and the splintering of the door.

c. Music.

Motion pictures, television, and radio rely much more heavily upon music in achieving climaxes than does the theatre; in the former media the human voice is heard over the same loud-speaker system as the music, and the audience is not conscious of any discrepancy between the two as is sometimes the case in the theatre when the music is not of high fidelity. However, there are times when music can appropriately be used to heighten, underline, or punctuate the climaxes, provided there is something in the text with which the director can justify the use of poetic license. In *Summer and Smoke*, for example, the overtones of sybolism suggest the appropriate use of two musical themes, a sensual and a spiritual *leitmotif* which surge to climax in many of the scenes and then diminuendo to serve as a bridge into the next scene.

E. The principle of economy of means.

Throughout the foregoing analysis of the means of building to climax, both inner and external, it will be observed that there was implicit the principle of economy of means.

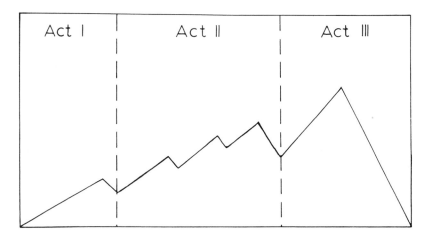

ONE PATTERN FOR A PLAY'S CLIMAXES

1. Saving the biggest effect for last.

   In arranging minor and major climaxes, the director must save his most powerful effect for last. If an actor gives too much emotional intensity to the Act I climax, he may have nothing left with which to top himself for the Act II and Act III climaxes. Having experienced the first act climax, the audience will not be satisfied with the same level of intensity for the next act—unless there is growth there will seem to be anticlimax and monotony. As an example, study Judith Anderson's handling of this problem in her masterful recording of *Medea*.

2. Deciding how many steps there are in the progression to climax.

   F. Cowles Strickland notes that King Richard repeats the word "down" five times in his descent speech from *Richard II*, Act III, Scene 3.[3] If the actor descends all the way on the first few "downs," he will have no movement left with which to make the final "down" climactic. Similarly Capulet threatens Juliet four times (*Romeo and Juliet*, Act III, Scene 5) and the actor must grow in intensity so that the fourth threat is most powerful.

3. Relating the number of steps in the progression to the blocking and movement.

   If the scene reaches its climax through a discernible number of intermediate steps, the physical blocking should as far as possible reflect this. The director should begin the progression in a weak area of the stage or with weak body positions, so as to give the scene room to build. If, for example, there are three intermediate steps in the build-up to climax, the director might use three movements; if he wishes the actor DRC for the climax, he might start the actor UL so that he can make three crosses—UR, DLC, and DRC.

4. Sustaining the climax when it is achieved.

   Having built up to the climax, it is important to sustain the high level of intensity long enough for its impact to be fully felt by the audience. Samuel Selden points out, for example, that in the climax of the play scene of *Hamlet* the king might cry, "Give me some light: away!" and make his exit before the audience could realize what happened.[4] The director must

3. F. Cowles Strickland, *The Technique of Acting* (New York: McGraw-Hill Book Company, Inc., 1956), p. 80.

4. Hubert C. Heffner, Samuel Selden and Hunton D. Sellman, *Modern Theatre Practice* (New York: Appleton-Century-Crofts, 1959), p. 301.

find ways to sustain this climactic moment while the audience's attention is directed to the panic of the king. A climax can be sustained for only a few moments, however; then the *diminuendo* or falling action should begin.

F. The principle of subordination.
   To deal effectively with his climaxes, the director must also apply the principle of subordination. In structuring the progression of the performance, he must seek out those moments, beats, or parts of scenes which are subordinate in importance and can be de-emphasized for the sake of contrast. The effective handling of these moments of a casual, relaxed, or transitional nature will make the climaxes seem even more intense.

   1. A build to climax is most powerful when it starts low, with a subordinate scene that can be "thrown away," played lightly or unemphatically. The inexperienced director sometimes tends to stress everything and work for too many climaxes; this would be the equivalent of playing an entire symphony *fortissimo*.

   2. After a climax has been achieved, there should be a subsiding of intensity or *diminuendo* to another subordinate moment before a new build-up begins.

   3. The *diminuendo* or subsiding action generally takes much less time than the progression to climax and, it is to be hoped, the audience's interest does not drop as low as it was at the beginning of the scene.

   4. A *diminuendo* can be accomplished by:

      a. A sudden drop from climax to a subdued, contrasting moment.

      b. A gradual descent or relaxation of tension through a reversal of the techniques used to build the scene—i.e., a decrease of intensity, weaker visual emphasis and picturization, weaker movement, vocal undercutting, decreases in volume, tempo, subdued theatrical elements such as lighting, sound, or music.

Example of the principles of climax and subordination, *Winterset*, Act III:

The final speech of Esdras, the father of Miriamne, as he and his son bend over her dead body and that of her beloved, Mio, is itself a resolution to the play rather than the climax (which was created by the attempted escape and machine-gunning of the lovers). Within the final speech itself, however, there must be a strong climax of recognition or awareness.

Choking back his tears, he starts softly with the realization of a new truth.	ESDRAS: Well, they were *wiser* than you and I. To die when you are young and untouched, that's *beggary* to a *miser* of *years*, but the *devils* locked in synod
Growing somewhat stronger.	*shake* and are *daunted* when men set their lives at hazard for the *heart's love*, and *lose*.
Drops back, with gentle wisdom.	And these, who were yet children, will weigh more than all a city's elders when the experiment is reckoned up in the end.
Builds with a sudden surge.	Oh, Miriamne, and Mio – Mio, my son – know this where you lie,
Clear and strong, "Why didn't I see it before?"	*this* is the *glory* of *earth-born men* and *women*, not to *cringe*, never to *yield*, but *standing*, take defeat *implacable* and *defiant*,
Minor climax.	die unsubmitting.
Then drops back with resignation.	I wish that I'd died so, long ago; before you're old you'll wish that you had died as they have.
Begins major build-up, growing emphatic.	On this *star*, in this hard star-*adventure*, knowing not what the fires *mean* to right and left, nor whether a meaning was *intended* or *presumed*, man can *stand up*, and look out *blind*, and say:
As a powerful cry of protest.	in all these turning *lights* I find no *clue*, Only a *masterless* night, and in my blood no certain answer,
Tops himself, in restrained triumph.	yet is my *mind* my *own*, yet is my *heart* a *cry* toward something *dim*
Strongly pointed as climax of speech	in *distance*, which is *higher* than *I* am and makes me *emperor* of the endless *dark* *even in seeking!*
Diminuendo begins.	What odds and ends of life men may live otherwise, let them live, and then go out, as I shall go, and you.
With quiet control of his emotions.	Our part is only to bury them. Come, take her up.
Gently and softly he bends over his daughter.	They must not lie here.

IV. Summary.

The need for structuring the tempo and climaxes of a performance is inherent in the nature of the theatre itself. Although a director must plan his tempo and climaxes in his preliminary blocking, he generally should wait until the last phase of the rehearsal period to tighten the tempo and heighten the climaxes. Tempo and climax are interrelated and have as their purpose to give to the audience the impression of speed and cumulative dramatic intensity.

A. Tempo.

    1. Ways to speed up the tempo of a play.
    2. Inner factors which affect tempo.
    3. External factors which affect tempo.
    4. Planning for tempo and achieving it in rehearsal.

B. Climax.

    1. Definition of climax.
    2. Finding climaxes in the script.
    3. Inner factors which can create a climax.
    4. External techniques which can create a climax.
    5. The principle of economy of means.
    6. The principle of subordination.

Selective Bibliography

Boleslavsky, Richard. *Acting: The First Six Lessons.* New York: Theatre Arts, Inc., 1933.

Dietrich, John E. *Play Direction.* New York: Prentice-Hall, Inc., 1953.

Heffner, Hubert C., Selden, Samuel, and Hunton D. Sellman, *Modern Theatre Practice.* New York: Appleton-Century-Crofts, 1959.

Klein, Rugh. *The Art and Technique of Play Directing.* New York: Rinehart, 1953.

McMullan, Frank. *The Director's Handbook.* Hamden, Conn.: Shoe String Press, 1964.

Strickland, F. Cowles. *The Technique of Acting.* New York: McGraw-Hill, Inc., 1956.

Wright, Edward A. and Downs, Lenthiel H. *A Primer for Playgoers.* Englewood Cliffs, N. J.: Prentice-Hall, Inc., 1969.

THE NIGHT THOREAU SPENT IN JAIL California State University, Long Beach. Directed by Harry E. Stiver. Designed by Ralph W. Duckwall (Sets), William French (Costumes) and Patrick Hadlock (Lights).

RING ROUND THE MOON California State University, Long Beach. Directed by Edward A. Wright. Designed by Ralph W. Duckwall (Sets) and Herbert L. Camburn (Costumes).

10 Casting and Rehearsing the Play

1 — designer *submit ideas*
2 — designer " *rendering.*
3 — *problems incounter*

I. Introduction.

Now that most of the fundamentals of directing have been thoroughly digested and the potential director has penetratingly prepared all phases of his director's book, he is ready for his artistic and practical work on the stage. No matter how great the talent of the director or his understanding of the principles of directing, the success of his production will depend to a great extent upon his ability to cast properly and to conduct orderly and organized rehearsals in which he applies his theory and insight. If the director is relatively inexperienced, then he will have all the more need for a systematic rehearsal procedure.

II. Casting the play.

This is perhaps the most critical time for the ultimate success of the play. The director should carefully prepare for this period so as to get the best possible cast and still leave each candidate with the feeling that he has had a fair chance and that the director has not played favorites. *auditions*

A. Preparation for casting.

The director should prepare the following in advance of tryouts:
1. A description of each character with both physical and psychological requirements (see Chapter 8). This should be pre-

California State University, Long Beach
Department of Theatre Arts

★★★★★ Casting Sheet ★★★★★

Name _____ Phone _____ Date _____

Address _____
　　　　　　(Street)　　　　　　　　　(City)　　　　　　　　　(State)

Year in School _____ Age _____ M _____ F _____ Ht. _____ Wt. _____

Color of Hair _____ Do you sing?_____ Dance? _____Play a musical instr.? _____

Voice Range _____ Foreign Languages spoken _____

Dialects _____ No. of units this semester _____

★★★★★★★★★★ Please fill out your program this semester in detail, putting an X ★★★★★★★★★★
in the box when you have a class or any outside work or commitment that would interfere
with rehearsal. We will build rehearsal schedules from this so fill in completely.

Hour	Monday	Tuesday	Wednesday	Thursday	Friday	Saturday	Sunday
9-10							
10-11							
11-12							
12-1							
1-2							
2-3							
3-4:30							
4:30-6							
7-8							
8-9							
9-10							

Please list on back of this sheet previous roles played and where.

— — — — — — — — Do Not Write Below This Line — — — — — — — — —

Juvenile _____ Ingenue _____ Character_____ Leads_____ Comedy _____ Heavy _____ Other_____

Appearance:　　　　　　　　　　　　　　Movement:

Speech:　　　　　　　　　　　　　　　　Emotion:

Voice:　　　　　　　　　　　　　　　　　Ability to Take Direction:

Interpretation:　　　　　　　　　　　　　Sense of Comedy:

Call Back for Role of: _____

sented to the group orally or on ditto sheets at the beginning of tryouts.
2. Announcement of date and place of tryouts.
3. A form to be filled out by candidates and used by director (see sample university theatre form illustrated).
4. Scripts of the play obtained in sufficient time for tryouts, with copies made available.
5. Tryout scenes, selected for:
   a. Variety of moods demanded in roles.
   b. Limit of three or four characters in each scene.
   (Some directors announce the tryout scenes ahead of time; others prefer not to.)

B. Methods of casting.

1. Open tryout method.
   Although this method is the most prevalent in educational and community theatres, it may be necessary to supplement it by other methods.

   a. A three to four minute scene is read from the stage by candidates. The first tryouts are devoted to a weeding out of the unsuitable and the working up of a list of "possibles" who are then placed on a "Callback" list for final readings. The decision as to whether to give each actor a thorough hearing or a quick screening at first must depend upon the number of applicants.
   b. Callbacks.
   The "possibles," sometmes as many as three to four for each major role, are called back for final readings which must be conducted more thoroughly and under less pressure than the first readings. The director now must consider how well people are matched who will be playing scenes together. (For romantic scenes, check the height of the lovers; check for family similarity and contrast if applicable.)
   c. Final readings.
   The director should assemble his final choices for another reading and careful scrutiny before announcing his cast. At this time he can fill in minor roles with some of the runners-up for the leads. He should make sure that anyone accepting a role understands and agrees to the obligations and responsibilities demanded, and that his schedule will permit his rehearsing at the time others in the same scenes are free.

2. Closed tryout method.

When a play is to be cast from a particular class or membership group, closed readings are held. This method requires that the director consider very carefully the potential of the group or class before selecting a play.

3. Personal audition and interview method.

Most professional productions are cast by private interview and reading, often in the director's office. For the nonprofessional theatre, however, this method is too time-consuming and not conducive to the feeling that the actors have been given fair and equal consideration. Often, however, a director will have to supplement open tryouts by personal auditions to complete his cast when the open tryouts fail to produce the certain type or quality of actor needed.

4. Use of other techniques to supplement the foregoing.

a. Memorized selections.

In the case of Shakespeare or other material that is difficult because of its language, the director may expedite tryouts by asking all applicants to memorize a given soliloquy.

b. Improvisations.

For actors with previous experience in the Stanislavski method, the reading tryout can be supplemented by an improvisation based on a situation in the play, or one even indirectly suggested by it, permitting the director to see the actors react spontaneously, freely and with an emotional truth that rarely can be shown in a first reading. The improvisation needs to be carefully structured to avoid the tensions of this type of tryout.

c. Physical movement.

Where the play requires style and heightened body control from the actors, this should be checked as part of the tryout by asking the actors to cross the stage, bow, turn, fall, or sit to a musical rhythm which can be played on the piano or with a drum.

5. What to look for in casting.

a. Some spark in the actor's personality which suggests the character.

b. The actor's voice and speech, particularly projection, variety, clarity, and suitability for the role.

c. The actor's physical appearance and its appropriateness for the role.

d. The actor's emotional intensity and sense of truth.

e. How the tryout audience responds to his reading. If a comedy, did he get any laughs?

f. The actor's sense of timing if the role is a comedy one.

g. The actor's stage presence and poise.

h. The actor's flexibility and ability to take direction.

i. Conflicts in the actor's schedule which might have a bearing on his attending rehearsals.

j. Special aptitudes required such as playing a musical instrument, singing, dancing or fencing.

k. In the case of minor roles, it is often sufficient to have only one or two specific requirements in mind, and to use ingenuity in taking advantage of the particular personalities of the actors available.

l. The theatrical requirements of the role.

    Whether a character is tall or short, blonde or brunette, deep voiced or high voiced, is often of less importance than whether he fulfills the theatrical requirements of the role as intended by the author. The director should have these requirements in mind during casting, and should return to them as he guides the actors in characterization. The kind of empathic response which he desires the audience to have to the character may have direct bearing on the choice of actors. Among the theatrical requirements, which can be fulfilled in more than one way by more than one "type" of actor, are:

(1) Positive identification. The audience must like him, find him sympathetic and want him to win. He must inspire confidence.

(2) Negative identification. The audience must dislike him, find him unpleasant, irritating, disgusting, or hateful.

(3) The audience must find him pathetic.

(4) The audience must find him comic. His purpose is to "get laughs."

(5) He must dominate other characters in the play. As this factor is relative, the strength or weakness of the other characters will determine how much strength it will take to dominate them.

(6) The character must be a foil or contrast to another character. Demetrius and Lysander in *A Midsummer Night's Dream,* for example, need to be as different physically as possible—what might be called relative characterization—in order that the audience can distinguish between them during the confusions of a night in a dark forest. In this play too, it is essential that Hermia be shorter in stature than Helena.

(7) The character is intended to supply atmosphere or local color.

(8) The character's only purpose is to convey information —messengers, for example—or perform other utility functions. Clarity of voice and diction may be the primary requisites of the role.

(9) The character may not be fully characterized by the playwright, and the actor must supply what the playwright omitted. Through astute casting the director can sometimes enrich his production by taking advantage of the special attributes of his actors.

(10) A special quality of dignity or maturity may be needed to avoid getting laughs in the wrong places. Lodovico, for example, in *Othello* is a relatively minor role in the last act, but he speaks the final speech of the play, and the director should save a strong and mature actor for this role.

C. The double cast.

Directors must decide whether or not to double cast. College or community theatre directors rarely use this method.

1. Its advantages are that more persons can participate in a production, and the roles are covered in case of the illness of an actor.

2. Its disadvantage is that it requires more of the director's time, doing in effect double coaching, and often results in a less polished performance than with a single cast. If the system is used, each actor should be required to attend every rehearsal, observing and learning while his alternate is being directed. Both actors should work in part of each rehearsal.

D. Understudies.

In the nonprofessional theatre, an actor often prefers not to devote the time to preparing a role which he is not assured of playing. At the first hint that an actor may be seriously ill, however, the director must have an understudy stand by. It is amazing how rapidly an actor can learn a part when the rest of the production has taken shape, provided the stage manager has carefully recorded all blocking.

E. Precasting.

Although the director must have one or more possible actors in mind when he selects a play which has a particularly demanding leading role, it is fatal to the morale of an educational or community theatre if it is suspected that the director has made promises or commitments to actors prior to tryouts. Someone much better may turn up at tryouts, and in any case actors must not feel that there is no use trying out, or that a little clique will always get the best parts.

III. The rehearsal schedule.

As soon as the play is cast, the director should list all the conflicts in time which his actors may have—hours when it is impossible for them to rehearse—and on the basis of this work out a rehearsal schedule adequate to his estimate of the difficulties of the play.

A. Factors that affect the making of a rehearsal schedule:

1. The schedule should be coordinated with the production staff and the master calendar for the use of the theatre. (Where the stage can be used only on certain nights, it is best to schedule the large group scenes on those nights.) Opening night should not be left uncertain, but fixed from the beginning.

2. The rehearsal schedule should be duplicated and distributed to all concerned—to the cast at the first rehearsal and to production staff and crew heads.

3. Rehearsals should be scheduled regularly and as close together as possible, to preclude the forgetting that occurs during a long interval.
   a. Daily rehearsals are the most efficient.
   b. Three times a week is minimal.
   c. Less than three rehearsals a week is an inefficient plan.

4. The total number of rehearsals needed will depend upon the difficulty of the material and the experience of the cast.
   a. Four to six weeks, with five rehearsals a week, is minimal for the average modern play with no special difficulties.
   b. Six to eight weeks may be necessary for Shakespeare and other classics, musicals and plays with special problems.
   c. Three to four weeks, with three or four 2-hour rehearsals per week, may be necessary for the average one-act play.

5. What can be accomplished in one rehearsal depends upon the size and experience of the cast, their fatigue level, the difficulty of the material, and the stimulation which the director can provide. A suggested allocation of time in the nonprofessional theatre is:

7:00 P.M. to 7:20	Warm-up (running lines, reviewing or getting familiar with new material).
7:20 P.M. to 8:15	Concentration on new material to be worked on.

8:15 P.M. to 8:25	Break.
8:25 to 9:00	Review and refine new material just worked on.
9:00 to 9:30 or 10:00	Repeat new material to fix it in actors' memory, or review previously learned material.

The director should be sensitive as to when the cast can be pushed, when they are fatigued, when they are on the verge of a creative discovery. When they are emotionally spent, the director should switch to less strenuous scenes. A play can also be over-rehearsed until the actors grow stale.

6. The director should schedule actors for particular scenes as needed, especially in a large cast play, and not expect busy students or working adults to give up time when not actually needed. Scenes involving certain characters or groups can be scheduled together on certain nights for more efficient use of the actors' time. (For example, the Friar scenes in *Romeo and Juliet* can, for the early weeks of rehearsal, be scheduled on nights when Benvolio, Tybalt and Mercutio are not present, and vice versa.) The director in the nonprofessional theatre is forced to be flexible in building his schedule around the conflicts, classes, and work commitments of his cast.

7. When the director finds that private coaching is necessary or that an actor is embarrassed to be coached in front of the group, individual sessions should be scheduled outside the regular rehearsals. Actors should not be pampered into expecting this, however, because of the demands made upon the director's time during the rehearsal period.

8. *Every rehearsal should have a purpose,* and both director and cast should bring something new to try out at each rehearsal. The purposes of each phase of the rehearsal period are shown in the suggested rehearsal schedule and explained in Section **V** in order to give the director an overview of the necessary steps between casting and opening night. The director must plan for what he hopes to accomplish at each rehearsal (though he need not necessarily announce his plans to the cast), adapting his strategy as he sees how the cast is progressing and how many rehearsals are left. Too often young directors arrive at rehearsal merely to "run through" an act, which, if it lacks a purpose, may prove to be merely running over the same mistakes again and again.

9. The principle of "the juggler."
   A scene that is not completely mastered cannot be left unrehearsed for more than two or three days without ill effects.

The director uses the principle of the juggler, throwing one ball (Act I) into the air, then adding a second one and keeping two going alternately, then adding a third and keeping all three going simultaneously.

B. A suggested rehearsal schedule.

On the basis of the aforesaid principles, following is a suggested rehearsal schedule (p. 260) that has been found workable (with modifications) at the university level for such modern full-length plays as *The Diary of Anne Frank, The Time of Your Life,* and *Summer and Smoke.* (Where a play is in a number of scenes rather than three acts, it is best to divide it into thirds for rehearsal purposes, based upon length rather than number of scenes.) Remember that various types of plays require different types of rehearsal schedules in which special problems peculiar to a particular play may receive ample rehearsal time and emphasis.

IV. General principles of rehearsal.

At the first rehearsal, it generally is desirable to make sure that the cast is familiar with the *traditions of the theatre* and understands the standard of discipline which the director will expect of them during the weeks to come.

A. Traditions of the rehearsal.

The rehearsal period is a special time in the daily life of theatre artists, a time for serious and concentrated creative work. To keep the theatre a place of awe and wonder, and make rehearsals efficient, an actor should either know or be told:

1. Come to the rehearsal prepared to work—physically, mentally and emotionally. (This includes bringing your script and a pencil to early rehearsals.)
2. Be prompt at all rehearsals and calls.
3. Share scenes rather than stealing them—each actor looks better with a strong partner. Never upstage your partner unless so directed.
4. Don't move, gesture, or face out front on another actor's line except as directed.
5. After the director stops to fix a line or piece of business, begin the rehearsal again by repeating the cue line or lines just before the one corrected so that the change can be rehearsed.
6. Counter-cross and dress stage without being told.
7. Stay in character—never talk under your breath or attempt to "break up" another actor. If you forget a line, remain in character and say to the prompter, "Line."

SUGGESTED REHEARSAL SCHEDULE

WEEK		PURPOSE	PERIOD
1st	Monday	Open tryouts	Casting
	Tuesday	Callbacks	,,
	Wednesday	Final casting	,,
	Thursday	Reading of whole play	Familiarization
	Friday	Reading, discussion and analysis of play	,,
2nd	Monday	Reading, discussion and analysis of play	,,
	Tuesday	Block Act I	Exploration
	Wednesday	Review Act I	,,
	Thursday	Block Act II	,,
	Friday	Act I for characterization and business	,,
3rd	Monday	Review Act II	Exploration
	Tuesday	Act I for enrichment	,,
	Wednesday	Act II for characterization and business	,,
	Thursday	Act I **WITHOUT BOOKS**	,,
	Friday	Acts I and II for enrichment	,,
4th	Monday	Block Act III	,,
	Tuesday	Polishing Act I	Discovery
	Wednesday	Act II **WITHOUT BOOKS**	Exploration
	Thursday	Review Act III for characterization	,,
	Friday	Run Acts II and III for polishing	,,
5th	Monday	Act III for business and enrichment	,,
	Tuesday	Act I for tempo and climax	Formalizing
	Wednesday	Act II for polishing	Discovery
	Thursday	Act III **WITHOUT BOOKS**	Exploration
	Friday	Run Acts II and III for continuity	Discovery
6th	Monday	Run Act I and II for tempo and climax	Formalizing
	Tuesday	Run Act III for tempo and climax	,,
	Wednesday	Act III and scenes that need polish	,,
	Thursday	Run through of entire play with hand props	Integration
	Friday	Run through of entire play for final polishing in rehearsal hall — stage used by technical crews	,,
	Saturday	Technical rehearsal for lights (without actors)	,,
7th	Sunday	1st Dress Rehearsal	,,
	Monday	2nd Dress Rehearsal with make-up	,,
	Tuesday	Preview Dress Rehearsal	,,
	Wednesday	Opening Night	Performance
	Thursday	Performance	,,
	Friday	Performance	,,
	Saturday	Performance	,,

(When performances are repeated the following weekend, a line-rehearsal is recommended as a refresher the day preceding.)

8. Don't give another actor a direction—let the director do that.
9. Learn your lines at home or offstage, not while everyone waits onstage. Learn the lines precisely and give cues consistently—don't rewrite the play or *ad lib*.
10. Protect your health, particularly when overtired or overheated.

B. Learning lines.

1. Inexperienced actors may need to be shown how to study lines, associating each line with its preceding cue. Some actors memorize best one way, some another, depending on individual differences and whether their visual or auditory memory is strong.

   a. One workable method is to use a blank piece of paper to cover up the line itself and reveal only the cue; the actor says the line, then uncovers it to see if it was correct.
   b. Another method is to have someone "cue" the actor, reading his cues and watching the script to see that he reads his lines correctly.
   c. Some actors have found it helpful to read their cues into a tape recorder, allowing pauses for their own lines to be spoken.
   d. When several actors have a long wait backstage, they can use the time profitably to "run lines," throwing each other their cues as quickly as they can without interpreting the lines.

2. It is unwise for the director to either expect or permit actors to learn their lines until after an act has been blocked. To do this would be learning by rote. Lines are easier to learn and retain when they are part of a "Gestalt," associating (1) cue, (2) line, (3) motivation, and (4) movement—all to be learned together.
3. The director should set a deadline for memorization of each act, and at this rehearsal scripts *must* be put aside whether or not actors are fumbling for lines. As a rough guide, the deadline for an act might well be after its third rehearsal, and deadlines for the other acts at least a week apart.
4. At the rehearsal when the actors lay their scripts aside for the first time, the director will have to be patient, expecting little if any progress from his cast in characterization, emotion, tempo or climax.

C. Understanding the actor.
When the cast assembles for the first reading, it will be a diversified collection of individuals whom the director must weld into a unified whole by opening night. The inanimate objects with

which the director affects the audience—the scenery, lights, costumes—can be made to do what he wants; yet the greatest impact upon the audience is made by an element that is far more complex, difficult to understand and elusive in control—the human beings who make up the cast. The director in the nonprofessional theatre must devote a major portion of his time to the problem of working with the actors, coaching them to give the performance he and they desire.

However experienced the actors or inexperienced the director, the latter has one great advantage—he can see the actors from out front as they cannot see themselves. The director need not be a better actor than his cast, but he must know how to communicate with them—how to talk the actor's language and to recognize the actor's problems. Here are some observations derived from the psychology of directing which may help the young director work more effectively with his actors:

1. Actors vary widely in their previous theatrical experience, in the methods which they use, and in the vocabulary with which they are used to having the director communicate with them. There is no reason why the director should use the same method or terminology with all.

2. Actors vary widely in their psychological background, emotional maturity, freedom and sense of security. They will also vary widely from rehearsal to rehearsal in their freshness or fatigue, emotional stability and interest in the problem at hand. There are some characteristics, however, which almost all actors share:

   a. Actors want to give a good performance. There is a high degree of *motivation* in the theatre. The director must use this and keep it alive.

   b. Actors want to have confidence in their director. They need to look to him as a source of support, trusting that he can guide them to a successful performance.

   c. Actors have heightened ego needs and are hypersensitive (or they would not be actors). They want to be praised by the director and assured that they are making progress. It is a sound rule to *praise the actor in front of the cast but criticize him in private*. There are exceptions to this, however: the overconfident actor who makes no progress until he is "taken down a peg," and criticism which can be made general and applied to the whole cast.

   d. Actors need to be accepted by the group to feel "belongingness" as a part of the team, no matter how small a role they play.

e. The shakier an actor is, the more he needs to be told that he is "coming along." A kind of panic can set in if an actor feels that the director is worried about him as the weak link in the cast. Often the director must do a bit of acting himself to convince an insecure actor that he can do the job if he will just believe in himself.

f. Actors need to be given something specific to think about at the end of a rehearsal so that they can bring something new to try at the next rehearsal. A healthy feeling with which an actor should leave rehearsal is that he accomplished something today and knows what specific problems to work on for tomorrow in order to polish his performance even more.

3. The actor needs inner *freedom.*
   For the most effective use of his body, voice and emotions, the actor must free himself from tensions. Unlike the musician, the actor is his own instrument, an instrument which must be tuned to respond to the most subtle command of its player's will. Freedom can be achieved by:

   a. Relaxation and muscular discipline.
       Dance movement, athletics and physical coordination all build up and aid in the development of relaxation. In performance, however, the actor is most apt to achieve relaxation through a control of his attention—through concentration.

   b. Concentration.
       (1) The actor's attention must not waver or drift out to the audience. It should be confined to the circumstances of the scene.
       (2) If the actor thinks the character's thoughts, he will respond in character and with truthful emotion. He should not say to himself, "I am pretending to be Hamlet," nor "I am Hamlet," nor even, "If I were Hamlet. . . ," but rather, "If that stupid idiot Polonius bothers me again I'll make him wish he hadn't."

   c. Spontaneity.
       Although the actor has rehearsed for weeks, he must respond as though each moment were occurring for the first time. He must avoid anticipating or premeditating reactions, attempting rather to create "the illusion of the first time."

4. The actor must play with a *sense of truth.*

He must make the audience believe in the truth of what he is saying and doing. Whether or not the actor's emotions are *actually* truthful, an audience of course has no way of knowing. It can evaluate only the impression of truth; but the spectator can be certain when the actor has evoked real emotional responses in him (the spectator) through empathy.

a. Acting can be said to have a sense of truth when it is convincing and believeable, when it rings true, when it corresponds with the audience's impression of how people would respond *if* the situation were actually taking place.

b. Although a master of acting technique might convince an audience of his sense of truth even though he were entirely devoid of feeling, the simplest and surest way for the young actor to seem convincing is for him really to respond truthfully. This is sometimes referred to as the Stanislavski or inner method of acting, because it is based upon what the actor discovers within himself rather than depending upon what previous actors have done to solve the same problems. The great advantage of the inner approach in the nonprofessional theatre, as many directors have observed, is that it works for the inexperienced actor; though he may lack technical skill, he can call upon his own freshness, vigor and emotions.

5. The actor must *motivate* whatever he does on stage.

   a. He should do nothing on stage without a purpose, or with what appears to be only a technical purpose.

   b. In life, human behavior is motivated by stimuli from within and from the outside. Although we do not always explain our motives and are sometimes not even conscious of our true motives, we seldom behave without some motivation.

   c. When no motive is supplied by the playwright or the director, the actor must find his own, consistent with his character.

   d. Actors who have difficulties in motivation are often so busy searching themselves introspectively that they fail to listen to what their co-actors are saying.

6. The actor must gain *access to his own emotions* and be able to reawaken them at will.

   An emotion aroused by accident is of little value compared with an emotion for which the actor finds some stimulation or preparation within himself, within the context of the scene, or within what his co-actors in the scene say or do. If he controls his concentration, he can then reawaken the same emotion at each performance. Exactly how the actor taps his own emotional resources is, in the final analysis, his own business— as long as it gets done. He may use one or more of the following approaches:

a. Emotion memory—the recollection of personal experiences which affected him in the past, and which can be reawakened by bringing to mind specific sensory images associated with the emotion.

b. Imagination—being able to visualize how the individual would feel if he were in the given circumstances.

c. Substitution of analogous emotions—never having committed a murder, for example, the actor may substitute a murderous impulse he once felt toward a buzzing mosquito.[1]

d. Autosuggestion or empathy for the character—having identified with the character, the actor lets the circumstances stimulate him as if he were the character. The actor's own identity is thus merged with that of the character. Stanislavski was aware that fine acting often draws from hidden resources and stands "on the threshold of the subconscious."

7. The actor must establish *relationships* to others.
The actor who focuses his attention exclusively within himself and his emotions has misinterpreted the Stanislavski system. His character does not exist in a vacuum, but has relationships to all of the other characters in the play.

a. The actor should know how his character feels about the others in the play—what they say and do at all times when he is on stage. He should know what he is doing on stage even when he has no lines. All too often a director might stop a scene, ask an actor what he is doing and be told (if the actor were candid), "Waiting for a cue." The actor who does this cuts himself off from the chance to be stimulated by what others are saying and doing so that when he gets his cue he will be emotionally ready.

b. The actor should let himself respond truthfully and in character to the moment-by-moment action and dialogue. He can do this only if he *listens* and *reacts*. The director may have to cut down responses that distract from the

1. This and many other valuable suggestions are contained in a slim book which actors and directors will find rewarding: Richard Boleslavsky, *Acting: The First Six Lessons* (New York: Theatre Arts, Inc., 1939), p. 44.

speaker, but it is easier to do this than to spark life in an unresponsive actor.

c. The actor who listens, responds and contributes to the interaction of the group not only builds rapport in the ensemble but also helps himself to prepare for his own emotional responses. Stanislavski called this "communion." An actor may even ask his co-actor for a reaction at a given moment so as to provide him with further motivation.

D. Understanding one's self as a director.

Directors, like actors, vary widely in background and training. There have been famous directors who were autocrats; others use passive, *laissez-faire* methods. Every director has yearned, as did Gordon Craig, for actors who would be "super-marionettes," responsive to every string pulled by the sole and supreme creative force, the director.

1. The director must assume that a communication failure between himself and his actors is a two-way street, and he may be as much at fault as his actors.
2. The director's goal should be the best possible production with the least amount of stress and strain at rehearsals.
3. He should not use his cast as outlets for his own frustrated impulses as an actor or need to be important. There is no place in the theatre for a director's temper tantrums. Moss Hart describes George S. Kaufman's modest method of directing professionals in *Act One*:

> . . . he seemed to allow the actors to use him as a sounding board. He watched and listened, and without seeming to impose his own preconceived ideas of how a scene should be played, he let each actor find a way of his own that was best for him; and slowly, with no more than a whispered word here and there, the scenes began to take on a directorial quality and flavor that was unmistakably his.[2]

4. The director in the nonprofessional theatre must be a teacher at the same time that he is a creative artist. This involves, as much as possible, telling the actors the reason for the instructions he gives them, so that they will learn and grow as actors as well as giving a particular performance.

2. Moss Hart, *Act One* (New York: Random House, 1959), p. 315.

3. James L. Mursell, *Educational Psychology* (New York: W. W. Norton and Company, 1939), p. 282.

5. The director should not betray to his cast his own anxieties, doubts, or fears for the success of the production.
6. A study in educational psychology[3] revealed that among the traits which pupils most objected to in their teachers were the following; the findings may have a valuable application for directors:

a. Failure to explain and make clear   e. Quick temper
b. Lack of discipline   f. Impatience
c. Favoritism   g. Sarcasm
d. Unfairness

7. The director's enthusiasm and confidence will be contagious. He can inspire the cast only to the extent that he himself feels enthusiasm for the play and confidence in his cast.
8. Professional modesty is an essental ingredient in the director. He will have done his work successfully if the reviews praise every actor in the cast, even though they scarcely take notice of the "direction."

E. Creating an environment in which the actor can do his best work. Rehearsals should be thought of as a very special time for actors and director to come together, not as inferior and superior, but as creative artists working together on a common task.
1. There should be freedom at rehearsals, an easy rapport and permissive environment which will encourage trial and error without fear of failure. Even a certain amount of "horsing around" may help the actors achieve spontaneity and release.
2. There must be sufficient discipline at rehearsals, however, so that time is not wasted by late arrivals, interruptions, or distractions by those offstage.
3. Directors and actors vary in their attitude toward visitors at rehearsals. A stranger in the auditorium can introduce tensions in the cast; but in rehearsing comedy the sound of a chuckle from out front may provide welcome encouragement.
4. The director himself must set an example of promptness and decorum at rehearsal. If the actors learn that the director is not ready to rehearse at the appointed time, they will soon grow careless themselves. Actors can hardly be expected to make progress if the director tells them to "run over their lines" in case he is late or fails to appear.
5. In the theatre actors should be encouraged to listen and watch when they are not onstage. Arthur Byron, a fine old actor who was president of Actors' Equity Association, once heard a grievance from a delegation of extras who had been kept

waiting to rehearse their scene. He replied to them, "But that is how I learned to act!"[4]

V. The periods of rehearsal.

Although different types of plays often require different approaches, generally rehearsing a play falls into fairly well-defined periods or phases, and the director needs to be aware of which period he is in—or should be in—so as not to move too soon to the next one or spend too much time on one particular phase to the neglect of the others.

A. Familiarization Period. (Reading the Play.)

    1. Creative aspects.

When the actors assemble for the first reading after casting is completed, there should be a considerable relaxation of tensions. The cast should know that it was chosen because it was the best possible one in the director's judgment. The task of digging into the content of the play begins.

    a. Round-table readings.

The director frequently will devote at least one and possibly as many as three days to reading and discussing the play. The director will discuss with the cast:

(1) His interpretation of the play, its theme, style, and impact.

(2) His concept of the characters and their interrelations.

(3) The spine, main actions in each act, and the changing beats.

    b. Seeing the whole before it is broken up into parts.

The director should help the cast to see the totality of the play, the relation of each character to the whole. Each actor should listen to the reading of scenes in which he himself may not appear; he may not hear these scenes again until dress rehearsal.

    c. Sharing with the cast the director's research into the period and background of the play.

    d. The actors should feel free to ask questions on the meaning of words, phrases, and speeches.

    2. Technical aspects.

    a. The director will show the cast the scene designs, ground

4. Edward Goodman, *Make Believe: The Art of Acting* (New York: Charles Scribner's Sons, 1956).

plans, and costume sketches, making sure that all are familiar with the ground plan of the set.

b. The director will check the rehearsal schedule with the cast, adjusting it for any conflicts, and distribute the schedule as finally agreed upon.

c. No technical comments on how to read lines should be given during this period.

d. The actors should underline the name of their character in their script each time they have a line, and note on the rehearsal schedule each scene in which they appear.

B. Exploration Period. (Blocking the Play.)

As the actors find out what the play is about and who their characters are, they begin to explore means of revealing these concepts to the audience. During this period the "blocking" or setting of physical positions on the stage is done, i.e., the director gives to the cast the picturization and movement which he has preplanned (as discussed in Chapters 4 and 5). This is a time of trial-and-error, and the actor should be encouraged to try and experiment without paying any penalties for error. Both actors and director must contribute to the establishment of a favorable environment for creative work, keeping an open-minded attitude and a willingness to explore.

1. General Principles:

a. During blocking rehearsals the actors should take time to write down all of their crosses, rises, sits, and positions opposite the lines on which they move.

b. One act is the most that usually should be blocked in one rehearsal, and sometimes even less. The act should be repeated several times so that the actors will remember whatever has been discovered in the rehearsal.

c. Time in communicating with the cast will be saved if the director works on the stage rather than from the auditorium.

d. The director should not expect results at this period. He is merely defining the problem and planting the seeds which will produce future solutions. Allow time for the incubation to take place.

e. The director should expect to deviate somewhat from his preplanned blocking because of (1) unforeseen problems, (2) his own spontaneous invention of better picturization or movement, and (3) the creative contribution of his actors. The director who comes to rehearsal without any preplanned blocking is asking for nothing but chaos and a waste of everyone's time.

f. As soon as the blocking of a scene is completed, the director should begin to urge actors to learn the lines of the scene. Complicated business with props, in fights and love scenes, should be postponed until books are out of the way.

2. Getting what the director wants from the actors.

This is actually the heart of play direction. Each director evolves his own method of working with actors, depending upon his background and training, the experience and training of the cast, the style and type of play, and the time remaining before opening night. A director may use different methods with different actors in the same scene, with different scenes and certainly with different plays. A continuum might be constructed to show directorial methods from complete permissiveness to complete authoritarianism:

Ideally the director should start near the left of the continuum, trying the most creative approach, allowing it sufficient time to work, before going on to the right. The last step at the right should be thought of as a last resort near opening night or with inexperienced actors. It should be kept in mind too that *when the director can't get what he wants from an actor, he may have to take what he gets and adapt it,* modifying his original interpretation and finding something within the actor's personality which can be substituted.

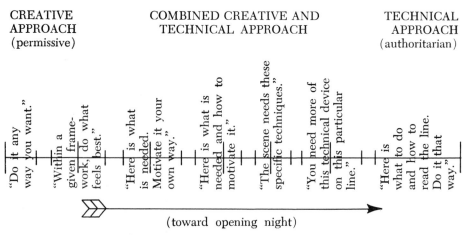

CONTINUUM

| CREATIVE APPROACH (permissive) | COMBINED CREATIVE AND TECHNICAL APPROACH | TECHNICAL APPROACH (authoritarian) |

"Do it any way you want." "Within a given frame-work, do what feels best." "Here is what is needed. Motivate it your own way." "Here is what is needed and how to motivate it." "The scene needs these specific techniques." "You need more of this technical device on this particular line." "Here is what to do and how to read the line. Do it that way."

(toward opening night)

a. Creative approach.

To rough in a framework or pattern for each scene and let the actors find the detailed moment-by-moment blocking. This method works best for serious and emotional drama, but requires experienced actors.

(1) Draw out through questions and discussion the actor's own interpretation of the scene. If it differs greatly from the director's, plant some questions in the actor's mind which may bring him to the desired interpretation. "How do you account for your behavior in the third act?" "What does your character want in life and in each act of the play?"

(2) Discuss the director's interpretation with the actor— the emotions and reactions of the character. Make sure the actor understands the inner aspects of the scene. Many faults of expression derive from a faulty understanding of what is to be expressed. Help the actor to live within the make-believe circumstances and to become aware of the full implications of the scene for his character. Sometimes outside readings can be suggested which will illuminate the play. The actor playing James Tyrone in O'Neill's *A Moon for the Misbegotten,* for example, must be thoroughly familiar with the same character in *Long Day's Journey Into Night.*

(3) Suggest avenues of observation for the actor—where he can go to find the character or emotion for which he is searching.

(4) Make sure the actor understands the breakdown of the scene into actions and beats—where each new beat begins and ends, and what his character is doing, both physically and psychologically, at each moment.

(5) Relate the emotions of the character to the actor's own experience. Find analogous situations which would be more familiar to the actor.

(6) Use improvisation, with the help of other actors, to recreate a prior situation in the life of the character which will help the actor understand the implications of the scene at hand. The scene itself may be improvised if the actors have not yet learned their lines. The scene should be structured just as in the author's script, listing the sequence of beats which answer the question, "What is . . . doing at this point?" The scene may be improvised several times, trying variations of the beats until the most effective ones are found. It should then be easier to stage the play formally with the author's words, retaining the spontaneity and "illusion of the first time."

(7) As an aid in identifying fully with his character, the actor might play his character in an improvised situation not written in the play: Hamlet as a carefree student at Wittenberg University, Blanche DuBois as the young wife before her husband's suicide, Anne Frank as a schoolgirl before she went into hiding.

(8) Visualize "offstage beats," the scenes described by the playwright but which take place offstage. Some scenes which might profitably be improvised as a means of helping the actors respond more fully to the succeeding scenes are:

(a) Amanda's shocking experience at the business college which she thought her daughter was attending (*The Glass Menagerie*).

(b) The day the cracked airplane cylinders are discovered at the factory (*All My Sons*).

(c) Romeo's unsuccessful efforts to woo Rosaline (*Romeo and Juliet*).

(d) Biff's interview with the man from whom he hopes to get a loan and from whom he steals a fountain pen (*Death of a Salesman*).

(9) By asking specific questions, draw out from the actor his moment-by-moment insight into the emotions of the character. "Are you glad about what you just said?" "Why did you do that?" "What are you thinking while he is speaking?" With actors trained in the Stanislavski system, whole scenes may be improvised in which the actors speak out loud their inner thoughts—the "sub-text."

(10) In classic or poetic plays where language may be a barrier to understanding, ask the actor temporarily to rephrase a speech in his own words.

(11) Make sure the actor knows the meaning of each line and word, to whom each line is addressed, and the motivation for the line.

(12) Indicate a general area of the stage for a scene and let the actor find his own movements within this framework. "This scene should play around the desk—see what feels comfortable to you."

b. Combined creative and technical approach.
To suggest to the actors specific positions and movements *along with their motivation*, helping the actors to justify and make their own the technical requirements of the scene.

(1) Suggest that somewhere in a particular speech the actor will want to rise or cross; let him find the exact spot for himself.

(2) Try a line or movement several ways and see which feels most comfortable to the actor or which looks better from out front.

(3) In big scenes of emotional climax, let the actor improvise his own movements as he feels them. Later they must be "set," repetitious movements eliminated and weak moments fixed.

(4) Tell the actor, "We need a movement here; what would your character do?"

(5) Tell the actor, "We need to have you cross DR to the fireplace. Can you find a motivation for yourself?"

(6) Give the actor both the specific movement and the motivation. "I think your character would turn away here because of his guilt feelings about what has just been said to him." "Try crossing to the mirror DR and adjusting your hair before saying the next line."

(7) Discuss with the actor what *effect* is desired. Use positive suggestion to help the actor visualize the technical result. An idea is more easily learned if it seems to come from the actor rather than the director. As F. Cowles Strickland expressed it, "Never tell an actor anything if you can make him think of it himself."[5] He cites as examples of this:

(a) Telling other actors to react to the humor of a particular line may make the speaker of the line aware for the first time that it is potentially funny.

(b) Telling an actor that his lines should come quickly because his partner is trying to build the scene to a climax may give the partner the first inkling that his scene is climactic.

(8) Use the physical to evoke the emotional. The so-called James-Lange effect is based on the power of the physical action to awaken emotion through autosuggestion. If the actor can't feel a particular emotion, give him physical business, movement, body positions or gestures which are characteristic, and the truthful *doing* may evoke the *feeling*.

(9) Show the actor the mood, feeling and intensity desired

5. F. Cowles Strickland, "Directing Amateurs," *Theatre Arts Monthly*, July, 1937, pp. 566-567.

without actually reading the lines for him. The director may improvise *around* the lines, paraphrasing the words or verbalizing the "sub-text" so that the actor will see the potentialities in the scene without being able to imitate directly what the director did.

c. Technical approach.

To give the actors the detailed blocking of positions, movement, crosses, turns, rises and seatings, letting the actors motivate or justify them for themselves as rehearsals progress. This method is the fastest, the best suited to comedy and stylized productions, and is necessarily used in summer stock companies.

(1) The technical approach to movement in relation to strong and weak lines is a great timesaver and frees the actor from having to solve problems that are best handled from out front by the director.

(2) Crosses, counter-crosses, turns, rises, and sits can be communicated to the cast verbally and generally do not need to be shown.

(3) With more than four actors on stage at once, picturization will present serious problems and the director dare not wait to face the actors in rehearsal without prior blocking of the scene in his director's book.

(4) Discuss with the actor in general what technical means he might use to achieve the effect he realizes is needed. Refer to possible:

   (a) Changes in tempo, volume, pitch, and quality to achieve variety.
   (b) Key words that need more emphasis.
   (c) Pointing of lines by movement, gesture, and pauses.
   (d) Transitions and where they should occur.
   (e) Topping and climax, and where they should occur.

(5) Tell the actor specifically where to use a technical device such as emphasis, inflection, pause, or variety in tempo, volume, pitch, and quality. Wherever possible give him the *motivation along with the mechanics*.

   (a) It is better to tell an actor, "Take a moment to think of an answer," rather than "Pause here," and more helpful to say, "You're ashamed to look him in the eye and so you turn away," rather than simply, "Turn away."

(b) The *question method* is a very useful one for correcting misplaced emphasis. If the actor says, "I *went* to the door," instead of "I went to the *door*," the director can ask him, "Where did you go?" His answer, "to the *door*" will have the correct emphasis, and this can be pointed out to the actor.

(c) Use positive rather than negative comments. "It needs more variety in pitch," is preferable to "It's monotonous," and "It needs more warmth," preferable to "It leaves me cold."

(d) It sometimes helps an actor enlarge his performance if the director stands at the back of the auditorium and calls his cues to him so that he will feel motivated to project his replies.

(6) If the director has a keen ear or sense of mimicry, he may try showing the actor two possible ways of playing a certain line—the way the actor has been doing it and the way the director thinks it should be done. He may then ask, "Which way was more effective?"

(7) When the director gives an actor a mechanical direction or piece of blocking the actor should try to find his own inner justification or motivation for the action, rather than to question the direction. The actor should thus be a flexible tool for the director, knowing that he is an element in the director's composition of stage pictures and vocal climaxes which he cannot see or hear from out front. He should be willing to accept a movement, position, or line reading for purely technical reasons, and only after he has made every effort to justify it should he ask the director for help if it still doesn't feel right.

(8) As a last resort when other techniques have failed or time has grown short, the director may legitimately try reading the line or doing the business for the actor. This technique presupposes (a) that the director is himself a competent actor and (b) that the actor will watch with an open mind and have enough technical awareness to recognize what the director is doing.

(a) Demonstration is an accepted method of teaching physical skills, and is perhaps the quickest way to convey a desired effect to the actor. Physical actions, movement, and the integration of lines with business lend themselves best to demonstration, but even line readings sometimes have to be given to the actor. Properly done this technique needs no apologies. Students of "the method" will be surprised to discover that Stanislavski himself used demonstration.[6]

(b) If the director is not sure of his acting technique, however, he is better off not trying to demonstrate than doing it and lamely apologizing afterwards, "That wasn't exactly right, but you get the idea."

C. Discovery Period. (Books out of hand.)

As soon as the blocking is set, the director should begin working with the actors for characterization, following the suggestions given in Chapter 8. The actor should be encouraged to try various psychological and physical elements to help him get into character.

1. Creative aspects.

 a. After the motivations and characterizations are grasped intellectually, the blocking set, and the lines learned, there will, ideally, be a rehearsal when the actor gets fully into character, is able to release the appropriate emotion, and the scene "plays."

 (1) The moment of discovery for a particular scene is sometimes sudden—a kind of "Eureka!" growing out of a flash of insight.

 (2) A high degree of concentration is necessary for the "Eureka" to take place. Creativity often happens at white heat. The actor must stay in character at these rehearsals and try to avoid breaking his or another actor's concentration.

 b. When the moment of creative discovery comes, make sure that the actor is praised after the scene is over and made aware of the fact that he has found something right for the performance.

 c. As the actor begins to find what he wants to do with several scenes as indicated in the foregoing, the director should clarify for himself and the actor which scenes yet remain to be worked on, narrowing down the number as rehearsals progress.

 d. As actors respond to each other in this period, new moti-

6. Nikolai M. Gorchakov, *Stanislavski Directs* (New York: Funk and Wagnalls Company, 1954), p. 259 and pp. 300-306.

vations will occur to them and to the director. Little moment-by-moment motivations and responses should be
added to fill up empty or dead spots, mechanical or inadequate reactions.

    e. An informal talk with an actor during a break or after re-
hearsal often may be a better way of suggesting what is
needed than to stop the rehearsal. The director should begin to make written or mental notes for this purpose. With
experience he learns when it is better not to stop the actors
and when to stop them.

2. Technical aspects.

    a. Add business and pantomime that enrich the scene and
and strengthen characterization.

    b. When the actor still has not found what the director wants,
technical suggestions must necessarily be given—relating to
key words, points to be "hit," variety in voice, topping and
undercutting, transitions.

    c. When books are out of hand for a particular scene, actors
may begin to work with rehearsal props (easy-to-find substitutes which may be in the prop room). These props often
assist in the discovery of the inner emotion. Character props
(canes, caps, etc.,) will help the actor get in character.

    d. The first few times the actor tries a scene without book,
the stage manager should be instructed to make detailed
corrections. Otherwise actors often will let lines become
fixed in their memory incorrectly. Later on the director may
choose to permit minor modifications except where the
rhythm, meaning or comic effect is weakened. In Shakespeare and other poetic drama, lines must be letter perfect.

D. Formalizing Period. (Polishing Rehearsals.)
This is the phase in which the director gives the production its
final shape in terms of tempo, climax, and the strength of the
individual actors' performances. At this point the director often
finds himself pushing the actors, demanding of them emotional
intensity which they do not know they have and sustained levels
for which they may lack the physical stamina and discipline.
Though he may feel himself a taskmaster, a slave driver at this
phase, the director's profession requires that he not settle for
anything less than the absolute best which he can get out of his
cast. If there are moments of resentment at the director's needling,
exhorting, demanding, they will all be forgotten in the aura of
opening-night success. This idea is aptly expressed by Anouilh in

his delightful play, *The Rehearsal,* when an actress complains to her director:

Hortensia: You're manipulating us like puppets! I warn you, we won't stand for it much longer!

Count: Count yourselves lucky that I don't bawl your heads off. There's no inspired production without tears. A play produced by a polite man rarely smacks of genius. . . .[7]

1. Creative aspects.

   a. At this stage, actors will benefit from going through a scene without interruption, letting the cumulative effect stimulate them to further growth. However many details can be fixed more efficiently as they happen rather than later from notes. Faced with the dilemma of "to stop or not to stop" a scene, the director can:

      (1) Alternate between detail rehearsals to stop and polish and continuity rehearsals in which the scene is repeated without stops so it can build to climax.

      (2) Use "sideline coaching," as Kenneth Graham has termed it: (i.e., without stopping the scene the director makes adjustments in composition, especially of large groups, and comments to the actors in a way that does not break them out of character).

   b. Now that the actors know their own lines and business, they should be encouraged to *listen* to their partner, react in character, and maintain eye-contact and rapport with the ensemble. Scenes come to life when they have group interplay rather than star acting—what Stanislavski called "stage interfluence." The actor must also be sure to give other actors adequate resistance in scenes of conflict.

   c. The actors must find a common style for the production. Each should watch the rest of the cast and attempt to find a style that is consistent. At this stage it is most helpful to rehearse with substitute costumes or makeshifts, to approximate the effect that will later be created by trains, capes, long skirts; rehearsing with the right kind of shoes is particularly helpful.

   d. The actor must heighten his emotions in proportion to the theatre in which they are to be projected, not by forcing artificially, but by making the emotion itself stronger, by wanting something more intensely, by drawing upon extra resources of vitality.

7. Jean Anouilh, *The Rehearsal,* in *Five Plays,* Vol. I (New York: Hill and Wang, 1958), p. 216.

e. Although many teachers of the Stanislavski method tell actors not to work for "results," the director must constantly keep results in mind. (*An Actor Prepares* is, after all, not *An Actor Rehearses*.) The rehearsal process means working for results, setting them when they are right, and anticipating the effect these results will have on the audience. Stanislavski's noted pupil, Vakhtangov, once said to Michael Chekhov when asked the secret of his success as a director, "I never rehearse without imagining that the theatre is already full. The imaginary audience is always there, from the very first rehearsal to the last."[8]

4. Technical aspects.

a. As the director nears dress rehearsal, his emphasis must grow increasingly technical. His concern should be with getting scenes up to tempo and with heightening climaxes. His approach now is apt to be:

"Keep what you've got—it's good—but make it even stronger."
"Take out the pauses."
"Pick up cues faster."
"Wait! Now! Hit it!"
"It's dragging. Faster."
"I lost that word."
"Top him!"

b. As the cast achieves what he has been seeking, the director should "set" or "fix" the scenes (in the sense of applying a fixative so that the scenes will keep their form intact) by letting the actors know immediately after a scene when it is just right, and perhaps repeating it immediately to solidify it in the actors' memories.

c. The actors must learn to play with control and consistency, so that emotions are the servant rather than the master, and so that the scene can be played the same at each run-through. When an actor says, "Don't worry, I'll get it right at the performance," the director has cause to worry aplenty. Too much emotion is as much a cause for worry as too little; even through real tears the actor must get his words out clearly and on cue.

d. The director should check the vocal projection of the actors from the back of the auditorium to make sure they can be heard and understood. The actors should use full voice to

8. Michael Chekhov, *To the Director and Playwright* (New York: Harper, 1963), p. 54.

see if they can sustain the role vocally without hoarseness or strain. (If hoarseness or sore throat develops, the actor should "save his voice" and the director may have to help him breathe correctly and relax his throat.)

e. Scenes and acts will be at varying degrees of completion. Act I will be ready to formalize and set while Act II is still in the Discovery Period and Act III in the Exploration Period. In the final week before dress rehearsal, the director should concentrate on Act III while at the same time keeping the other acts alive by run-throughs.

f. As the play takes shape, the director will see which scenes or which actors need more intensive work. This period is the director's last chance to work with his cast and to correct whatever is necessary.

g. The director should polish, revise, and perfect each detail, anticipating as much as possible the problems which the introduction of scenery, props and costumes will add.

h. As a practical necessity, the director may have to settle for less than he had conceived, abandon some ideas that did not shape up, relax the pressure on some actors who may be doing their best yet are falling short, and make a choice as to which elements are most amenable to improvement so as to make the best investment of the time remaining before opening night.

E. Integration Period. (Dress rehearsals.)

1. Creative aspects.

a. The director should not expect the best performance from the actors at the first dress rehearsal when they are getting accustomed to lights, scenery, props, and costumes. It sometimes happens that the technical elements, particularly costume, stimulate an actor to a new inner quality of performance. Often, however, the actors are so busy adjusting to new elements that both inner emotion and external tempo suffer temporarily.

b. There should be at least one dress rehearsal, however, when all the technical elements are integrated so that the actors can restore their inner concentration and bring the play up to performance level.

c. During the dress rehearsal period the actors might profitably restudy their scripts; they may discover new shades of meaning or lines that they have been misreading.

d. The old adage that "a bad dress rehearsal means a good opening night" is far from reliable; it all depends on whether the things that went wrong at the dress rehearsal are fixed before the opening. Nothing should be left to chance on opening night nor any new technical elements introduced that the actors have not rehearsed with; wishful thinking is no substitute for painstaking rehearsal.

e. At the end of the last dress rehearsal, the director should leave the cast with a feeling of confidence.

2. Technical aspects.

a. The director should work with the technical crews as much as possible without the cast in order to save the actors' energies and have all technical elements "set" and perfected before the actors work with them.

b. Technical elements should be added in the following order:
   (1) A rehearsal for the actors with all hand props.
   (2) A rehearsal for the actors with the scenery, lights and furniture (sometimes where necessary without using costumes).
   (3) A "costume parade" (if a costume play) in order to view and check each actor's costumes before dress rehearsal and get him used to wearing and moving in them.
   (4) A "dress rehearsal" using scenery, costumes, props, lights, music, and sound.
   (5) At least two final dress rehearsals using all elements plus make-up.

c. During dress rehearsals the director should interrupt as little as possible—where necessary to fix light or sound cues that are wrong, but rarely, if ever, for purely acting problems. The director instead should make copious notes to be given to the cast afterwards. A telephone from auditorium to stage manager is invaluable.

d. Integrating the technical elements and the actors into a unified production requires that the director remain calm during dress rehearsals and in control of a group of tense and perhaps overtired actors and crews.

   (1) When a cue goes wrong, the director should be able to note specifically what was wrong about it and how it can be fixed. Temperamental directors often communicate the fact that they are displeased but not how to remedy the error.
   (2) Although there is a constant temptation to break this rule, it is a wise practice to go through channels during dress rehearsal—communicating with the electrical

and stage crews through the technical director, through the costumer on costume matters, and with the cast and prop crew through the stage manager. Conversely, technical director and costumer should not instruct cast except via director.

(3) When the hour grows late and people are overwrought, making notes to discuss the next day is the best way to deal with apparently insoluble problems.

e. At one of the last dress rehearsals, the curtain call should be planned and rehearsed. The mood of the play will determine the kind of curtain call, from "gag" calls in a farce to a dignified "tableau" call in a tragedy. It is traditional to allow the audience to show its appreciation to the live actor.

f. If the play is a comedy, the cast should be reminded to *hold for laughs,* and how to do this correctly. Where feasible, a preview audience invited to the last dress rehearsal will give a sample of laugh reactions and help the cast set their timing.

g. In going over final notes with the cast before the last dress rehearsal, it is often a good idea to remind them of the *traditions of the theatre.* In addition to the specific rules pertaining to smoking backstage, etc., there are theatre traditions which give a cast a sense of pride to know they will be expected to honor:

h. Traditions of the performance.

(1) Every audience—large or small—is entitled to the best performance you are capable of giving.

(2) "The show must go on." Neither fog, snow, rain nor flood, sick babies nor flat tires are valid excuses for failing to be on stage on time. A trouper never lets his fellows or his audience down.

(3) Be in your dressing room at least one hour before curtain.

(4) Never peek out front nor appear in the lobby areas in costume or make-up.

(5) The stage manager is in absolute authority backstage, but it is each actor's personal responsibility to make his entrance on time. Never leave the area where you can hear the play without the permission of the stage manager. When the stage manager calls "Places," respond immediately.

(6) Actors—respect the backstage crews; your performance depends on them. Although there are costume

and prop crews assigned, this does not relieve the actor of personal responsibility to take pride in his costume, to keep it clean, to obtain his hand props and return them to the designated place.

(7) Crew members—respect the actors; the performance depends on their emotional control, concentration and confidence. Do nothing that will interfere with these factors.

(8) Absolute quiet backstage is a necessity for the audience's enjoyment and the participant's work; never do anything that might distract a performer.

(9) Never break out of character when in view of the audience; keep the show going somehow—in an emergency *ad lib* a line or help a co-actor who forgets a line.

(10) There is no place in the theatre for alcoholic beverage in any form.

(11) Leave personal problems at the stage door. Stanislavski best expressed this when he wrote in "Toward an Ethics for the Theatre":

> Never come into the theatre with mud on your feet. Leave your dust and dirt outside. Check your little worries, squabbles, petty difficulties with your outside clothing—all the things that ruin your life and draw your attention away from your art.[9]

F. Performance Period.

1. Creative aspects.

    a. On opening night, the director must avoid the appearance of nervousness at all costs. He should give the cast quiet reassurance that he has confidence in them.

    b. The second performance is the time when there is often a let-down, and the director might well have a pep talk to fix loose ends, remind actors to pick up cues and polish things that weren't right on opening night.

    c. On every succeeding performance, the actors should be kept alert and disciplined by the director's watching the performance and bringing back notes, comments, and praise for a scene that went particularly well. He should continue polishing the reading of lines, the pointing for laughs, and the adjustment of tempo to the audience response. The director's presence in the auditorium has a desirable effect

9. Constantin Stanislavski, *Building a Character* (New York: Theatre Arts Books: MacGregor, Robert M., 1949), p. 244.

upon the morale of cast and crew, discouraging "fooling around," carelessness, *ad libbing*, or a let-down after opening night. Even with the best of intentions, actors tend to lengthen their pauses in dramatic scenes or add comic business which they find audiences enjoy though it may distract from the dialogue. The director will want to keep his production in its original shape by discouraging these tendencies—or an even worse one, the addition of "gags." For the director to condone this or fail to deal firmly with it would be to open a Pandora's box which might undo all the painstaking work of rehearsal.

2. Technical aspects.

The director by now should have every performance responsibility covered by crew heads. Nothing makes a production staff more nervous than a director's last-minute fiddling with lights or scenery. The director should ascertain that his cast and crew heads are in the building on time, and leave them free to do their rehearsed tasks.

G. Post-performance period.

Responsibilities of the director after the production closes include:

1. To give the cast and particularly the crews his expression of appreciation and praise for a job well done.
2. To evaluate objectively the success of the production, taking into account all available evidence from audience reaction (of primary value) and such evidence as ticket sales and critics' reviews, which while less reliable cannot be discounted.

VI. Suggested standards for play production evaluation.

Although evaluating a production becomes highly complex with many subjective factors interwoven, a set of criteria for evaluation such as the following may be helpful to the director in his own personal growth and in attempting to appraise the theatrical value of the production for all concerned:

A. Audience response.

1. Did the audience indicate by its laughter, absorbed silence, or rustling and coughing, that it was entertained, moved, held in suspense, or bored? If the director is alert to these subtle but unmistakable clues, he will learn far more about the success of the production than he will from flattering intermission well-wishers. What actually happened in the auditorium—did the production communicate to the audience and did the au-

dience respond to it as intended? Many critics fail to report this paramount fact, and give only personal impressions, oblivious to the audience around them.

    2. Did the ticket sales and box office revenue indicate that the public wanted to see the play and gave it favorable word-of-mouth publicity?

B. Choice of play.
Did the play prove to be a wise choice in terms of audience interest, values, abilities of the cast and staff to do it justice?

C. Standards of acting.
    1. Did the actors realize the playwright's intent and bring the material to life?
    2. Did the actors play with a sense of truth, motivating their actions and gaining access to their own emotions?
    3. Did the actors create convincing, believable and consistent characters?
    4. Did the actors play and respond together as an ensemble and with a unity of style?
    5. Could the actors be seen, heard, and understood?
    6. Did the actors supply vocal and visual variety, tempo, and climax?
    7. If a comedy, did the actors point their laughs effectively?
    8. Was there a freshness and imagination in the conception and execution of the performance?
    9. Was there growth and heightened accomplishment by the individual performers?

D. Standards of the technical elements.
    1. Did the scenery appropriately reflect the playwright's intent and contribute to the total aesthetic impression? Were the shifts of scenery handled quickly and quietly?
    2. Did the costumes seem appropriate for the characters, the playwright's intent and the requirements of the actors for movement? Did they make a positive contribution to the total aesthetic impresson?
    3. Did the lighting contribute unobtrusively to the total aesthetic impression and give adequate visibility to the actors?
    4. Did the make-up express the characters and appear convincing?
    5. Were the other elements—properties, sound effects, and music—appropriate and did they make a positive, unobtrusive contribution?

E. Standards of direction.
    1. If the answers to most of the foregoing questions are affirma-

tive, the director has done his work well. Many laymen are not aware of "direction" and it is just as well that they should not be. Even to the trained eye, it is often impossible to distinguish between the contributions of director, actors, and designer. If the director has coordinated all the elements of the production effectively, there will be a unity of impression that permits the audience to become absorbed in the play.

2. Did the director, in addition, supply an imaginative, perceptive appreciation of the playwright's intent, and reflect this inventively and effectively in the production, with good taste and sensitivity?
3. Were the ensemble elements of tempo, crowd scenes, fights effectively handled?
4. Was the director efficient in his handling of rehearsals and economical in his requirements for budget and man-hours? (The audience will not be able to assess this aspect, but the participants will be well aware of it.)
5. Finally, the best test of direction is the absence of negative factors—if no glaring moments were noticeable to the audience in which actors stumbled over lines, a performer was conspicuously unable to meet the demands of the role, cues were missed, laughter came in the wrong places, or an element of scenery, props, costumes, lighting or make-up attracted attention to itself or was allowed to distract from the performance.

VII. Summary.

The success of the play will depend to a great extent upon the director's ability to conduct systematic rehearsals and to discover ways of drawing out the creative abilities of his cast while at the same time giving the play a technical form and shape which will make it most effective to the audience.

A. Casting the play.
   1. Preparation for casting.
   2. Methods of casting.
   3. The double cast.
   4. Understudies.
   5. Precasting.
B. The rehearsal schedule.
   1. Factors that affect the making of a rehearsal schedule.
   2. A suggested rehearsal schedule.
C. General principles of rehearsal.
   1. Traditions of the rehearsal.
   2. Learning lines.

3. Understanding the actor.
4. Understanding one's self as a director.
5. Creating an environment in which the actor can do his best work.

D. The periods of rehearsal.
1. Familiarization Period. (Reading the play.)
2. Exploration Period. (Blocking the play.)
3. Discovery Period. (Books out of hand.)
4. Formalizing Period. (Polishing rehearsals.)
5. Integration Period. (Dress rehearsals.)
6. Performance Period.
7. Post-performance Period.

E. Suggested standards for play production evaluation.
1. Audience response.
2. Choice of play.
3. Standards of acting.
4. Standards of technical elements.
5. Standards of direction.

Selective Bibliography

Working with Actors

Cole, Toby and Chinoy, Helen K., eds. *Directing the Play: A Source Book of Stagecraft.* Indianapolis: Bobbs-Merrill, 1953.

Dean, Alexander and Carra, Lawrence. *Fundamentals of Play Directing.* rev. ed. New York: Holt, Rinehart & Winston, Inc., 1965.

"Directing Amateurs," series of articles by Valentine Windt, F. Cowles Strickland, Alexander Dean, Bernard Szold, Frederick Burleigh and Edwin Duerr, *Theatre Arts Monthly,* July, October, November, 1937.

Eustis, Morton. "The Director Takes Command," *Theatre Arts Monthly.*
    I. "Guthrie McClintic," February, 1936.
    II. "Max Reinhardt, Robert Sinclair," March, 1936.
    III. "John Murray Anderson, Harold Clurman," April, 1936.

———. *"The Man Who Came to Dinner* with George Kaufman Directing," *Theatre Arts Monthly,* vol. 23, no. 11, November, 1939.

Gorchakov, Nikolai. *Stanislavski Directs.* New York: Funk and Wagnalls, 1954.

Hart, Moss. *Act One.* New York: Random House, 1959.

Hopkins, Arthur. *How's Your Second Act?* New York: Samuel French, 1948.

Isaacs, Hermine Rich. "First Rehearsals: Elia Kazan Directs a Modern Legend," *Theatre Arts Monthly,* vol. 28, no. 3, March, 1944. Reprinted in *Theatre Arts Anthology.* New York: Theatre Arts Books: Robert M. MacGregor, 1950.

McGaw, Charles. *Acting Is Believing.* New York: Rinehart and Co., 1955.

Moore, Sonia. *The Stanislavski Method.* New York: The Viking Press, 1960.

Spolin, Viola. *Improvisation for the Theatre.* Evanston: Northwestern University Press, 1963.

Stanislavski, Constantin. *An Actor Prepares.* New York: Theatre Arts, Inc., 1936.

———. *Creating a Role.* New York: Theatre Arts Books, 1961.

External Techniques

Franklin, Miriam. *Rehearsal: The Principles and Practice of Acting for the Stage*. Englewood Cliffs, N. J.: Prentice Hall, Inc., 1963.

Funke, Lewis, and John E. Booth. *Actors Talk About Acting*. New York: Random House, 1961. (Abridged) Avon Paperback, 1963.

Kahan, Stanley. *Introduction to Acting*. New York: Harcourt, Brace and Co., 1962.

Olivier, Sir Laurence. Interview on his approach to *Othello, Life,* vol. 56, no. 18, May 1, 1964.

Seyler, Athene, and Stephen, Haggard. *The Craft of Comedy*. New York: Theatre Arts, Inc., 1946.

Stanislavski, Constantin. *Building a Character*. New York: Theatre Arts Books: Robert M. MacGregor, 1949.

Strickland, F. Cowles. *The Technique of Acting*. New York: McGraw-Hill Book Co., 1956.

White, Edwin C., and Battye, Margueriet. *Acting and Stage Movement*. New York: Arc Books, 1963.

Lane, Yoti. *The Psychology of the Actor*. London: Secker and Warburg, 1959.

Rehearsal Techniques, Cincinnati: The National Thespian Society, 1948.

Shaw, George Bernard. *The Art of Rehearsal*. New York: Samuel French, 1928.

Webster, Margaret. "Credo of a Director," *Theatre Arts Monthly,* May, 1938, vol. 22, no. 5.

Inner Techniques

Carnovsky, Morris. "Design for Acting: The Quest of Technique," in *The Context and Craft of Drama,* by Robert W. Corrigan and James H. Rosenberg. San Francisco: Chandler Publishing Co., 1964.

Chekhov, Michael. *To the Actor: On the Technique of Acting*. New York: Harper and Brothers, 1953.

Cole, Toby, ed. *Acting: A Handbook of the Stanislavski Method*. New York: Lear Publishers, 1947.

Funke, Lewis and John E. Booth. *Actors Talk About Acting*. New York: Random House, 1961. (Abridged) Avon Paperback, 1963.

Gourfinkel, Nina. "The Actor Sets to Work on His Part," *World Theatre,* VIII 1, Spring, 1959.

Lewis, Robert. *Method or Madness?* New York: Samuel French, Inc., 1958.

Magarshack, David. *Stanislavski on the Art of the Stage*. New York: Hill and Wang, 1961.

Appendix A

A List of 500 Recommended Plays

for the Theatre

Following is a list of approximately 500 plays which represent a wide diversity of tastes and styles. The plays chosen are either modern plays or noteworthy modern adaptations or translations of classics such as Molière, Chekhov, etc. The plays of the Greeks, Shakespeare and the Elizabethans, and other established classics *readily available* in anthologies, are excluded.

The following information is included for your use in choosing plays and determining the basic scope of the works listed:

1. Play title
2. Author
3. Type of play—i.e., comedy, drama, etc.
4. Number of characters identified by sex
5. Number of interior and exterior Settings
6. Play-leasing company holding rights
7. Fee for performance (First figure indicates fee for first performance, second figure for each subsequent performance.)

You may keep the list current by getting on the mailing list of the play-leasing companies which publish catalogues. The principal ones are as follows:

General

Samuel French, Inc. (French)
7623 Sunset Blvd.

Hollywood, California 90046
or
25 West 45th Street
New York, New York 10036

Walter H. Baker Company
100 Summer Street
Boston, Massachusetts 02110

Dramatists Play Service, Inc. (DPS)
440 Park Avenue South
New York, New York 10016

The Dramatic Publishing Company
86 East Randolph Street
Chicago, Illinois 60601

Plays for Children

The Children's Theatre Press
Cloverlot
Anchorage, Kentucky

The Coach House Press
53 West Jackson Blvd.
Chicago, Illinois

Six or Fewer Characters

Play	Author	Type	Number of Characters	Sets	Leasing Co.	Royalty
Krapp's Last Tape	Samuel Beckett	Drama	1 man,	Interior	French	$20-15
Dear Liar	Jerome Kilty (Shaw)	Comedy	1 man, 1 woman	Interior	French	$35-25
Hello and Goodbye	Athol Fugard	Drama	1 m, 1 w	Interior	French	$50-25
The Owl and the Pussycat	Bill Manhoff	Comedy	1 m, 1 w	Interior	French	$50-25
Two for the Seesaw	William Gibson	Comedy	1 m, 1 w	Interior	French	$50-25
The Fourposter	Jan de Hartog	Comedy	1 m, 1 w	Interior 1890-1925	French	on app.
Happy Days	Samuel Beckett	Drama	1 m, 1 w	Exterior	French	$35-25
The Only Game in Town	Frank D. Gilroy	Drama	2 m, 1 w	Interior	French	$50-25
The Slave (1 hour)	Le Roi Jones	Drama	2 m, 1 w	Interior	French	$35-30
Dutchman (1 hour)	Le Roi Jones	Drama	2 m, 1 w	Interior (Subway)	French	$35-30
The Private Ear and the Public Eye	Peter Shaffer	Comedy	2 m, 1 w	2 plays	French	$25-15 ea. or $50-25 together
Butterflies Are Free	Leonard Gershe	Comedy	2 m, 2 w	Interior	French	on app.
The Knack	Ann Jellicoe	Comedy	3 m, 1 w	Interior	French	$50-25

Six or Fewer Characters (Continued)

Play	Author	Type	Number of Characters	Sets	Leasing Co.	Royalty
The Hollow Crown	John Barton	Comedy-Drama	3 m, 1 w	Concert Stage	French	$35-25
The Second Man	S. N. Behrman	Comedy	2 m, 2 w	Interior	French	$50-25
No Exit	Jean-Paul Satre	Drama	2 m, 2 w	Interior	French	$25-20
The Marriage-Go-Round	Leslie Stevens	Comedy	2 m, 2 w	Interior	French	$50-25
Springtime for Henry	Benn W. Levy	Comedy	2 m, 2 w	Interior	French	$50-25
A Moon for the Misbegotten	Eugene O'Neill	Drama	3 m, 1 w	Exterior	French	$50-25
Endgame	Samuel Beckett	Drama	3 m, 1 w	Interior	French	$35-25
There's Always Juliet	John van Druten	Comedy	2 m, 2 w	Interior	French	$35-25
Private Lives	Noel Coward	Comedy	2 m, 3 w	1 Interior, 1 Exterior	French	$50-25
Hail, Srawdyke	David Halliwell	Comedy-Drama (Mature)	4 m, 1 w	Interior	French	$50-25
Five Finger Exercise	Peter Shaffer	Tragedy	3 m, 2 w	Interior	French	$50-25
Tchin-Tchin	Sidney Michaels	Comedy	3 m, 2 w	Multiple Sets	French	$50-25
Janus	Carolyn Green	Farce	3 m, 2 w	Interior	French	$50-25

Six or Fewer Characters (Continued)

Play	Author	Type	Number of Characters	Sets	Leasing Co.	Royalty
Red Magic	Michel de Ghelderode	Melodrama	5 m, 1 w (extras)	Interior	French	$35-25
Spoon River Anthology	Charles Aidman (Masters)	Staged Reading	3 m, 2 w	Concert Stage	French	$50-25
Angel Street	Patrick Hamilton	Melodrama	2 m, 3 w	Interior	French	$50-25
Duet for Two Hands	Mary Hayley Bell	Melodrama	2 m, 3 w	Interior	French	$35-25
Fortune and Men's Eyes	John Herbert	Drama	5 men	Interior	French	$50-25
The Days Between	Robert Anderson	Drama	4 m, 2 w	Combined Set	French	$50-25
The Birthday Party	Harold Pinter	Melodrama	4 m, 2 w	Interior	French	$50-25
A Delicate Balance	Edward Albee	Drama	2 m, 4 w	Interior	French	$50-25
Exit the King	Eugene Ionesco	Drama	3 m, 3 w	Interior	French	$50-25
Joe Egg	Peter Nichols	Comedy-Drama	2 m, 3 w	Interior	French	$50-25
The Homecoming	Harold Pinter	Drama	5 m, 1 w	Interior	French	$50-25
In White America	Martin B. Duberman	History	3 black: 2 m, 1 w 3 white: 2 m, 1 w	Concert Stage	French	$35-25
A Thousand Clowns	Herb Gardner	Comedy	4 m, 1 w boy, 12 yrs.	Interior	French	$50-25

Six or Fewer Characters (Continued)

Play	Author	Type	Number of Characters	Sets	Leasing Co.	Royalty
Barefoot in the Park	Neil Simon	Comedy	4 m, 2 w	Interior	French	$50-25
Oh Dad, Poor Dad, Mamma's Hung You in the Closest and I'm Feeling So Sad	Arthur Kopit	Farce	4 m, 2 w	2 Interiors	French	$50-25
The Innocents	William Archibald (H. James)	Melodrama	1 m, 3 w 1 boy, 1 girl	Interior	French	$50-25
Affairs of State	Louis Verneuil	Comedy	4 m, 2 w	Interior	French	$50-25
Papa Is All	Patterson Greene	Comedy	3 m, 3 w	Interior	French	$35-25
Silent Night, Lonely Night	Robert Anderson	Serious	2 m, 3 w, 1 child	Interior	French	$50-25
The Silver Cord	Sidney Howard	Drama	2 m, 4 w	Interior	French	$25-20
I Have Been Here Before	J. B. Priestly	Drama	4 m, 2 w	Interior	French	$25-20
The Square Root of Wonderful	Carson McCullers	Drama	2 m, 3 w, 1 boy	Interior	French	$50-25
The Effect of Gamma Rays on Man-in-the-Moon Marigolds	Paul Zindel	Drama	5 women	Interior	DPS	$50-25
The Price	Arthur Miller	Drama	3 m, 1 w	Interior	DPS	$50

Six or Fewer Characters (Continued)

Play	Author	Type	Number of Characters	Sets	Leasing Co.	Royalty
Summertree	Ron Cowen	Drama	3 m, 2 w, 1 child	Area Staging	DPS	$35-25
The Star Spangled Girl	Neil Simon	Comedy	2 m, 1 w	Interior	DPS	$50-25
And Things That Go Bump in the Night	Terrence McNally	Drama	4 m, 2 w	Interior	DPS	$35-25
Tiny Alice	Edward Albee	Drama	4 m, 1 w	2 Interiors	DPS	$50-25
Luv	Murray Schisgal	Comedy	2 m, 1 w	Exterior	DPS	$50-25
Hughie	Eugene O'Neill	Drama	2 men	Interior	DPS	$25
Slow Dance on the Killing Ground	William Hanley	Drama	2 m, 1 w	Interior	DPS	$50-25
Mary, Mary	Jean Kerr	Comedy	3 m, 2 w	Interior	DPS	$50-25
Who's Afraid of Virginia Woolf?	Edward Albee	Drama	2 m, 2 w	Interior	DPS	$50
The Caretaker	Harold Pinter	Comedy-Drama	3 men	Interior	DPS	$50-25
Long Day's Journey into Night	Eugene O'Neill	Drama	3 m, 2 w	Interior	DPS	$50
Everybody Loves Opal	John Patrick	Comedy	4 m, 2 w	Interior	DPS	$50-25
Gallows Humor	Jack Richardson	Comedy-Drama	2 m, 1 w	2 Interiors	DPS	$50-25

295

Six or Fewer Characters (Continued)

Play	Author	Type	Number of Characters	Sets	Leasing Co.	Royalty
Under the Yum Yum Tree	Laurence Roman	Comedy	3 m, 2 w	Interior	DPS	$50-25
The Rivalry	Norman Corwin	Drama	2 m, 1 w, 3 bit parts	Platforms	DPS	$50-25
Waiting for Godot	Samuel Beckett	Comedy-Tragedy	4 men, 1 boy	Exterior	DPS	$50-25
The Little Hut	Andre Roussin	Comedy	4 m, 1 w	Exterior	DPS	$50-25
Dial "M" for Murder	Frederick Knott	Melodrama	5 m, 1 w	Interior	DPS	$50-25
Kind Sir	Norman Krasna	Comedy	3 m, 3 w	Interior	DPS	$50-25
The Moon is Blue	F. Hugh Herbert	Comedy	3 m, 1 w	1 Interior 1 Exterior	DPS	$50-25
Bell, Book and Candle	John van Druten	Comedy	3 m, 2 w	Interior	DPS	$50-25
The Glass Menagerie	Tennessee Williams	Drama	2 m, 2 w	Unit Set	DPS	$50-25
Sleuth	Anthony Shaffer	Melodrama	2 men	Interior	French	$50-25
Last of the Red Hot Lovers	Neil Simon	Comedy	1 m, 3 w	Interior	French	$50-25
The Prisoner of Second Avenue	Neil Simon	Comedy	2 m, 4 w	Interior	French	$50-25

Seven Characters

Play	Author	Type	Number of Characters	Sets	Leasing Co.	Royalty
There's a Girl in My Soup	Terence Frisby	Comedy	4 m, 3 w	Interior	French	$50-25
Hedda Gabler	Henrik Ibsen	Drama	3 m, 4 w	Interior	—	—
The Lion in Winter	James Goldman	Drama	5 m, 2 w	Multiple Sets	French	$50-25
The Confidential Clerk	T. S. Eliot	Comedy	4 m, 3 w	2 Interiors	French	$50-25
All Summer Long	Robert Anderson	Drama	3 m, 2 w, 2 juveniles	Combination Set	French	$50-25
The Rainmaker	N. Richard Nash	Comedy	6 m, 1 w	Combination Set	French	$50-25
Mr. Pim Passes By	A. A. Milne	Comedy	3 m, 4 w	Interior	French	$50-25
Come Blow Your Horn	Neil Simon	Comedy	3 m, 4 w	Interior	French	$50-25
Blithe Spirit	Noel Coward	Farce	2 m, 5 w	Interior	French	$50-25
Gigi	Anita Loos	Comedy	2 m, 5 w	2 Interiors	French	$50-25
Dangerous Corner	J. B. Priestly	Melodrama	3 m, 4 w	Interior	French	$25-20
The Flowering Cherry	Robert Bolt	Drama	4 m, 3 w	Interior	French	$25-20
The Living Room	Graham Greene	Melodrama	2 m, 5 w	Interior	French	$50-25
Goodbye Charlie	George Axelrod	Farce	4 m, 3 w	Interior	French	$50-25
Summer of the Seventeenth Doll	Ray Lawler	Drama	3 m, 4 w	Interior	French	$50-25

297

Seven Characters (Continued)

Play	Author	Type	Number of Characters	Sets	Leasing Co.	Royalty
Brecht on Brecht	Bertolt Brecht	Revue	4 m, 3 w (any mixture)	Concert Stage	French	$50-25
No Time for Comedy	S. N. Behrman	Comedy	4 m, 3 w	2 Interiors	French	$35-25
O Mistress Mine	Terence Rattigan	Comedy	2 m, 5 w	2 Interiors	French	$35-25
Big Fish, Little Fish	Hugh Wheeler	Comedy	5 m, 2 w	Interior	DPS	$50-25
Critics Choice	Ira Levin	Comedy	2 m, 4 w, 1 boy	Interior	DPS	$50-25
The Pleasure of His Company	Samuel Taylor	Comedy	5 m, 2 w	Interior	DPS	$50-25
Suddenly Last Summer	Tennessee Williams	Drama	2 m, 5 w	Exterior	DPS	$35-25
I Am a Camera	John van Druten	Drama	3 m, 4 w	Interior	DPS	$50-25
I've Got Sixpence	John van Druten	Drama	3 m, 4 w	Multiple Sets	DPS	$50-25
An Inspector Calls	J. B. Priestley	Drama	4 m, 3 w	Interior	DPS	$50-25
Ladies in Retirement	Percy and Denham	Mystery	1 m, 6 w	Interior	DPS	$35-25

Eight Characters

Play	Author	Type	Number of Characters	Sets	Leasing Co.	Royalty
Little Murders	Jules Feiffer	Comedy	6 m, 2 w	Interior	French	$50-25
Black Comedy	Peter Shaffer	Farce	5 m, 3 w	Interior	French	$50-25
The Odd Couple	Neil Simon	Comedy	6 m, 2 w	Interior	French	$50-35
The Elder Statesman	T. S. Eliot	Comedy-Drama	5 m, 3 w	Interior Exterior	French	$50-25
A Shot in the Dark	Marcel Achard	Comedy	5 m, 3 w	Interior	French	$50-25
The Chinese Prime Minister	Enid Bagnold	Comedy	5 m, 3 w	Interior	French	$50-25
The Two Mrs. Carrolls	Martin Vale	Melodrama	3 m, 5 w	2 Interiors	French	$50-25
The Mousetrap	Agatha Christie	Melodrama	5 m, 3 w	Interior	French	$50-25
The Reluctant Debutante	William Douglas Home	Comedy	3 m, 5 w	Interior	French	$50-25
Lo and Behold	John Patrick	Comedy	5 m, 3 w	Interior	French	$50-25
Toys in the Attic	Lillian Hellman	Drama	4 m, 4 w, (3 extras)	Interior, Exterior	French	$50-25
Strictly Dishonorable	Preston Sturgis	Comedy	7 m, 1 w	2 Interiors	French	$25-20
Portrait in Black	Ivan Goff and Ben Roberts	Melodrama	5 m, 3 w	Interior	French	$35-25

Eight Characters (Continued)

Play	Author	Type	Number of Characters	Sets	Leasing Co.	Royalty
Susan Slept Here	Steve Fisher and Alex Gottlieb	Comedy	4 m, 4 w	Interior	French	$25-20
Abie's Irish Rose	Anne Nichols	Comedy	6 m, 2 w	2 Interiors	French	$25-20
Separate Rooms	Carole, Dinehart, Gottlieb and Joseph	Comedy	5 m, 3 w	Interior	French	$25-20
Biography	S. N. Behrman	Comedy	5 m, 3 w	Interior	French	$35-25
Claudia	Rose Franken	Comedy-Drama	3 m, 5 w	Interior	French	$50-25
Will Success Spoil Rock Hunter?	George Axelrod	Farce	6 m, 2 w	2 Interiors	French	$50-25
Dracula	Deane and Balderston (Stoker)	Melodrama	6 m, 2 w	3 Interiors	French	$25-20
Mandragola	Machiavelli (trans. Eric Bentley)	Comedy	5 m, 3 w	Unit Set	French	$25-20
Deep Blue Sea	Terence Rattigan	Drama	5 m, 3 w	Interior	French	$50-25
To Be Young, Gifted and Black	Lorraine Hansberry (adapt. Nemiroff)	Biography	3 m, 5 w	Platform Stage	French	$50-25
Invitation to a March	Arthur Laurents	Comedy	3 m, 4 w, 1 boy	2 Exteriors	DPS	$50-25
A Loss of Roses	William Inge	Drama	4 m, 4 w	Interior	DPS	$50-25

Eight Characters (Continued)

Play	Author	Type	Number of Characters	Sets	Leasing Co.	Royalty
Bus Stop	William Inge	Comedy	5 m, 3 w	Interior	DPS	$50-25
The Tender Trap	Shulman and Smith	Comedy	4 m, 4 w	Interior	DPS	$50-25
The Love of Four Colonels	Peter Ustinov	Comedy	6 m, 2 w	Multiple Sets	DPS	$50-25
The Country Girl	Clifford Odets	Drama	6 m, 2 w	5 Interiors	DPS	$50-25
The Hairy Ape	Eugene O'Neill	Drama	6 m, 2 w extras	5 Interiors, 2 Exteriors	DPS	$35-25

Nine Characters

Play	Author	Type	Number of Characters	Sets	Leasing Co.	Royalty
The Firebugs	Max Frisch (trans. Gorelik)	Drama	6 m, 3 w extras	Composite Interiors	French	$50-25
The Boys in the Band	Mart Crowley	Comedy	9 men	Interior	French	$50-25
The Millionairess	G. Bernard Shaw	Comedy	6 m, 3 w	3 Interiors	French	$25
The Constant Wife	W. Somerset Maugham	Comedy	4 m, 5 w	Interior	French	$50-25
The Sign in Sidney Brustein's Window	Lorraine Hansberry	Drama	6 m, 3 w	Interior	French	$50-25
A Thurber Carnival	James Thurber	Revue	5 m, 4 w (more if desired)	Multiple Sets	French	$50-25
Never Too Late	Sumner Arthur Long	Farce	6 m, 3 w	Interior	French	$50-25
The Show-Off	George Kelly	Comedy	6 m, 3 w	Interior	French	$50-25
East Lynne	Brian J. Burton	Melodrama	4 m, 5 w	Interior	French	$25-20
Hotel Universe	Philip Barry	Comedy-Drama	5 m, 4 w	Exterior	French	$50-25
Hay Fever	Noel Coward	Comedy	4 m, 5 w	Interior	French	$50-25
Noah	Audrey Obey	Fantasy	5 m, 4 w extras	3 Exteriors	French	$25-20
The Chalk Garden	Enid Bagnold	Comedy-Drama	2 m, 7 w	Interior	French	$50-25

Nine Characters (Continued)

Play	Author	Type	Number of Characters	Sets	Leasing Co.	Royalty
A Murder Has Been Arranged	Emlyn Williams	Melodrama	4 m, 5 w	Interior	French	$25-20
The Loud Red Patrick	John Boruff	Comedy	4 m, 5 w	Interior	French	$50-25
The Rope Dancers	Morton Wishengrad	Drama	5 m, 4 w	Interior	French	$50-25
Rashomon	Fay and Michael Kanin	Drama	6 m, 3 w	Exterior	French	$50-25
The Late Christopher Bean	Sidney Howard	Comedy	5 m, 4 w	Interior	French	$25-20
Laburnum Grove	J. B. Priestly	Comedy	6 m, 3 w	Interior	French	$25-20
Peg O' My Heart	J. Hartley Manners	Comedy	5 m, 4 w	Interior	French	$25-20
Uncle Vanya	Anton Chekhov (adapt. Young)	Drama	5 m, 4 w	3 Interiors	French	$25-20
Purlie Victorious	Ossie Davis	Comedy	6 m, 3 w	2 Composite Exteriors	French	$50-25
Pink String and Sealing Wax	Roland Pertwee	Melodrama	4 m, 5 w	Interior	French	$25-20
Morning's at Seven	Paul Osborn	Comedy	4 m, 5 w	Exterior	French	$25-20
The Damask Cheek	John van Druten and Lloyd Morris	Comedy	3 m, 6 w	Interior	French	$35-25
A Hatful of Rain	Michael V. Gazzo	Drama	7 m, 2 w	Interior	French	$50-25

303

Nine Characters (Continued)

Play	Author	Type	Number of Characters	Sets	Leasing Co.	Royalty
The Cocktail Party	T. S. Eliot	Comedy-Drama	5 m, 4 w	2 Interiors	French	$50-25
The Animal Kingdom	Philip Barry	Comedy	5 m, 4 w	2 Interiors	French	$50-25
Night Must Fall	Emlyn Williams	Melodrama	4 m, 5 w	Interior	French	$25-20
Alice Sit-by-the-Fire	J. M. Barrie	Comedy	3 m, 6 w	2 Interiors	French	$35-25
Doctor in the House	Richard Gordon and Ted Willis	Comedy	5 m, 4 w	Interior	French	$35-25
The Beautiful People	William Saroyan	Comedy	7 m, 2 w	Interior	French	$25-20
Outward Bound	Sutton Vane	Comedy-Drama	6 m, 3 w	Interior	French	$25-20
The Play's the Thing	Ferenc Molnar (Adapt. Wodehouse)	Comedy	8 m, 1 w	Interior	French	$50-25
The Lilies of the Field	F. Andrew Leslie	Drama	4 m, 5 w	Open Stage	DPS	$35-25
Years Ago	Ruth Gordon	Comedy	4 m, 5 w	Interior	DPS	$35-25
The School for Wives	Moliere (trans. Wilbur)	Comedy	7 m, 2 w	Unit Set	DPS	$50-25
The Milk Train Doesn't Stop Here Anymore	Tennessee Williams	Drama	5 m, 4 w	Unit Set	DPS	$50-25
Period of Adjustment	Tennessee Williams	Drama	4 m, 5 w	Interior	DPS	$50-25

Nine Characters (Continued)

Play	Author	Type	Number of Characters	Sets	Leasing Co.	Royalty
Once More with Feeling	Harry Kurnitz	Comedy	8 m, 1 w	Interior	DPS	$50-25
Edwin Booth	Milton Geiger	Drama	5 m, 3 w, 1 boy	Unit Set	DPS	$50-25
A Roomful of Roses	Edith Sommer	Comedy-Drama	3 m, 5 w, 1 boy	Interior	DPS	$50-25
The Trip to Bountiful	Horton Foote	Drama	6 m, 3 w extras	Multiple Sets	DPS	$50-25
The Heiress	Ruth and Augustus Goetz	Drama	3 m, 6 w	Interior	DPS	$50-25
The Hasty Heart	John Patrick	Comedy-Drama	8 m, 1 w	Interior	DPS	$50-25

Ten Characters

Play	Author	Type	Number of Characters	Sets	Leasing Co.	Royalty
The White House Murder Case	Jules Feiffer	Comedy-Drama	9 m, 1 w	Interior, Exterior	French	$50-25
Celimare	Labiche and Delucour (adapt. Hoffman)	Comedy-Drama	5 m, 3 w, 2 extras	3 Interiors	French	$25-20
Medea	Robinson Jeffers	Tragedy	5 m, 5 w, extras	Exterior	French	$50-25
Petticoat Fever	Mark Reed	Comedy	6 m, 4 w	Interior	French	$25-20
The Cat and the Canary	John Willard	Melodrama	6 m, 4 w	2 Interiors	French	$25-20
The Bat	Mary Roberts Rinehart and Avery Hopwood	Melodrama-Comedy	7 m, 3 w	2 Interiors	French	$25-20
Dear Brutus	J. M. Barrie	Comedy	4 m, 6 w	Interior, Exterior	French	$35-25
Rain from Heaven	S. N. Behrman	Drama	6 m, 4 w	Interior	French	$35-25
Time of the Cuckoo	Arthur Laurents	Comedy	5 m, 5 w	Exterior	French	$50-25
Charley's Aunt	Brandon Thomas	Farce	6 m, 4 w	1 Exterior, 2 Interiors	French	$25
A Doll's House	Henrik Ibsen (adapt. Ginsbury)	Drama	5 m, 5 w	Interior	French	$15
The Linden Tree	J. B. Priestly	Drama	4 m, 6 w	Interior	French	$50-25

Ten Characters (Continued)

Play	Author	Type	Number of Characters	Sets	Leasing Co.	Royalty
French Without Tears	Terence Rattigan	Comedy	7 m, 3 w	Interior	French	$25-20
Heartbreak House	G. B. Shaw	Comedy	6 m, 4 w	Interior	French	$25
The Ninth Guest	Owen Davis	Melodrama	7 m, 3 w	Interior	French	$25-20
The Dover Road	A. A. Milne	Comedy	6 m, 4 w	Interior	French	$50-25
La Ronde	Arthur Schnitzler (adapt. Bentley)	Comedy	5 m, 5 w	Multiple Sets	French	$25-20
Time and the Conways	J. B. Priestly	Drama	4 m, 6 w	Interior	French	$25-20
The Far Off Hills	Lennox Robinson	Comedy-Drama	5 m, 5 w	2 Interiors	French	$25-20
The Diary of Anne Frank	Goodrich and Hackett	Drama	5 m, 5 w	Interior	DPS	$50-25
Time Out for Ginger	Ron Alexander	Comedy	5 m, 5 w	Interior	DPS	$50-25
A Touch of the Poet	Eugene O'Neill	Drama	7 m, 3 w	Interior	DPS	$50-25
The Dark at the Top of the Stairs	William Inge	Drama	3 m, 3 boys, 2 w, 2 girls	Interior	DPS	$50-25
Visit to a Small Planet	Gore Vidal	Comedy	8 m, 2 w	Interior	DPS	$50-25
A Clearing in the Woods	Arthur Laurents	Drama	5 m, 1 w, 1 child	Unit Set	DPS	$50-25

Ten Characters (Continued)

Play	Author	Type	Number of Characters	Sets	Leasing Co.	Royalty
My Three Angels	Sam and Bella Spewack	Comedy	7 m, 3 w	Interior	DPS	$50-25
All My Sons	Arthur Miller	Drama	6 m, 4 w	Interior	DPS	$35-25
The Little Foxes	Lillian Hellman	Drama	6 m, 4 w	Interior	DPS	$25
Beyond the Horizon	Eugene O'Neill	Drama	6 m, 4 w	1 Interior, 2 Exteriors	DPS	$35-25
Of Mice and Men	John Steinbeck	Drama	9 m, 1 w	2 Interiors, 1 Exterior	DPS	$25
Anna Christie	Eugene O'Neill	Drama	8 m, 2 w extras	2 Interiors, 1 Exterior	DPS	$35-25
The House of Blue Leaves	John Guare	Farce	4 m, 6 w	Interior	French	$50-35

Eleven Characters

Play	Author	Type	Number of Characters	Sets	Leasing Co.	Royalty
Play It Again, Sam	Woody Allen	Comedy	3 m, 8 w	Interior	French	$50-35
Forty Carats	Jay Allen	Comedy	5 m, 6 w	3 Interiors	French	Applica.
The Great White Hope	Howard Sackler	Tragedy	8 m, 3 w	Multiple Sets	French	$50-35
The Cactus Flower	Abe Burrows	Comedy	7 m, 4 w	4 Settings	French	$50-35
Andorra	Max Frisch (trans. Bullock)	Drama	8 m, 3 w	Area Staging	French	$50-25
A Raisin in the Sun	Lorraine Hansberry	Drama	7 m, 3 w, 1 child	Interior	French	$50-25
Come Back, Little Sheba	William Inge	Drama	8 m, 3 w	Interior	French	$50-25
Middle of the Night	Paddy Chayefsky	Drama	3 m, 8 w	Interior	French	$50-25
The Potting Shed	Graham Greene	Drama	6 m, 5 w	3 Interiors	French	$50-25
The Waltz of the Toreadors	Jean Anouilh (trans. Hill)	Farce	4 m, 7 w	Interior	French	$50-25
Craig's Wife	George Kelly	Drama	5 m, 6 w	Interior	French	$50-25
What Every Woman Knows	J. M. Barrie	Comedy	7 m, 4 w	4 Interiors	French	$35-25
Ten Little Indians	Agatha Christie	Comedy-Melodrama	8 m, 3 w	Interior	French	$50-25

Eleven Characters (Continued)

Play	Author	Type	Number of Characters	Sets	Leasing Co.	Royalty
Corruption in the Palace of Justice	Ugo Betti	Drama	9 m, 2 w	Interior	French	$35-25
Lord Pengo	S. N. Behrman	Comedy	7 m, 4 w	2 Interiors	French	$50-25
Separate Tables	Terence Rattigan	Drama	3 m, 8 w	2 Interiors	French	$50-25
Merton of the Movies	Kaufman and Connelly	Comedy	7 m, 4 w extras	5 sets	French	$25-20
The Family Reunion	T. S. Eliot	Drama	7 m, 4 w	Interior	French	$25-20
Present Laughter	Noel Coward	Comedy	5 m, 6 w	Interior	French	$50-25
Tea and Sympathy	Robert Anderson	Drama	9 m, 2 w	Composite Set	French	$50-25
The Shadow of a Gunman	Sean O'Casey	Tragedy	8 m, 3 w	Interior	French	$25-20
Another Language	Rose Franken	Comedy	6 m, 5 w	2 Interiors	French	$35-25
Tobacco Road	Jack Kirkland	Comedy	6 m, 5 w	Exterior	French	$50-25
The Curious Savage	John Patrick	Comedy	5 m, 6 w	Interior	DPS	$35-25
I Never Sang for My Father	Robert Anderson	Drama	7 m, 4 w	Area Staging	DPS	$50-25
The Misanthrope	Molière (trans. Wilbur)	Comedy	8 m, 3 w	Interior	DPS	$35-25
Third Best Sport	Eleanor and Leo Bayer	Comedy	7 m, 4 w	Interior	DPS	$50-25

Eleven Characters (Continued)

Play	Author	Type	Number of Characters	Sets	Leasing Co.	Royalty
The Flowering Peach	Clifford Odets	Comedy-Drama	7 m, 4 w	Interior, Exterior	DPS	$50-25
Picnic	William Inge	Drama	4 m, 7 w	Exterior	DPS	$50-25
Venus Observed	Christopher Fry	Comedy	7 m, 4 w	1 Interior, 1 Exterior	DPS	$35-25
The Seven Year Itch	George Axelrod	Comedy	6 m, 5 w	Interior	DPS	$50-25
Amphitryon 38	Jean Giraudoux (adapt. Behrman)	Comedy	6 m, 5 w	Interior, 3 Exteriors	DPS	$25
The Lady's Not for Burning	Christoper Fry	Comedy	8 m, 3 w	Interior	DPS	$50-25
The Winslow Boy	Terence Rattigan	Drama	7 m, 4 w	Interior	DPS	$50-25

311

Twelve Characters

Play	Author	Type	Number of Characters	Sets	Leasing Co.	Royalty
Let's Get a Divorce	Sardou and Narjac (adapt. Goldsby)	Comedy	7 m, 5 w extras	1 Interior, 1 Exterior	French	$25-20
After the Rain	John Bowen	Drama	9 m, 3 w	1 Exterior	French	$50-25
Plaza Suite	Neil Simon	Comedy	7 m, 5 w	Interior	French	Applica.
Send Me No Flowers	Barasch and Moore	Comedy	9 m, 3 w	Interior	French	$50-25
A Far Country	Henry Denker	Drama	6 m, 6 w	Interior	French	$50-25
Little Women	Marion DeForrest	Comedy	5 m, 7 w	Interior	French	$25-20
The Girls in 509	Howard Teichman	Comedy	9 m, 3 w	Interior	French	$50-25
The Killer	Eugene Ionesco	Drama	10 m, 2 w	Multiple Sets	French	$35-25
Pygmalion	G. B. Shaw	Comedy	6 m, 6 w	3 Interiors	French	$25
Leonce and Lena	Georg Buchner (adapt. Bentley)	Farce	9 m, 3 w extras	3 Interiors, 3 Exteriors	French	$25-20
The Torch-Bearers	George Kelly	Comedy	6 m, 6 w	2 Interiors	French	Applica.
Mr. Mergenthwirker's Lobblies	Nelson Bond	Comedy	9 m, 3 w extras	2 Interiors	French	$35-25
Tartuffe	Molière (adapt. Malleson)	Comedy	8 m, 4 w	Interior	French	$25-20
The Playboy of the Western World	J. M. Synge	Comedy	7 m, 5 w	Interior	French	$25-20

Twelve Characters (Continued)

Play	Author	Type	Number of Characters	Sets	Leasing Co.	Royalty
The Imaginary Invalid	Molière (adapt. Malleson)	Farce	8 m, 4 w	Interior	French	$25-20
Holiday	Philip Barry	Comedy	7 m, 5 w	2 Interiors	French	$50-25
Autumn Crocus	C. L. Anthony	Drama	4 m, 8 w	Interior	French	$25-20
Plaza Suite	Neil Simon	Comedy	7 m, 5 w	Interior	French	$50-35
Gramercy Ghost	John Cecil Holm	Comedy	6 m, 6 w	Interior	DPS	$35-25
Ivory Tower	Weidman and Yaffe	Drama	11 m, 1 w	2 Interiors	DPS	$35-25
The Gazebo	Alec Coppel	Comedy-Melodrama	9 m, 3 w	Interior	DPS	$50-25
Bad Seed	Maxwell Anderson	Melodrama	7 m, 4 w, 1 girl	Interior	DPS	$50-25
Anniversary Waltz	Chodorov and Fields	Comedy	7 m, 5 w	Interior	DPS	$50-25
The Happy Time	Samuel Taylor	Comedy	8 m, 4 w	2 Interiors	DPS	$50-25
A Streetcar Named Desire	Tennessee Williams	Drama	6 m, 6 w	Interior	DPS	$50-25
Harvey	Mary Chase	Comedy	6 m, 6 w	2 Interiors	DPS	$50-25

Thirteen Characters

Play	Author	Type	Number of Characters	Sets	Leasing Co.	Royalty
The Sea Gull	Anton Chekhov (trans. Goodman)	Drama	8 m, 5 w	2 Exteriors	French	$25-20
The Balcony	Jean Genet	Drama	9 m, 4 w	Several Scenes	French	$35-25
Philadelphia, Here I Come	Brian Friel	–Comedy	9 m, 4 w	Composite Sets	French	$50-25
The Servant of Two Masters	Goldoni (adapt. Dept.)	Farce	9 m, 4 w	3 Interiors, 1 Exterior	French	$25-20
The Male Animal	James Thurber and Elliott Nugent	Comedy	8 m, 5 w	Interior	French	$50-25
The Butter-and-Egg Man	George S. Kaufman	Comedy	8 m, 5 w	2 Interiors	French	$50-25
Thieves Carnival	Jean Anouilh (adapt. Hill)	Comedy	10 m, 3 w	2 Exteriors, 1 Interior	French	$35-25
The Tenth Man	Paddy Chayefsky	Comedy	12 m, 1 w	Composite Sets	French	$50-25
Seven Keys to Baldpate	George M. Cohan	Melodrama	9 m, 4 w	Interior	French	$25-20
Anastasia	Guy Bolton	Drama	8 m, 5 w	Interior	French	$50-25
Poor Bitos	Jean Anouilh	Drama	10 m, 3 w, 1 child	Interior	French	$50-25
Death Takes a Holiday	Aberto Cassella (adapt. Ferris)	Melodrama	7 m, 6 w	Interior	French	$50-25

Thirteen Characters (Continued)

Play	Author	Type	Number of Characters	Sets	Leasing Co.	Royalty
Patterns	James Reach	Drama	7 m, 6 w	Interior	French	$25-20
The Goose Hangs High	Lewis Beach	Comedy	7 m, 6 w	Interior	French	$25
I Killed the Count	Alec Coppell	Melodrama	10 m, 3 w	Interior	French	$25-20
They Knew What They Wanted	Sidney Howard	Comedy-Drama	9 m, 4 w, extras	Interior	French	$25-20
Mr. Barry's Etchings	Bullock and Archer	Comedy	7 m, 6 w	Interior	DPS	$25
Duel of Angels	Jean Giraudoux (adapt. Fry)	Comedy	8 m, 5 w, extras	Exterior, Interior	DPS	$50-25
Romanoff and Juliet	Peter Ustinov	Comedy	9 m, 4 w	Unit Set	DPS	$50-25
The Climate of Eden	Moss Hart	Drama	8 m, 5 w	Unit Set	DPS	$50-25
The Member of the Wedding	Carson McCullers	Drama	6 m, 7 w	Unit Set	DPS	$50-25
Ring Round the Moon	Jean Anouilh	Comedy	6 m, 7 w	Exterior	DPS	$50-25
Death of a Salesman	Arthur Miller	Drama	8 m, 5 w	Unit Set	DPS	$50-25
An Enemy of the People	Henrik Ibsen (adapt. Miller)	Drama	10 m, 3 w	3 Interiors	DPS	$25
Light Up the Sky	Moss Hart	Comedy	9 m, 4 w	Interior	DPS	$50-25
Another Part of the Forest	Lillian Hellman	Drama	8 m, 5 w	Interior	DPS	$50-25

315

Thirteen Characters

Play	Author	Type	Number of Characters	Sets	Leasing Co.	Royalty
A Month in the Country	Ivan Turgenev (adapt. Williams)	Comedy	7 m, 5 w, 1 child	Interior, Exterior	French	$35-25

Fourteen Characters

Play	Author	Type	Number of Characters	Sets	Leasing Co.	Royalty
The Blacks	Jean Genet	Drama	9 m, 5 w	Composite Sets	French	$35-25
A Flea in Her Ear	Georges Feydeau (trans. Mortimer)	Farce	9 m, 5 w	3 Interiors	French	$50-25
The Impossible Years	Fisher and Marx	Farce	9 m, 5 w	Interior	French	$50-25
The Amen Corner	James Baldwin	Comedy	4 m, 10 w	Composite Interior	French	$50-25
The Miracle Worker	William Gibson	Drama	7 m, 7 w	Unit Set	French	$50-25
The Desperate Hours	Joseph Hayes	Melodrama	11 m, 3 w	Unit Set	French	$50-25
One Way Pendulum	N. F. Simpson	Comedy	10 m, 4 w	Composite Interior	French	$35-25
A Majority of One	Leonard Spigelgass	Comedy	6 m, 8 w	4 Interiors	French	$50-25
A Man for All Seasons	Robert Bolt	Tragedy	11 m, 3w	Unit Set	French	$50-25
The Tavern	George M. Cohan	Melodrama	10 m, 4 w	Interior	French	$25-20
A Case of Libel	Henry Denker	Melodrama	11 m, 3w 3 extras	Interior inset	French	$50-25
Kind Lady	Edward Chodorov	Melodrama	6 m, 8 w	Interior	French	$25-20
Clerambard	Marcel Ayme (adapt. Kerz)	Comedy	7 m, 7 w	2 Interiors, Exterior	French	$50-25

Fourteen Characters (Continued)

Play	Author	Type	Characters	Sets	Leasing Co.	Royalty
All the Way Home	Tad Mosel	Drama	6 m, 7 w, 1 child	Composite Interior-Exterior Sets	French	$50-25
The Fighting Cock	Jean Anouilh	Comedy	9 m, 3 w	Interior, Exterior	French	$50-25
The Cradle Song	G. Martinez-Sierra (adapt. Underhill)	Drama	4 m, 10 w extras	2 Interiors	French	$50-25
The Cave Dwellers	William Saroyan	Comedy	9 m, 5 w	Bare Stage	French	$50-25
The Old Maid	Zoe Akins	Drama	5 m, 9 w	3 Interiors	French	$25-20
The Miser	Molière (adapt. Malleson)	Farce	11 m, 3 w	Interior	French	$25-20
Green Grow the Lilacs	Lynn Riggs	Drama	10 m, 4 w extras	Multiple Sets	French	$50-25
Guest in the House	Wilde and Eunson	Comedy-Drama	6 m, 8 w	Interior	French	$35-25
An Italian Straw Hat	Labiche and Marc-Michel (adapt. Hoffman)	Comedy	9 m, 5 w extras	4 Interiors	French	$25
The Flies	Jean-Paul Sartre	Tragedy	8 m, 6 w extras	2 Interiors, 2 Exteriors	French	$25-20

Fourteen Characters (Continued)

Play	Author	Type	Characters	Sets	Leasing Co.	Royalty
Deadwood Dick	Tom Taggart	Melodrama	7 m, 7 w extras	Interior	French	$25-20
Celestina	Fernando de Rojas (adapt. Bentley)	Melodrama	8 m, 6 w	5 Interiors, 3 Exteriors	French	$25-20
Jenny Kissed Me	Jean Kerr	Comedy	4 m, 10 w	Interior	DPS	$25
The Night of the Iguana	Tennessee Williams	Drama	8 m, 6 w	Exterior	DPS	$50-25
Purple Dust	Sean O'Casey	Comedy	11 m, 3 w	Interior	DPS	$50-25
Sabrina Fair	Samuel Taylor	Comedy	7 m, 7 w	Exterior	DPS	$50-25
Edward, My Son	Morley and Langley	Drama	10 m, 4 w	6 Interiors	DPS	$25
Summer and Smoke	Tennessee Williams	Drama	8 m, 6 w	Unit Set	DPS	$50-25
Arsenic and Old Lace	Joseph Kesselring	Comedy	11 m, 3 w	Interior	DPS	$35-25
On Borrowed Time	Paul Osborn	Drama	11 m, 3 w	Unit Set	DPS	$35-25
The Children's Hour	Lillian Hellman	Drama	2 m, 12 w	2 Interiors	DPS	$35-25
Room Service	Murray and Boretz	Comedy	12 m, 2 w	Interior	DPS	$25

Fifteen or More Characters

Play	Author	Type	Number of Characters	Sets	Leasing Co.	Royalty
We Bombed in New Haven	Joseph Heller	Drama	16 m, 1 w	3 Sets	French	$50-25
The Man in the Glass Booth	Robert Shaw	Drama	18 m, 3 w	3 Interiors	French	$50-35
The Resistible Rise of Arturo Ui	Bertolt Brecht	Drama	30 m, 5 w	Multiple Sets	French	$50-25
In the Matter of J. Robert Oppenheimer	Heinar Kipphardt	Drama	14 m, 9 w extras	Interior	French	$50-35
The Front Page	Hecht and MacArthur	Comedy-Melodrama	17 m, 5 w	Interior	French	$50-25
The Trial	Gide and Barrault	Tragedy	21 m, 3w extras	Multiple Sets	French	$50-25
The Drunkard	Brian J. Burton	Melodrama	7 m, 8 w	Multiple Sets	French	$25-20
Futz	Rochelle Owens	Drama	10 m, 5 w	Multiple Sets	French	$50-25
The Devils	John Whiting	Melodrama	17 m, 6 w extras	Composite Sets	French	$50-25
Back to Methuselah	G. Bernard Shaw (adapt. Moss)	Comedy-Drama	17 speaking roles	Composite Sets	French	$35-25
Galileo	Bertolt Brecht (trans. Laughton)	Drama	27 m, 4 w extras	Composite Sets	French	$50-25

Fifteen or More Characters (Continued)

Play	Author	Type	Number of Characters	Sets	Leasing Co.	Royalty
Viet Rock	Megan Terry	Drama	8-20 characters	Composite Sets	French	$35-25
The Royal Hunt of the Sun	Peter Shaffer	Drama	22 m, 2 w extras	Multiple Sets	French	$50-25
Androcles and the Lion	G. Bernard Shaw	Comedy	14 m, 2 w extras	1 Interior, 2 Exteriors	French	$25
Dark of the Moon	Richardson and Berney	Drama	28 roles	Multiple Sets	French	$50-35
The Unknown Soldier and His Wife	Peter Ustinov	Comedy	15 m, 2 w	Platform Set	French	$50-25
Hostile Witness	Jack Roffey	Melodrama	14 m, 2 w extras	Courtroom 2 Insets	French	$50-25
Don't Drink the Water	Woody Allen	Farce	12 m, 4 w	Interior	French	$40-25
Rosencrantz and Guildenstern Are Dead	Tom Stoppard	Comedy	14 m, 2 w extras	Unit Set	French	$50-35
The Chinese Wall	Max Frisch (trans. Rosenberg)	Drama	16 m, 7 w extras	A Stage	French	$35-25
The Blue Bird	Maurice Maeterlinck (trans. Matos)	Fantasy	7 m, 7 w, 10 children	Interior, 4 Exteriors	French	$25-20
Caesar and Cleopatra	G. Bernard Shaw	Comedy	20 m, 5 w extras	6 Exteriors, 3 Interiors	French	$25

Fifteen or More Characters (Continued)

Play	Author	Type	Number of Characters	Sets	Leasing Co.	Royalty
Saint Joan	G. Bernard Shaw	Comedy-Drama	21 m, 2 w extras	6 Interiors, 1 Exterior	French	$25
Hogan's Goat	William Alfred	Tragedy	10 m, 5 w extras	Composite Sets	French	$50-25
Alice in Wonderland	Eva LeGallienne	Fantasy	50 characters	Multiple Sets	French	$25-20
The Desk Set	William Marchant	Comedy	8 m, 8 w	Interior	French	$50-25
J. B.	Archibald MacLeish	Drama	12 m, 9 w	Interior	French	$50-25
The Matchmaker	Thornton Wilder	Farce	9 m, 7 w	4 Interiors	French	Applica.
Witness for the Prosecution	Agatha Christie	Melodrama	17 m, 5 w extras	2 Interiors	French	$50-25
Our Town	Thornton Wilder	Drama	17 m, 7 w extras	Bare Stage	French	$25-20
Peter Pan	J. M. Barrie	Fantasy	25 characters	Multiple Scenes	French	$35-25
The Magnificent Yankee	Emmet Lavery	Comedy	15 m, 2 w	Interior	French	$50-25
The Physicists	Friedrich Duerrenmatt	Melodrama	16 m, 4 w	Interior	French	$50-25
Anatomy of a Murder	Elihu Winer	Melodrama	16 m, 2 w	4 Interiors 2 Insets	French	$50-25

Fifteen or More Characters (Continued)

Play	Author	Type	Number of Characters	Sets	Leasing Co.	Royalty
The Deputy	Rolf Hochhuth	Tragedy	22 m, 2 w	Multiple Sets	French	$50-25
Time Remembered	Jean Anouilh	Comedy	13 m, 2 w	Interior, 2 Exteriors	French	$50-25
Rhinoceros	Eugene Ionesco	Comedy	11 m, 6 w extras	Exterior, 2 Interiors	French	$50-25
The Gang's All Here	Lawrence and Lee	Drama	15 m, 4 w	4 Interiors	French	$50-25
Juno and the Paycock	Sean O'Casey	Tragedy	14 m, 5 w	Interior	French	$25
Dylan	Sidney Michaels	Drama	15 m, 13 w	Multiple Sets	French	$50-25
Mother Courage and Her Children	Bertolt Brecht	Drama	18 m, 5 w extras	Interior, 5 Exteriors	French	$50-25
The Skin of Our Teeth	Thornton Wilder	Drama	5 m, 5 w extras	1 Interior, 1 Exterior	French	$50-25
Ondine	Jean Giraudoux (adapt. Valency)	Tragedy	17 m, 11 w	3 Sets	French	$50-25
Berkeley Square	John Balderston	Fantasy	7 m, 8 w	2 Interiors	French	$25-20
Tovarich	Jacques Deval	Comedy	8 m, 7 w	4 Interiors	French	$35-20
Becket	Jean Anouilh (trans. Hill)	Drama	15 m, 3 w	Multiple Sets	French	$50-25
A Country Scandal	Anton Chekhov (adapt. Szogyi)	Comedy	11 m, 5 w	2 Interiors, 2 Exteriors	French	$35-25

323

Fifteen or More Characters (Continued)

Play	Author	Type	Number of Characters	Sets	Leasing Co.	Royalty
The Hostage	Brendan Behan	Comedy-Drama	11 m, 7 w	Composite Set	French	$50-25
Blues for Mr. Charlie	James Baldwin	Drama	16 m, 7 w	Bare Stage	French	$50-25
Look Homeward, Angel	Ketti Frings	Comedy-Drama	10 m, 9 w extras	Exterior and 2 Insets	French	$50-25
The Ponder Heart	Fields and Chodorov	Comedy	20 m, 10 w extras	2 Interiors, Exterior	French	$50-25
The Visit	Friedrich Duerrenmatt (adapt. Valency)	Drama	25 m, 5 w, 2 children	Multiple Sets	French	$50-25
As You Desire Me	Luigi Pirandello (trans. Abba)	Drama	11 m, 7 w	2 Interiors	French	$50-25
The Death of Doctor Faust	Michel deGhelderode (trans. Haugh)	Drama	12 m, 4 w extras	2 Interiors, Exterior	French	$35-25
The Egg	Felicien Marceau	Comedy	19 m, 14 w	Multiple Sets	French	$50-25
Ah, Wilderness	Eugene O'Neill	Comedy	9 m, 6 w	3 Interiors, 1 Exterior	French	$50-25
Quality Street	J. M. Barrie	Comedy	6 m, 9 w extras	2 Interiors	French	$35-25
Lorenzaccio	Alfred de Musset (adapt. Bruce)	Drama	36 m, 4 w extras	7 Exteriors	French	$25-20

324

Fifteen or More Characters (Continued)

Play	Author	Type	Number of Characters	Sets	Leasing Co.	Royalty
Hotel Paradiso	Feydeau and Desvallieres (trans. Glenville)	Farce	13 m, 8 w extras	2 Interiors	French	$50-25
Under Milkwood	Dylan Thomas	Drama	17 m, 17 w	Area Set	French	$50-25
The Enchanted	Jean Giraudoux (adapt. Valency)	Comedy	9 m, 11 w	Interior, Exterior	French	$50-25
Blood Wedding	F. Garcia Lorca	Tragedy	9 m, 9 w extras	5 Interiors, 2 Exteriors	French	$35-25
Family Portrait	Coffee and Cowen	Drama	12 m, 10 w	Interior, 3 Exteriors	French	$25-20
Camille	Alexandre Dumas, fils	Drama	11 m, 6 w extras	3 Interiors	French	$25-20
Darkness At Noon	Sidney Kingsley	Tragedy	18 m, 3 w	Composite Interior	French	$50-25
The Good Woman of Setzuan	Bertolt Brecht (adapt. Bentley)	Morality	18 m, 11 w extras	4 Interiors	French	$50-25
Tiger at the Gates	Christopher Fry	Comedy-Tragedy	15 m, 7 w	Exterior	French	$50-25
Major Barbara	G. Bernard Shaw	Comedy	9 m, 7 w	2 Exteriors, 1 Interior	French	$25

Fifteen or More Characters (Continued)

Play	Author	Type	Number of Characters	Sets	Leasing Co.	Royalty
Caligula	Albert Camus (adapt. O'Brien)	Drama	13 m, 2 w	Exterior	French	$50-25
Fuente Ovejuna	Lope de Vega (adapt. Campbell)	Drama	18 m, 4 w extras	5 Interiors, 3 Exteriors	French	$25-20
Spring's Awakening	Frank Wedekind (adapt. Bentley)	Drama	31 m, 8 w extras	6 Interiors, 5 Exteriors	French	$25-20
Point of No Return	Paul Osborn	Comedy	14 m, 7 w, 2 children	4 Interiors	French	$50-25
Chicken Every Sunday	J. and P. Epstein	Comedy	12 m, 9 w	Interior	French	$50-25
My Heart's in the Highlands	William Saroyan	Fantasy	13 m, 2 w extras	Multiple Sets	French	$25-20
Dinner at Eight	George S. Kaufman and Edna Ferber	Drama	14 m, 11 w	Interior	French	$50-25
The Caine Mutiny Court-Martial	Herman Wouk	Drama	19 men	Interior	French	$50-25
Ladies of the Jury	Fred Ballard	Comedy	12 m, 10 w	2 Interiors	French	$50-25
The Caucasian Chalk Circle	Bertolt Brecht (adapt. Bentley)	Tragedy-Comedy	39 m, 14 w, 3 children	Composite Interior-Exterior	French	$50-25
Time of Your Life	William Saroyan	Comedy	18 m, 7 w	2 Interiors	French	$35-25

326

Fifteen or More Characters (Continued)

Play	Author	Type	Number of Characters	Sets	Leasing Co.	Royalty
The Slaughter of the Innocents	William Saroyan	Drama	17 m, 6 w, 1 child	Interior	French	$25-20
Career	James Lee	Comedy	11 m, 4 w	Multiple Sets	French	$35-25
The Philadelphia Story	Philip Barry	Comedy	9 m, 6 w	Interior, Exterior	French	$50-25
Mary of Scotland	Maxwell Anderson	Drama	22 m, 5 w	4 Interiors, Exterior	French	$25-20
Elizabeth the Queen	Maxwell Anderson	Drama	16 m, 7 w extras	4 Interiors, 1 Exterior	French	$25-20
The Royal Family	Kaufman and Ferber	Comedy	11 m, 6 w	Interior	French	$35-25
The Admirable Crichton	J. M. Barrie	Comedy	13 m, 12 w	Exterior, 2 Interiors	French	$35-25
The Three Sisters	Anton Chekhov (trans. Young)	Drama	9 m, 5 w	2 Interiors, 1 Exterior	French	$25-20
R. U. R.	Karel Capek	Fantasy	13 m, 4 w	2 Interiors	French	$25-20
Pantagleize	Michel deGhelderode (trans. Hauger)	Fantasy	14 m, 2 w extras	4 Interiors, Exterior	French	$35-20
The Cherry Orchard	Anton Chekhov (trans. Young)	Comedy-Drama	10 m, 5 w	Exterior, 2 Interiors	French	$25-20

327

Fifteen or More Characters (Continued)

Play	Author	Type	Number of Characters	Sets	Leasing Co.	Royalty
The Insect Comedy	J. and K. Capek	Comedy	21 m, 9 w extras	Composite Set	French	$25-20
The Inspector General	Nikolai Gogol	Farce	15 m, 4 w	2 Interiors	French	$25-20
The Apple Cart	G. Bernard Shaw	Comedy	10 m, 5 w	2 Interiors, Exterior	French	$25
He Who Gets Slapped	Leonid Andreyev	Drama	20 m, 13 w		French	$25-20
The Diary of a Scoundrel	Alexander Ostrovsky	Comedy	9 m, 7 w	3 Interiors	French	$25-20
The Private Life of the Master Race	Bertolt Brecht (adapt. Bentley)	Melodrama	Multiple characters	Multple Sets	French	$50-25
Woyzeck	Georg Buchner (trans. Hoffman)	Tragedy	13 m, 4 w, 5 children	Multple Sets	French	$10
Street Scene	Elmer Rice	Drama	16 m, 11 w	Exterior	French	$50-25
The Plough and the Stars	Sean O'Casey	Drama	10 m, 5 w	3 Interiors	French	$25-20
Yerma	F. G. Lorca	Tragedy	6 m, 17 w	2 Interiors, 3 Exteriors	French	$35-25
Murder in the Cathedral	T. S. Eliot	Tragedy	10 m, 9 w	3 Interiors	French	$35-25

328

Fifteen or More Characters (Continued)

Play	Author	Type	Number of Characters	Sets	Leasing Co.	Royalty
Peer Gynt	Henrik Ibsen (adapt. Green)	Fantasy	8 m, 12 w	Multiple Sets	French	$35-25
The Adding Machine	Elmer Rice	Drama	14 m, 9 w	5 Interiors, 2 Exteriors	French	$50-25
Beggar on Horseback	Connelly and Kaufman	Fantasy	16 m, 5 w	Multiple Sets	French	$50-25
The House of Connelly	Paul Green	Drama	4 m, 6 w 20 extras	Interior, 2 Exteriors	French	$25-20
Tonight We Improvise	Luigi Pirandello	Drama	Approximately 50 characters	Interior, Exterior	French	$50-25
Libel	Edward Wooll	Melodrama	20 m, 4 w	Interior	French	$25-20
The Night Thoreau Spent in Jail	Lawrence and Lee	Drama	11 m, 5 w extras	Platform Stage	French	$50-35
The Lower Depths	Maxim Gorky (trans. Szogyi)	Drama	12 m, 5 w extras	Interior	French	$50-25
The Prime of Miss Jean Brodie	Jay Allen	Comedy	4 m, 15 w	Platform Stage	French	$50-25
Splendor in the Grass	F. Andrew Leslie	Drama	10 m, 9 w	Unit Set	DPS	$35-25
Father of the Bride	Caroline Francke	Comedy	11 m, 7 w extras	Interior	DPS	$35-25

329

Fifteen or More Characters (Continued)

Play	Author	Type	Number of Characters	Sets	Leasing Co.	Royalty
I Remember Mama	John van Druten	Comedy	9 m, 13 w, (inc. children)	Unit Set	DPS	$25
My Sister Eileen	Fields and Chodorov	Comedy	21 m, 6 w	Interior	DPS	$25
Junior Miss	Fields and Chodorov	Comedy	11 m, 6 w	Interior	DPS	$25
The Barretts of Wimpole Street	Rudolf Besier	Comedy-Drama	12 m, 5 w	Interior	DPS	$50-25
You Can't Take It With You	Kaufman and Hart	Comedy	9 m, 7 w extras	Interior	DPS	$25
Stage Door	Ferber and Kaufman	Comedy	11 m, 21 w	Interior	DPS	$25
Jimmy Shine	Murray Schisgal	Comedy	9 m, 9 w	Unit Set	DPS	$50-25
A Cry of Players	William Gibson	Drama	15 m, 3 w 1 girl, extras	Area Staging	DPS	$50-25
Mister Johnson	Norman Rosten	Drama	22 m, 5 w	Multiple Sets	DPS	$35-25
Compulsion	Meyer Levin	Drama	24 m, 5 w	Unit Set	DPS	$50-25
Incident at Vichy	Arthur Miller	Drama	21 men	Interior	DPS	$50-25
After the Fall	Arthur Miller	Drama	12 m, 11 w extras	Unit Set	DPS	$50-25
The Ballad of the Sad Cafe	Edward Albee	Drama	14 m, 6 w	Unit Set	DPS	$55-30

Fifteen or More Characters (Continued)

Play	Author	Type	Number of Characters	Sets	Leasing Co.	Royalty
Romulus	Gore Vidal	Comedy	18 m, 2 w	Exterior	DPS	$50-25
The Andersonville Trial	Saul Levitt	Drama	28 men	Interior	DPS	$50-25
The Best Man	Gore Vidal	Drama	14 m, 6 w	Interiors	DPS	$50-25
Sweet Bird of Youth	Tennessee Williams	Drama	15 m, 7 w	Interiors	DPS	$50-25
All the King's Men	Robert Penn Warren	Drama	14 m, 4 m extras	Open Stage	DPS	$35-25
Auntie Mame	Lawrence and Lee	Comedy	25 m, 12 w, 3 boys	Interiors, Exteriors	DPS	$50-25
Tall Story	Lindsay and Crouse	Comedy	21 m, 8 w, 1 boy	Interiors	DPS	$50-25
Inherit the Wind	Lawrence and Lee	Drama	21 m, 6 w 3 children	Unit Set	DPS	$50-25
Sunrise at Campobello	Dore Schary	Drama	19 m, 5 w	Interiors	DPS	$50-25
Who Was That Lady I Saw You With?	Norman Krasna	Comedy	15 m, 6 w	Interior	DPS	$50-25
No Time for Sergeants	Ira Levin	Comedy	34 m, 3 w	Unit Set	DPS	$50-25
The Happiest Millionaire	Kyle Crichton	Comedy	9 m, 6 w	Interior	DPS	$50-25
Orpheus Descending	Tennessee Williams	Drama	10 m, 9 w	Interior	DPS	$50-25

Fifteen or More Characters (Continued)

Play	Author	Type	Number of Characters	Sets	Leasing Co.	Royalty
The Lark	Jean Anouilh (adapt. Hellman)	Drama	15 m, 5 w	Platforms	DPS	$50-25
A View from the Bridge	Arthur Miller	Drama	12 m, 3 w	Unit Set	DPS	$50-25
The Great Sebastians	Lindsay and Crouse	Comedy-Melodrama	15 m, 6 w	Interior	DPS	$50-25
Cat on a Hot Tin Roof	Tennessee Williams	Drama	8 m, 5 w, 4 children	Interior	DPS	$50-25
Red Roses for Me	Sean O'Casey	Comedy-Drama	21 m, 9 w	Interior, 2 Exteriors	DPS	$35-25
The Dark is Light Enough	Christopher Fry	Drama	12 m, 3 w	Interior	DPS	$50-25
Mrs. McThing	Mary Chase	Comedy-Fantasy	9 m, 10 w	Interior	DPS	$50-25
In the Summer House	Jane Bowles	Drama	5 m, 10 w	Interior and Exterior	DPS	$50-25
The Solid Gold Cadillac	Teichmann and Kaufman	Comedy	11 m, 6 w	Multiple Sets	DPS	$50-25
The Teahouse of the August Moon	John Patrick	Comedy	18 m, 8 w, 3 children	Multiple Sets	DPS	$50-25
Madam, Will You Walk?	Sidney Howard	Comedy-Fantasy	11 m, 4 w extras	Multiple Sets	DPS	$50-25

332

Play	Author	Type	Number of Characters	Sets	Leasing Co.	Royalty
Camino Real	Tennessee Williams	Fantasy	26 m, 10 w extras	Multiple Sets	DPS	$50-25
Mister Roberts	Heggen and Logan	Comedy	19 m, 1 w	Multiple Sets	DPS	$50-25
Bernardine	Mary Chase	Comedy	13 m, 6 w	Stylized Setting	DPS	$50-25
The Shrike	Joseph Kramm	Drama	17 m, 5 w	Unit Setting	DPS	$50-25
The Crucible	Arthur Miller	Drama	10 m, 10 w	Multiple Sets	DPS	$50-25
The Rose Tattoo	Tennessee Williams	Drama	9 m, 14 w	Unit Set	DPS	$50-25
The Grass Harp	Truman Capote	Comedy	10 m, 8 w	1 Interior, 1 Exterior	DPS	$50-25
The Wingless Victory	Maxwell Anderson	Tragedy	8 m, 8 w	2 Interiors	DPS	$25
Billy Budd	Coxe and Chapman	Tragedy	22 men	2 Interiors, Exterior	DPS	$50-25
Detective Story	Sidney Kingsley	Drama	24 m, 8 w extras	Interior	DPS	$50-25
Stalag 17	Bevan and Trzcinski	Comedy-Melodrama	21 men	Interior	DPS	$50-25
Anne of the Thousand Days	Maxwell Anderson	Drama	11 m, 5 w extras	Unit Set	DPS	$50-25
Life with Mother	Clarence Day	Comedy	8 m, 8 w	2 Interiors	DPS	$50-25

Fifteen or More Characters (Continued)

Play	Author	Type	Number of Characters	Sets	Leasing Co.	Royalty
Idiot's Delight	Robert E. Sherwood	Drama	17 m, 10 w	Interior	DPS	$25
Born Yesterday	Garson Kanin	Comedy	12 m, 4 w	Interior	DPS	$50-25
The Silver Whistle	Robert E. McEnroe	Comedy	10 m, 5 w	Exterior	DPS	$50-25
The Madwoman of Chaillot	Jean Giraudoux (adapt. Valency)	Comedy-Drama	17 m, 8 w	1 Interior, 1 Exterior	DPS	$50-25
There Shall be No Night	Robert E. Sherwood	Drama	13 m, 4 w	3 Interiors	DPS	$50-25
The Corn is Green	Emlyn Williams	Drama	10 m, 5 w extras	Interior	DPS	$35-25
Three Men on a Horse	Holm and Abbott	Comedy	11 m, 4 w	3 Interiors	DPS	$25
Abe Lincoln in Illinois	Robert E. Sherwood	Drama	25 m, 7 w	7 Interiors, 3 Exteriors	DPS	$25
George Washington Slept Here	Kaufman and Hart	Comedy	9 m, 8 w	Interior	DPS	$25
The Man Who Came to Dinner	Kaufman and Hart	Comedy	15 m, 9 w extras	Interior	DPS	$25
Winterset	Maxwell Anderson	Drama	16 m, 3 w extras	Interior, Exterior	DPS	$25
The Petrified Forest	Robert E. Sherwood	Drama	18 m, 3 w	Interior	DPS	$25

Fifteen or More Characters (Continued)

Play	Author	Type	Number of Characters	Sets	Leasing Co.	Royalty
Cyrano de Bergerac	Edmond Rostand (trans. Hooker)	Comedy-Drama	10 m, 3 w many "bits"	2 Interiors, 3 Exteriors	DPS	$25
The Women	Clare Boothe	Comedy	35 women	11 Interiors	DPS	$25
Boy Meets Girl	Sam and Bella Spewack	Comedy	14 m, 5 w	2 Interiors	DPS	$25
Golden Boy	Clifford Odets	Drama	17 m, 2 w	4 Interiors, 2 Exteriors	DPS	$25
High Tor	Maxwell Anderson	Romantic Comedy	14 m, 2 w extras	Exterior	DPS	$35-25

Appendix B

A List of Recordings for Voice

ALBEE, EDWARD
    Who's Afraid of Virginia Woolf?   Columbia
    (Complete) Uta Hagen, Arthur Hill, George   DOS-687
    Grizzard, etc. Original Broadway production.
    4 Records.

    Zoo Story (Complete)   Spoken Arts
    Mark Richman. 1 Record.   S-608

ARISTOPHANES
    Lysistrata (Complete)   Caedmon
    Hermione Gingold, Stanley Holloway. 2 Records.   TRS-313

BECKETT, SAMUEL
    Krapp's Last Tape (Complete)   Spoken Arts
    1 Record.   788

    Waiting for Godot (Complete)   Caedmon
    Bert Lahr, E. G. Marshall, etc. 2 Records.   TRS-352

BEHAN, BRENDAN
    The Hostage (Complete)   Columbia
    Julie Harris, etc. 3 Records.   CDOS-729

BERRIGAN, DANIEL J., S. J. (Complete)
    The Trial of the Catonsville 9   Caedmon
    Center Theatre Group Production. 3 Records.   TRS-353

BÉSIER, RUDOLPH
    The Barretts of Wimpole Street   Caedmon
    (Excerpts) Katharine Cornell. 1 Record.   1071

BRECHT, BERTOLT
    Brecht on Brecht — Columbia O2S-203
    Original Broadway Cast. 2 Records.

    Man's a Man (Excerpts) — Spoken Arts 870
    1 Record.

CHEKHOV, ANTON
    The Cherry Orchard (Complete) — Caedmon TRS-314
    Jessica Tandy, Guthrie Theatre, etc. 3 Records.

    Ivanov (Complete) — Victor VDS-109
    Sir John Gielgud, Vivien Leigh. 2 Records.

    The Sea Gull (Excerpts) — Library Edition 4012
    Kirkland Acting Group. 1 Record.

    Three Sisters (Complete) — Caedmon TRS 325
    Siobhan McKenna, etc. 3 Records.

    Uncle Vanya (Complete) — Phillips 2-701
    Lord Laurence Olivier, Sir Michael Redgrave, Dame Sybil Thorndike, Sir Lewis Casson, Rosemary Harris, Joan Plowright. 2 Records.

COCTEAU, JEAN
    The Infernal Machine (Complete) — Caedmon TRS 321
    Margaret Leighton, Diane Cilento, Jeremy Brett. 3 Records.

CONGREVE, WILLIAM
    Love for Love (Complete) — Victor VDS-112
    British National Theatre. 3 Records.

    The Way of the World (Complete) — Caedmon TRS-339
    British National Theatre. 3 Records.

    The Way of the World (Excerpts) — Library Edition 4006
    Robert Culp, etc. 1 Record.

CROWLEY, MART
    Boys in the Band (Complete) — A & M 6001
    Original Broadway Cast. 2 Records.

DRYDEN, JOHN
    All for Love (Excerpts) — Library Edition 4007
    Robert Culp, etc. 1 Record.

DUBERMAN, MARTIN B.
    In White America (Excerpts) — Columbia KOS-2430
    1 Record.

DUMAS, ALEXANDRE, *fils*
    Camille (Excerpts) — Caedmon 1175
    Eva Le Gallienne, etc. 1 Record.

ELIOT, T. S.
  Family Reunion (Complete)   Caedmon
  Dame Flora Robson, Paul Scofield, etc. 3 Records.   TRS-308

  Murder in the Cathedral (Complete)   Angel
  Robert Donat, etc. 2 Records.   3505

  Murder in the Cathedral (Complete)   Caedmon
  Paul Scofield, etc. 2 Records.   TRS-330

EURIPIDES
  Medea (Complete)   Caedmon
  Dame Judith Anderson, Anthony Quayle. 2 Records.   TRS-302

  ———— *Everyman* (Slightly Abridged)   Caedmon
  Burgess Meredith, etc. 1 Record.   1031

FRY, CHRISTOPHER
  The Lady's Not for Burning (Complete)   Decca
  Sir John Gielgud, Pamela Brown, Richard Burton.   DX-110
  2 Records.

GENET, JEAN
  The Balcony (Complete)   Caedmon
  Cyril Cusack, Patrick Magee. 3 Records.   TRS-316

GILROY, FRANK D.
  The Subject Was Roses (Complete)   Columbia
  Jack Albertson, etc. 3 Records.   DOS-708

GOLDSMITH, OLIVER
  She Stoops to Conquer (Complete)   Caedmon
  Alastair Sim, Claire Bloom. 3 Records.   TRS-309

  She Stoops to Conquer (Excerpts)   Library
  Robert Culp, etc. 1 Record.   Edition
                                                                 4010

HECHT, BEN
  The Front Page (Complete)   Caedmon
  Robert Ryan, Bert Convy, Peggy Cass. 3 Records.   TRS-351

IBSEN, HENRIK
  A Doll's House (Complete)   Caedmon
  Claire Bloom, Donald Madden. 3 Records.   TRS-343

  A Doll's House (Excerpts)   Library
  The Kirkland Group. 1 Record.   Edition
                                                                 4013

IBSEN, HENRIK/MILLER, ARTHUR
  An Enemy of the People (Complete)   Caedmon
  (Miller adaptation) 3 Records.   TRS-349

IBSEN, HENRIK
  Ghosts (Excerpts)   Library
  Robert Culp, etc. 1 Record.   Edition
                                                                 4002

Hedda Gabler (Complete)	Caedmon
Joan Plowright, Anthony Quayle, Patrick Magee,	TRS-322
etc. 3 Records.	
The Master Builder (Complete)	Caedmon
Sir Michael Redgrave, etc. 2 Records.	TRS-307

IONESCO, ENGENE

The Chairs (Complete)	Caedmon
Siobhan McKenna, Cyril Cusack. 2 Records.	TRS-323

KIPPHARDT, HEINAR

In the Matter of J. Robert Oppenheimer (Complete)	Caedmon
Joseph Wiseman, Lincoln Center Repertory	TRS-336
Theatre. 3 Records.	

MARLOWE, CHRISTOPHER

Dr. Faustus (Abridged)	Caedmon
Frank Silvera, etc. 1 Record.	1033
Dr. Faustus (Abridged)	Library
Robert Culp, etc. 1 Record.	Edition
	4005

MICHAELS, SIDNEY

Dylan (Complete)	Columbia
Sir Alec Guiness and Broadway Cast. 3 Records.	DOS-701

MILLER, ARTHUR

After the Fall (Complete)	Caedmon
Original Broadway Cast. 4 Records.	TRS-326
The Crucible (Excerpts)	Spoken Arts
1 Record.	704
Death of a Salesman (Slightly Abridged)	Decca
Original Broadway Cast except Thomas Mitchell	DX-102
plays Willy Loman. 2 Records.	
Death of a Salesman (Complete)	Caedmon
Lee J. Cobb, Mildred Dunnock, etc. 3 Records.	TRS-310
Incident at Vichy (Complete)	Caedmon
Hal Holbrook, David Wayne, Joseph Wiseman.	TRS-318
2 Records.	
A View From the Bridge (Complete)	Caedmon
Broadway Cast revival. 2 Records.	TRS-317

MOLIERE

The Doctor in Spite of Himself	Library
(Excerpts) Robert Culp, etc. 1 Record.	Edition
	4009
The Misanthrope (Complete)	Caedmon
APA-Phoenix Production. 2 Records.	TRS-337

The Miser (Complete) Lincoln Center Production. 2 Records.	Caedmon TRS-338
The School for Wives (Complete) Brian Bedford, etc. 3 Records.	Caedmon TRS-344
Tartuffe (Complete) Stratford, Canada Production. 3 Records.	Caedmon TRS-332

O'CASEY, SEAN

Juno and the Paycock (Complete) Siobhan McKenna, Cyril Cusack. 2 Records.	Seraphim 6014

O'NEILL, EUGENE

Ah, Wilderness (Complete) 3 Records.	Caedmon TRS-340
The Emperor Jones (Complete) James Earl Jones, etc. 2 Records.	Caedmon TRS-341
Long Day's Journey into Night (Complete) Robert Ryan, Stacy Keach, Geraldine Fitzgerald. 4 Records.	Caedmon TRS-350
A Moon for the Misbegotten (Complete) Salome Jens, etc. 3 Records.	Caedmon TRS-333
More Stately Mansions (Complete) Ingrid Bergman, Colleen Dewhurst, Arthur Hill. 3 Records.	Caedmon TRS-331
Mourning Becomes Electra (Complete) Jane Alexander, Sada Thompson. 4 Records.	Caedmon DOS-688
Strange Interlude (Complete) Actor's Studio with Franchot Tone, etc. 5 Records.	Columbia TRS-331

ROSTAND, EDMOND

Cyrano de Bergerac (Complete) Sir Ralph Richardson, etc. 3 Records.	Caedmon TRS-306
Cyrano de Bergerac (Excerpts) Jose Ferrer. 1 Record.	Capitol W-283

SACKLER, HOWARD

The Great White Hope (Complete) Original Broadway Cast. 3 Records.	Tetra 5200

SATRE, JEAN-PAUL

No Exit (Complete) Donald Pleasence, Anna Massey, etc. 2 Records.	Caedmon TRS-327

SCHISGAL, MURRAY

Luv (Complete) Eli Wallach, Anne Jackson, etc. 2 Records.	Columbia CDOS-718

_____ *The Second Shepherd's Play* (Complete)   Caedmon
1 Record.   1032

SHAKESPEARE, WILLIAM
    All's Well that Ends Well (Complete)   Argo
    Marlowe Society. 3 Records.   354/6

    All's Well that Ends Well (Complete)   Caedmon
    Claire Bloom, Dame Flora Robson, etc. 3 Records.   SRS-212

    Antony and Cleopatra (Complete)   Caedmon
    3 Records.   SRS-235

    Antony and Cleopatra (Complete)   Argo
    Marlowe Society. 4 Records.   307/10

    As You Like It (Complete)   Argo
    Marlowe Society. 3 Records.   125/7

    As You Like It (Complete)   Caedmon
    Vanessa Redgrave, etc. 3 Records.   SRS-210

    The Comedy of Errors (Complete)   Caedmon
    Anna Massey, etc. 2 Records.   SRS-205

    The Comedy of Errors (Complete)   Argo
    Marlowe Society. 2 Records.   311/2

    Coriolanus (Complete)   Argo
    Marlowe Society. 4 Records.   135/8

    Coriolanus (Complete)   Caedmon
    Jessica Tandy, Richard Burton. 3 Records.   SRS-236

    Cymbeline (Complete)   Caedmon
    Boris Karloff, etc. 3 Records.   SRS-236

    Cymbeline (Complete)   Argo
    Marlowe Society. 4 Records.   265/8

    Hamlet (Abridged)   Victor
    Sir John Gielgud, Pamela Brown. 2 Records.   LM-6007

    Hamlet (Complete)   Columbia
    Richard Burton, Hume Cronyn, etc. 4 Records.   DOS-702

    Hamlet (Complete)   Caedmon
    Paul Scofield, etc. 4 Records.   SRS-232

    Hamlet (Excerpts)   Victor
    Lord Laurence Olivier (Film version) 1 Record.   LM-1924

    Henry IV, Part I (Complete)   Argo
    Marlowe Society. 4 Records.   208/11

    Henry IV, Part I (Complete)   Caedmon
    Pamela Brown, Anthony Qualye. 3 Records.   SRS-217

    Henry IV, Part II (Complete)   Argo
    Marlowe Society. 4 Records.   212/15

Henry IV, Part II (Complete) Max Adrian, Harry Andrews. 4 Records.	Caedmon SRS-218
Henry V (Complete) Marlowe Society. 4 Records.	Argo 261/4
Henry V (Complete) Sir John Gielgud, etc. 4 Records.	Caedmon SRS-219
Henry V (Excerpts) Lord Laurence Olivier (Film version) 1 Record.	Victor LM-1924
Henry VI, Part I (Complete) Marlow Society. 3 Records.	Argo 368/8
Henry VI, Part II (Complete) Marlowe Society. 4 Records.	Argo 389/92
Henry VI, Part III (Complete) Marlowe Society. 4 Records.	Argo 393/6
Henry VIII (Complete) Marlowe Society. 4 Records.	Argo 303/6
Henry VIII (Excerpts) Dame Sybil Thorndike, Sir Lewis Casson. 1 Record.	Spoken Arts 881
Julius Caesar (Complete) Marlowe Society. 3 Records.	Argo 132/4
Julius Caesar (Complete) Sir Ralph Richardson, John Mills, Anthony Quayle. 3 Records.	Caedmon SRS-230
Julius Caesar (Slightly Abridged) Mercury Theatre, Orson Welles, etc. 2 Records.	Lexington 7570/75
King John (Complete) Marlowe Society. 4 Records.	Argo 168/71
King John (Complete) Sir Donald Wolfit, etc. 3 Records.	Caedmon SRS-215
King Lear (Complete) Dublin Gate Theatre. 4 Records.	Spoken Word A9
King Lear (Complete) Marlowe Society. 4 Records.	Argo 280/3
King Lear (Complete) Paul Scofield, etc. 4 Records.	Caedmon SRS-215
Love's Labour's Lost (Complete) Marlowe Society. 3 Records.	Argo 313/5
Macbeth (Complete) Marlowe Society. 3 Records.	Argo 175/7

Macbeth (Complete) Old Vic Company. 2 Records.	Victor LM6010
Macbeth (Complete) Anthony Quayle, Gwen Ffrangcon-Davies. 3 Records.	Caedmon SRS-231
Macbeth (Excerpts of above) 1 Record.	Caedmon 1167
Measure for Measure (Complete) Marlowe Society. 4 Records.	Argo 164/7
Measure for Measure (Complete) Sir John Gielgud, Margaret Leighton, Sir Ralph Richardson. 3 Records.	Caedmon SRS-204
Merchant of Venice (Complete) Marlowe Society. 4 Records.	Argo 160/3
Merchant of Venice (Complete) Dorothy Tutin, Harry Andrews, Hugh Griffith. 3 Records.	Caedmon SRS-209
Merry Wives of Windsor (Complete) Marlowe Society. 3 Records.	Argo 351/3
Merry Wives of Windsor (Complete) Anthony Quayle, Michael MacLiammoir. 3 Records.	Caedmon SRS-203
A Midsummer Night's Dream (Complete) Marlowe Society. 3 Records.	Argo 250/2
A Midsummer Night's Dream (Complete) Paul Scofield, etc. 3 Records.	Caedmon SRS-208
Much Ado About Nothing (Complete) Marlowe Society. 3 Records.	Argo 300/2
Much Ado About Nothing (Complete) British National Theatre. 3 Records.	Victor VDS-104
Much Ado About Nothing (Complete) Rex Harrison, etc. 3 Records.	Caedmon SRS-206
Othello (Complete) Paul Robeson, Jose Ferrer, Uta Hagen, etc. 3 Records.	Columbia CSL-153
Othello (Complete) Marlowe Society. 4 Records.	Argo 121/4
Othello (Complete) Lord Laurence Olivier, etc. 4 Records.	Victor VDS-100
Othello (Complete) Frank Silvera, Anna Massey. 3 Records.	Caedmon SRS-225

Pericles (Complete) Marlowe Society. 3 Records.	Argo 411/3	

Pericles (Complete)
Paul Scofield, Sir Felix Aylmer, etc. 3 Records.

Caedmon
SRS-237

Richard II (Complete)
Marlowe Society. 3 Records.

Argo
139/41

Richard II (Complete)
Sir John Gielgud, Sir Ralph Richardson,
etc. 3 Records.

Caedmon
SRS-216

Richard III (Complete)
Marlowe Society. 4 Records.

Argo
407/10

Richard III (Complete)
Robert Stephens, Dame Peggy Ashcroft,
etc. 4 Records.

Caedmon
SRS-223

Romeo and Juliet (Complete)
Marlowe Society. 4 Records.

Argo
200/3

Romeo and Juliet (Complete)
Claire Bloom, Dame Edith Evans,
Albert Finney. 3 Records.

Caedmon
SRS-228

The Taming of the Shrew (Complete)
Marlowe Society. 3 Records.

Argo
348/50

The Taming of the Shrew (Complete)
Trevor Howard, Margaret Leighton. 3 Records.

Caedmon
SRS-211

The Tempest (Complete)
Marlowe Society. 3 Records.

Argo
216/8

The Tempest (Complete)
Sir Michael and Vanessa Redgrave, etc. 3 Records.

Caedmon
SRS-201

Timon of Athens (Complete)
Marlowe Society. 3 Records.

Argo
253/5

Titus Andronicus (Complete)
Marlowe Society. 3 Records.

Argo
357/9

Titus Andronicus (Complete)
Anthony Qualye, Michael Hordern, etc. 3 Records.

Caedmon
SRS-227

Troilus and Cressida (Complete)
Marlowe Society. 4 Records.

Argo
128/31

Troilus and Cressida (Complete)
Diane Cilento, Jeremy Brett, Cyril Cusack, etc.
3 Records.

Caedmon
SRS-234

Twelfth Night (Complete)
Marlowe Society. 3 Records.

Argo
284/6

Twelfth Night (Complete)
Siobhan McKenna, Paul Scofield, John Neville,
etc. 3 Records.

Caedmon
SRS-213

Two Gentlemen of Verona (Complete)
Marlowe Society. 3 Records.

Argo
172/4

Two Gentlemen of Verona (Complete)
3 Records.

Caedmon
SRS-S-202

The Winter's Tale (Complete)
Marlowe Society. 4 Records.

Argo
204/7

The Winter's Tale (Complete)
Sir John Gielgud, Dame Peggy Ashcroft.

Caedmon
SRS-214

SHAW, GEORGE BERNARD

Caesar and Cleopatra (Abridged)
2 Records.

Caedmon
TRS-304

Don Juan in Hell (Complete)
(3rd Act of *Man and Superman*)
Charles Boyer, Agnes Moorehead, Charles
Laughton, Sir Cedric Hardwick. 2 Records.

Columbia
QSL-166

Heartbreak House (Complete)
Jessica Tandy, etc. 3 Records.

Caedmon
TRS-335

Major Barbara (Complete)
Robert Morley, etc. 4 Records.

Caedmon
TRS-319

Pygmalion (Complete)
Sir Michael Redgrave, Lynn Redgrave. 2 Records.

Caedmon
TRS-354

Saint Joan (Complete)
Siobhan McKenna, Donald Pleasance,
Felix Aylomer. 4 Records.

Caedmon
TRS-311

Saint Joan (Complete)
Barbara Jefford, Max Adrian, etc. 3 Records.

Argo
5470/2

SHERIDAN, RICHARD BRINSLEY

The Rivals (Complete)
Dame Edith Evans, etc. 2 Records.

Caedmon
TC-2020

The Rivals (Abridged)
Robert Culp, etc. 1 Record.

Library
Edition
4004

The School for Scandal (Complete)
Sir John Gielgud, Sir Ralph Richardson. 3 Records.

Command
S-13002

The School for Scandal (Complete)
Sir John Gielgud, Sir Ralph Richardson. 3 Records.

Caedmon
TRS-305

The School for Scandal (Complete)
Swan Theatre Players. 3 Records.

Spoken Arts
968/70

SOPHOCLES

Antigone (Complete)

Caedmon

Dorothy Tutin, Max Adrian, Jeremy Brett, etc. 2 Records.	TRS-320
Oedipus Rex (Complete) Douglas Campbell, Stratford Players. 2 Records.	Caedmon 2012

SYNGE, JOHN MILLINGTON

Playboy of the Western World (Complete) Siobhan McKenna, Cyril Cusack, etc. 2 Records.	Seraphim 6013
Riders to the Sea (Complete) Eireann Players. 1 Record.	Spoken Arts 743
Shadow of the Glen (Complete) Radio Eireann Players. 1 Record.	Spoken Arts 743

THOMAS, DYLAN

Under Milkwood (Complete) Richard Burton, Hugh Griffith, etc. 2 Records.	Argo 21/22
Under Milkwood (Complete) B. B. C. Cast. 2 Records.	Spoken Arts 991/2

WEBSTER, JOHN

The Duchess of Malfi (Complete) Barbara Jefford, Alec McCowen, etc. 3 Records.	Caedmon TRS-344

WEISS, PETER

Marat/Sade (Complete) Royal Shakespeare Company. 3 Records.	Caedmon TRS-312

WILDE, OSCAR

The Importance of Being Earnest (Complete) Sir John Gielgud, Dame Edith Evans, Pamela Brown, etc. 2 Records.	Angel 3504
The Importance of Being Earnest (Complete) Joan Greenwood, Lynn Redgrave, etc. 2 Records.	Caedmon TRS-329
Lady Windermere's Fan (Excerpts) 1 Record.	Library Edition 4001
Salome (Abridged) Kirkland Acting Group. 1 Record.	Library Edition 4011

WILLIAMS, TENNESSEE

The Glass Menagerie (Complete) Montgomery Clift, Julie Harris, Jessica Tandy, David Wayne. 2 Records.	Caedmon TRS-301
The Rose Tattoo (Complete) Maureen Stapleton, Harry Guardino. 3 Records.	Caedmon TRS-324

Index